ISBN 0-8373-2845-4

C-2845   **CAREER EXAMINATION SERIES**

This is your
PASSBOOK® for...

Assessment of
Teaching Assistant

Skills (ATAS)

Test Preparation Study Guide

Questions & Answers

N L C

NATIONAL LEARNING CORPORATION™

ISBN 0-8373-2845-4

C-2845   CAREER EXAMINATION SERIES

This is your
PASSBOOK® for...

Teaching Assistant

Test Preparation Study Guide

Questions & Answers

NLC

NATIONAL LEARNING CORPORATION

Copyright © 2005 by

National Learning Corporation

212 Michael Drive, Syosset, New York 11791

(516) 921-8888
Outside N.Y.: 1(800) 645-6337
ORDER FAX: 1(516) 921-8743
www.passbooks.com
email: passbooks @ aol.com
sales @ passbooks.com
info @ passbooks.com

PRINTED IN THE UNITED STATES OF AMERICA

PASSBOOK®

NOTICE

This book is *SOLELY* intended for, is sold *ONLY* to, and its use is *RESTRICTED* to *individual*, bona fide applicants or candidates who qualify by virtue of having seriously filed applications for appropriate license, certificate, professional and/or promotional advancement, higher school matriculation, scholarship, or other legitimate requirements of educational and/or governmental authorities.

This book is *NOT* intended for use, class instruction, tutoring, training, duplication, copying, reprinting, excerption, or adaptation, etc., by:

(1) Other Publishers

(2) Proprietors and/or Instructors of "Coaching" and/or Preparatory Courses

(3) Personnel and/or Training Divisions of commercial, industrial, and governmental organizations

(4) Schools, colleges, or universities and/or their departments and staffs, including teachers and other personnel

(5) Testing Agencies or Bureaus

(6) Study groups which seek by the purchase of a single volume to copy and/or duplicate and/or adapt this material for use by the group as a whole without having purchased individual volumes for each of the members of the group

(7) Et al.

Such persons would be in violation of appropriate Federal and State statutes.

PROVISION OF LICENSING AGREEMENTS. — Recognized educational commercial, industrial, and governmental institutions and organizations, and others legitimately engaged in educational pursuits, including training, testing, and measurement activities, may address a request for a licensing agreement to the copyright owners, who will determine whether, and under what conditions, including fees and charges, the materials in this book may be used by them. In other words, a licensing facility *exists* for the legitimate use of the material in this book on other than an individual basis. However, it is asseverated and affirmed here that the materials in this book *CANNOT* be used without the receipt of the express permission of such a licensing agreement from the Publishers.

NATIONAL LEARNING CORPORATION
212 Michael Drive
Syosset, New York 11791

Inquiries re licensing agreements should be addressed to:
The President
National Learning Corporation
212 Michael Drive
Syosset, New York 11791

PASSBOOK SERIES®

THE *PASSBOOK SERIES®* has been created to prepare applicants and candidates for the ultimate academic battlefield—the examination room.

At some time in our lives, each and every one of us may be required to take an examination—for validation, matriculation, admission, qualification, registration, certification, or licensure.

Based on the assumption that every applicant or candidate has met the basic formal educational standards, has taken the required number of courses, and read the necessary texts, the *PASSBOOK SERIES®* furnishes the one special preparation which may assure passing with confidence, instead of failing with insecurity. Examination questions—together with answers—are furnished as the basic vehicle for study so that the mysteries of the examination and its compounding difficulties may be eliminated or diminished by a sure method.

This book is meant to help you pass your examination provided that you qualify and are serious in your objective.

The entire field is reviewed through the huge store of content information which is succinctly presented through a provocative and challenging approach—the question-and-answer method.

A climate of success is established by furnishing the correct answers at the end of each test.

You soon learn to recognize types of questions, forms of questions, and patterns of questioning. You may even begin to anticipate expected outcomes.

You perceive that many questions are repeated or adapted so that you gain acute insights, which may enable you to score many sure points.

You learn how to confront new questions, or types of questions, and to attack them confidently and work out the correct answers.

You note objectives and emphases, and recognize pitfalls and dangers, so that you may make positive educational adjustments.

Moreover, you are kept fully informed in relation to new concepts, methods, practices, and directions in the field.

You discover that you are actually taking the examination all the time: you are preparing for the examination by "taking" an examination, not by reading extraneous and/or supererogatory textbooks.

In short, this PASSBOOK®, used directedly, should be an important factor in helping you to pass your test.

TEACHING ASSISTANT

INTRODUCTION

Purpose of This Preparation Guide

This preparation guide is designed to help familiarize candidates with the content and format of the Assessment of Teaching Assistant Skills (ATAS). Educators may also find the information in this guide useful as they discuss the test with candidates.

This preparation guide illustrates some of the types of ATAS questions; however, the set of sample questions does not necessarily define the content or difficulty of an entire actual test. All test components (e.g., directions, content, and question formats) may differ from those presented here. The program is subject to change.

Organization of This Preparation Guide

The ATAS objectives appear on the pages following this introduction. The objectives list the content that is eligible to be assessed by the ATAS. Each objective is followed by focus statements that provide examples of the range, type, and level of content that may appear on the ATAS. Following the objectives is information about the sample questions for the ATAS and a set of sample directions for the ATAS.

The sample multiple-choice questions are presented next. The correct answer and an explanation of the correct answer follow at the end.

The Assessment of Teaching Assistant Skills (ATAS)

The purpose of the Assessment of Teaching Assistant Skills (ATAS) is to assess knowledge and skills in the following four areas:

- Reading
- Writing
- Mathematics
- Instructional Support

The Assessment of Teaching Assistant Skills consists of 100 multiple-choice questions.

Strategies for Taking the ATAS

Be On Time
Arrive at the test center on time so that you are rested and ready to begin the test when instructed to do so.

Follow Directions
At the beginning of the test session and throughout the test, follow all directions carefully. This includes the oral directions that will be read by the test administrator and any written directions in the test booklet. If you do not understand something about the directions, do not hesitate to raise your hand and ask your test administrator.

Pace Yourself
The test schedule is designed to allow sufficient time for completion of the test. Each test session is three hours in length. Furthermore, the test is designed to allow you to

allocate your time within the session as you need. You will be required to return your materials at the end of the three-hour session.

Since the allocation of your time during the test session is largely yours to determine, planning your own pace for taking the test is very important. There will be 100 multiple-choice questions for the ATAS. Do not spend a lot of time with a multiple-choice test question that you cannot answer promptly; skip that question and move on. If you skip a question, be sure to skip the corresponding row of answer choices on your answer sheet. Mark the question in your test booklet so that you can return to it later, but be careful to appropriately record on the answer sheet the answers to the remaining questions.

You may find that you need less time than the three hours allotted in a test session, but you should be prepared to stay for the entire time period. Do not make any other commitments for this time period that may cause you to rush through the test.

Read Carefully
Read the directions and the questions carefully. Read all response options. Remember that the test questions call for the "best answer"; do not choose the first answer that seems reasonable. Read and evaluate all choices to find the best answer. Read the questions closely so that you understand what they ask. For example, it would be a waste of time to perform a long computation when the question calls for an approximation.

Read the test questions, but don't read into them. The questions are designed to be straightforward, not tricky. Often your first and most direct opinion, based on your knowledge, is the best answer.

Mark Answers Carefully
Your answers for the multiple-choice questions will be scored electronically; therefore, the answer you select must be clearly marked and the only answer marked. If you change your mind about an answer, erase the old answer completely. Do not make any stray marks on the answer sheet; these may be misinterpreted by the scoring machine. You may use any available space in the test booklet for notes, but **your answers must be clearly marked on your answer sheet. ONLY ANSWERS THAT APPEAR ON YOUR ANSWER SHEET WILL BE SCORED.** Answers in your test booklet will not be scored.

IF YOU SKIP A QUESTION, BE SURE TO SKIP THE CORRESPONDING ROW OF ANSWER CHOICES ON YOUR ANSWER SHEET.

Guessing
As you read through the response options, do your best to find the best answer. If you cannot quickly find the best answer, try to eliminate as many of the others as possible. Then guess among the remaining answer choices. Your score on each test is based on the number of test questions you have answered correctly. There is no penalty for incorrect answers; therefore, it is better to guess than not to respond at all.

Reading Passages
Some test questions are based on reading passages. You may want to employ some of the following strategies while you are completing these test questions.

One strategy is to read the passage thoroughly and carefully and then answer each question, referring to the passage only as needed. Another strategy is to read the questions first, gaining an idea of what is sought in them, and then read the passage with the questions in mind. Yet another strategy is to review the passage to gain an overview of its content, and then answer each question by referring back to the passage for the specific answer. Any of these strategies may be appropriate for you. You should not answer the questions on the basis of your own opinions but rather on the basis of the ideas and opinions expressed in the passage.

Check Accuracy

Use any remaining time at the end of the test session to check the accuracy of your work. Go back to the test questions that gave you difficulty and verify your work on them. Check the answer sheet, too. Be sure that you have marked your answers accurately and have completely erased changed answers.

ATAS OBJECTIVES

Sub-area I—Reading

0001   Understand the meaning of general vocabulary words
For example:

- Determining the meaning of commonly encountered words presented in context
- Identifying appropriate synonyms or antonyms for words
- Recognizing the correct use of commonly misused pairs of words (e.g. their/there, to/too)

0002   Understand the stated main idea of a reading passage
For example:

- Identifying the stated main idea of a passage
- Identifying the topic sentence of a passage
- Recognizing introductory and summary statements of a passage
- Selecting an accurate restatement of the main idea of a passage

0003   Understand the sequence of ideas in a reading passage
For example:

- Identifying the order of events or steps described in a passage
- Organizing a set of instructions into their proper sequence
- Identifying the cause-and-effect relationships described in a passage

0004   Interpret textual and graphic information
For example:

- Interpreting information from tables, line and bar graphs, and pie charts
- Recognizing appropriate representations of written information in graphic or tabular form
- Recognizing differences between fact and opinion

Sub-area II—Writing

0005   Understand the standard use of verbs
For example:

- Identifying standard subject-verb agreement (e.g. number, person)
- Identifying verb tense (e.g. present, past)
- Recognizing consistency of verb tense (e.g. verb endings)

0006   Understand the standard use of pronouns and modifiers
For example:

- Identifying agreement (number, gender, person) between a pronoun and its antecedent
- Using possessive pronouns (e.g. its vs. it's), relative pronouns (e.g. that, which) and demonstrative pronouns (e.g. this, that)
- Using comparative and superlative modifiers (e.g. good/better/best)

0007   Understand standard sentence structure and punctuation
For example:
- Distinguishing between sentence fragments and complete sentences
- Distinguishing between run-on sentences and correctly divided sentences
- Identifying correct and incorrect punctuation

0008   Understand the standard use of capitalization and spelling
For example:
- Identifying standard capitalization at the beginning of sentences
- Identifying standard capitalization of proper words and titles
- Recognizing standard spelling of commonly encountered words presented in context

Sub-area III—Mathematics

0009   Understand number concepts
For example:
- Identifying the place value of digits (e.g. hundreds, tens, ones, tenths)
- Identifying correctly rounded numbers
- Identifying equivalent weights and measures in different units (e.g. feet and inches, quarts and pints, kilograms and grams)
- Estimating the solution to a measurement problem (e.g. height, perimeter)

0010   Understand the addition and subtraction of whole numbers
For example:
- Solving problems involving the addition of whole numbers
- Solving problems involving the subtraction of whole numbers
- Applying principles of addition and subtraction of whole numbers to solve problems encountered in every day life

0011   Understand multiplication and division of whole numbers
For example:
- Solving problems involving the multiplication of whole numbers
- Solving problems involving the division of whole numbers
- Applying principles of multiplication and division of whole numbers to solve problems encountered in every day life

0012   Understand operations involving fractions, decimals and percents
For example:
- Solving problems involving fractions, decimals and percents
- Solving problems involving conversions between fractions, decimals and percents

0013   Understand classroom instruction related to reading

For example:

- Providing support under the guidance of classroom teachers to match student needs, styles of learning and background experiences (e.g. drilling, using pictorial or video materials, relating reading materials to real-life contexts)

- Helping students use instructional resources (dictionaries, encyclopedias, multimedia) to support reading

- Helping students use a variety of approaches to understand what they read (e.g. skimming, questioning to tap prior knowledge, monitoring understanding, reviewing, summarizing)

- Gathering information about students' progress as readers to support the teacher's planning, assessment and instruction

0014   Understand classroom instruction related to writing

For example:

- Understanding drafting, editing and proofreading written work

- Helping students focus their writing

- Helping students use instructional resources (dictionaries, grammar books, library and technological resources) to support writing

- Gathering information about students' progress as writers to support the teacher's planning, assessment and instruction

0015   Understand classroom instruction related to mathematics

For example:

- Relating mathematics to everyday situations

- Identifying and correcting basic errors in addition, subtraction, multiplication and division

- Helping students use instructional resources (hands-on materials, rulers, money, charts, graphs) to support mathematical learning

- Gathering information about students' progress in mathematics to support the teacher's planning, assessment and instruction

Along with each sample question, this guide presents the correct response and an explanation of why the correct response is the best available response. Keep in mind when reviewing the questions and response options that there is one *best* answer to each question. Remember, too, that each explanation offers one of perhaps many perspectives on why a given response is correct or incorrect in the context of the question; there may be other explanations as well.

EXAMINATION SECTION

DIRECTIONS: Each question or incomplete statement is followed by several suggested answers or completions. Select the one that BEST answers the question or completes the statement. *PRINT THE LETTER OF THE CORRECT ANSWER IN THE SPACE AT THE RIGHT.*

Questions 1 through 3 refer to the following passage:

Children can benefit greatly from learning how to play chess. Through studying and playing chess, they strengthen their thinking, learn how to deal with competitive situations and develop important social skills.

Playing chess requires hard thinking. Players must analyze moves and decide on the best one to play. Then they must live with their decision no matter how good or bad the move.

Players must set goals and fight their way toward achieving them. Usually, the first player to make a bad move loses the game, but not always. Staying focused on winning the game and overcoming setbacks are valuable experiences for young people.

Chess also helps children improve their social skills. Learning to win graciously is just as important as learning to be a good loser. Both of these skills help children interact successfully with other people.

Chess can be a great deal of fun to play. It can also teach children valuable skills that they can use for the rest of their lives.

1. Read the sentence below, taken from the fourth paragraph of the   1._____
   passage; then complete the exercise that follows:

   "Learning to win graciously is just as important as learning to be a good loser."

   Select the best definition of the word <u>graciously</u> as it is used in the sentence above.
   A. quietly
   B. courteously
   C. happily
   D. humorously

2. What is the *topic sentence* of the passage?
   A. Children can benefit greatly from learning how to play chess
   B. Through studying and playing chess, they strengthen their thinking, learn how to deal with competitive situations and develop important social skills
   C. Chess can be a great deal of fun to play
   D. It can also teach children valuable skills that they can use for the rest of their lives

2._____

3. According to the passage, how do children develop social skills while playing chess?
   A. By staying focused on winning the game and overcoming setbacks they encounter
   B. By having fun playing with other children
   C. By living with the decisions they make during each game
   D. By learning how to behave appropriately whether they win or lose a game

3._____

4. Use the graph below to answer the question:

4._____

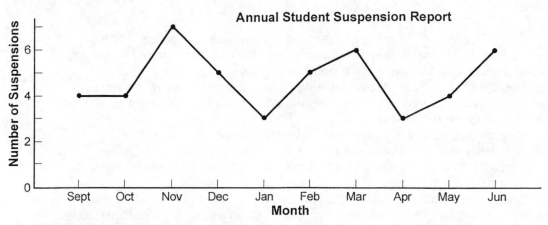

What was the total number of student suspensions during the three-month period of September, October and November?
   A. 8
   B. 11
   C. 12
   D. 15

5. Which sentence is in the present tense?
   A. The grocery bag still stood where he left it.
   B. Melissa asks for a little more sugar in her tea.
   C. Conrad reflected on the meaning of the story.
   D. He came home soon after we arrived.

5._____

6. Choose the best word to complete the sentence below:

The new principal, _____ speaks four languages, has some exciting ideas to suggest.
   A. that
   B. whom
   C. which
   D. who

6._____

7. Which of the following is NOT a complete sentence?   7._____
    A. Making a lesson plan is necessary.
    B. First, define the objectives.
    C. The usual standards for evaluation.
    D. Nothing is more important.

8. Which word is spelled *incorrectly*?   8._____
    A. critisism
    B. judicial
    C. scholastic
    D. recognition

9. How many centimeters are in 7 meters?   9._____
    A. 10
    B. 70
    C. 100
    D. 700

10. A cashier has $42 in his cash drawer at the beginning of his shift. During   10._____
    his shift, he collects $815. How much money is in his drawer at the end
    of his shift?
    A. $773
    B. $815
    C. $839
    D. $857

11. What is the remainder when 53 is divided by 9?   11._____
    A. 6
    B. 7
    C. 8
    D. 9

12. What is 60% written as a fraction?   12._____
    A. 2/5
    B. 3/5
    C. 2/3
    D. 5/6

13. A teaching assistant in a second-grade class is taking a small group of   13._____
    students to the school library to find information needed to complete an
    assignment on whales. Which of the following would be the best way for
    the teaching assistant to help the students with their project?
    A. Make sure the students remain quiet and behave appropriately
       while they are in the library
    B. Have the students choose information resources on their own, and
       help them use the resources to complete their assignments
    C. Show the students how to find the entry on whales in a dictionary,
       and transfer that information to their notebooks
    D. Find a story about whales, read it aloud to the students, then have
       them discuss what they learned from the story

14. Ms. Perrotta, a teaching assistant in a seventh-grade English class, has been asked to supervise a small group of students while they each edit the first drafts of short stories they are writing based on personal experiences. Which of the following pieces of information would be most helpful for Ms. Perrotta to provide to the teacher about the students' work during this session?

    A. What kinds of help the students needed
    B. Which story Ms. Perrotta thinks is the most creative
    C. Which student Ms. Perrotta thinks is the best writer
    D. How well the students worked together

14._____

15. Mr. Barry has just introduced his third-grade class to the concept of division. After several days, most of the students seem to have grasped the concept, but Louisa is still confused. Mr. Barry asks Ms. Salem, his teaching assistant, to help Louisa. Which of the following approaches would best help Louisa understand the basic idea of division?

    A. Show Louisa how to do division problems using a calculator
    B. Have Louisa read the section in the textbook on division and ask Ms. Salem if she has any questions
    C. Have Louisa separate a large pile of pennies into smaller piles of equal numbers
    D. Give Louisa a worksheet with several simple division problems

15._____

ANSWERS AND EXPLANATIONS

1. B

   To be gracious is to behave in a kind and polite manner to others. Thus, of the choices available, "courteously" most closely fits the meaning of the word graciously as it appears in the passage.

2. A

   The topic sentence of a passage introduces the central idea that the rest of the passage develops. This passage talks about a variety of ways in which playing chess benefits children. Therefore, A best states the central idea.

3. D

   In the fourth paragraph, the author points out that, whether children win or lose at chess, they gain experience in interacting with other people.

4. D

   The graph indicates that there were four students suspended in September, four more in October, and seven more in November. Thus, the total was 15.

5. B

   When a verb is in the present tense, it expresses action that is taking place right now, rather than in the past or in the future. To express the present tense with a singular noun, an *s* or an *es* is usually added to the verb. Among the alternatives, only B contains a verb in the present tense.

6. D

   The pronouns "that" and "which" are generally used to refer to a thing or an idea. The pronouns "who" and "whom" are used to refer to a person. Specifically, the pronoun "who" is used when the person being referred to is the subject of a phrase or sentence, and the pronoun "whom" is used when the person being referred to is the object of a phrase or sentence. In this sentence, "who" refers to "principal," which is the subject of the opening phrase.

7. C

   A complete sentence is a group of words that expresses a complete thought. Only C does not express a complete thought.

8. A

   Choice A, "critisism," is not spelled correctly. The correct spelling is "criticism."

9. D

   There are 100 centimeters in a meter, therefore there are 700 centimeters in 7 meters.

10. D

   In order to determine how much money the cashier has in his cash drawer at the end of the day, add the amount at the beginning of the day ($42) to the amount added during the day ($815). The result is $857.

11. C

The remainder is what is left over when one number is divided by another number. When 53 is divided by 9, the result is 5, with 8 left over.

12. B

Sixty percent means 60 out of 100, or 60/100, which is the same as 6/10, which is the same as 3/5.

13. B

The goal of this activity is to have the students use the school library to gather information to complete an assignment on whales. By allowing the students to select information resources on their own, then showing them how to use these resources effectively, the teaching assistant helps students learn basic research skills while providing the assistance needed to complete their assignments.

14. A

The fundamental purpose of the work that the teacher has assigned is to help students learn how to edit their own work, a complex skill that the students will continue to learn and practice over many years. Response A, providing information on the kinds of problems that the students are experiencing as they try to edit their own work, represents the best way of helping the teacher plan the continuing instruction that the students will need.

15. C

The teacher has asked his teaching assistant to provide extra help to a student who is having difficulty understanding a new mathematical concept. The activity described in Response C is best suited to this goal because it introduces the concept of division in a simple, concrete manner. By using familiar objects in a hands-on activity, Louisa can more easily grasp the fundamental idea of division before applying the concept to specific problems.

HOW TO TAKE A TEST

I. YOU MUST PASS AN EXAMINATION
   A. *WHAT EVERY CANDIDATE SHOULD KNOW*

   Examination applicants often ask us for help in preparing for the written test. What can I study in advance? What kinds of questions will be asked? How will the test be given? How will the papers be graded?

   As an applicant for a civil service examination, you may be wondering about some of these things. Our purpose here is to suggest effective methods of advance study and to describe civil service examinations.

   Your chances for success on this examination can be increased if you know how to prepare. Those "pre-examination jitters" can be reduced if you know what to expect. You can even experience an adventure in good citizenship if you know why civil service examinations are given.

   B. *WHY ARE CIVIL SERVICE EXAMINATIONS GIVEN?*

   Civil service examinations are important to you in two ways. As a citizen, you want public jobs filled by employees who know how to do their work. As a job-seeker, you want a fair chance to compete for that job on an equal footing with other candidates. The best known means of accomplishing this two-fold goal is the competitive examination.

   Examinations are widely publicized throughout the nation. They may be administered for jobs in federal, state, city, municipal, town, or village governments or agencies.

   Any citizen may apply, with some limitations, such as the age or residence of applicants. Your experience and education may be reviewed to see whether you meet the requirements for the particular examination. When these requirements exist, they are reasonable and are applied consistently to all applicants. Thus, a competitive examination may cause you some uneasiness now, but it is your privilege and safeguard.

   C. *HOW ARE CIVIL SERVICE EXAMINATIONS DEVELOPED?*

   Examinations are carefully written by trained technicians who are specialists in the field known as "psychological measurement," in consultation with recognized authorities in the field of work that the test will cover. These experts recommend the subject matter areas or skills to be tested; only those knowledges or skills important to your success on the job are included. The most reliable books and source materials available are used as references. Together, the experts and technicians judge the difficulty level of the questions.

   Test technicians know how to phrase questions so that the problem is clearly stated. Their ethics do not permit "trick" or "catch" questions. Questions may have been tried out on sample groups, or subjected to statistical analysis, to determine their usefulness.

   Written tests are often used in combination with performance tests, ratings of training and experience, and oral interviews. All of these measures combine to form the best known means of finding the right man for the right job.

II. HOW TO PASS THE WRITTEN TEST

A. *NATURE OF THE EXAMINATION*

To prepare intelligently for civil service examinations, you should know how they differ from school examinations you have taken. In school you were assigned certain definite pages to read or subjects to cover. The examination questions were quite detailed and usually emphasized memory. Civil service examinations, on the other hand, try to discover your present ability to perform the duties of a position, plus your potentiality to learn these duties. In other words, a civil service examination attempts to predict how successful you will be. Questions cover such a broad area that they cannot be as minute and detailed as school examination questions.

In the public service similar kinds of work, or positions, are grouped together in one "class." This process is known as "position-classification." All the positions in a class are paid according to the salary range for that class. One class title covers all these positions, and they are all tested by the same examination.

B. *FOUR BASIC STEPS*

1. Study the Announcement.--How, then, can you know what subjects to study? Our best answer is: "Learn as much as possible about the class of positions for which you have applied." The examination will test the knowledge, skills, and abilities needed to do the work.

Your most valuable source of information about the position you want is the official announcement of the examination. This announcement lists the training and experience qualifications. Check these standards and apply only if you come reasonably close to meeting them.

The brief description of the position in the examination announcement offers some clues to the subjects which will be tested. Think about the job itself. Review the duties in your mind. Can you perform them, or are there some in which you are rusty? Fill in the blank spots in your preparation.

Many jurisdictions preview the written test in the examination announcement by including a section called "Knowledge and Abilities Required," "Scope of Examination," or some similar heading. Here you will find out specifically what fields will be tested.

2. Review Your Own Background.-- Once you learn in general what the position is all about, and what you need to know to do the work, ask yourself which subjects you already know fairly well and which need improvement. You may wonder whether to concentrate on improving your strong areas or on building some background in your fields of weakness. When the announcement has specified "some knowledge" or "considerable knowledge," or has used adjectives such as "beginning principles of ...." or "advanced .....methods," you can get a clue as to the number and difficulty of questions to be asked in any given field. More questions, and hence broader coverage, would be included for those subjects which are more important in the work. Now weigh your strengths and weaknesses against the job requirements and prepare accordingly.

3. Determine the Level of the Position.-- Another way to tell how intensively you should prepare is to understand the level of the job for which you are applying. Is it the entering level? In other words, is this the position in which beginners in a field of work are hired? Or is it an intermediate or advanced level? Sometimes this is indicated by such words as "Junior" or "Senior" in the class title.Other jurisdictions use Roman numerals to designate the level: Clerk I,

Clerk II, for example. The word "Supervisor" sometimes appears in the title. If the level is not indicated by the title, check the description of duties. Will you be working under very close supervision, or will you have responsibility for independent decisions in this work?

4. Choose Appropriate Study Materials.-- Now that you know the subjects to be examined and the relative amount of each subject to be covered, you can choose suitable study materials. For beginning level jobs, or even advanced ones, if you have a pronounced weakness in some aspect of your training, read a modern, standard textbook in that field. Be sure it is up-to-date and has general coverage. Such books are normally available at your library, and the librarian will be glad to help you locate one. For entry level positions, questions of appropriate difficulty are chosen -- neither highly advanced questions, nor those too simple. Such questions require careful thought but not advanced training.

If the position for which you are applying is technical or advanced, you will read more advanced, specialized material. If you are already familiar with the basic principles of your field, elementary textbooks would waste your time. Concentrate on advanced textbooks and technical periodicals. Think through the concepts and review difficult problems in your field.

These are all general sources. You can get more ideas on your own initiative, following these leads. For example, training manuals and publications of the government agency which employs workers in your field can be useful, particularly for technical and professional positions. A letter or visit to the government department involved may result in more specific study suggestions, and certainly will provide you with a more definite idea of the exact nature of the position you are seeking.

III. KINDS OF TESTS

Tests are used for purposes other than measuring knowledge and ability to perform specified duties. For some positions, it is equally important to test ability to make adjustments to new situations or to profit from training. In others, basic mental abilities not dependent upon information are essential. Questions which test these things may not appear as pertinent to the duties of the position as those which test for knowledge and information. Yet they are often highly important parts of a fair examination. For very general questions, it is almost impossible to help you direct your study efforts. What we can do is to point out some of the more common of these general abilities needed in public service positions and describe some typical questions.

1. General Information

Broad, general information has been found useful for predicting job success in some kinds of work. This is tested in a variety of ways, from vocabulary lists to questions about current events. Basic background in some field of work, such as sociology or economics, may be sampled in a group of questions. Often these are principles which have become familiar to most persons through "exposure" rather than through formal training. It is difficult to advise you how to study for these questions; being alert to the world around you is our best suggestion.

2. Verbal Ability

An example of an ability needed in many positions is verbal or language ability. Verbal ability is, in brief, the ability to use and understand words. Vocabulary and grammar tests are typical measures of this ability. "Reading comprehension" or "paragraph interpretation" questions are common in many kinds of civil service tests. You are given a paragraph of written material and asked to find its central meaning.

3. Numerical Ability

Number skills can be tested by the familiar arithmetic problem, by checking paired lists of numbers to see which are alike and which are different, or by interpreting charts and graphs. In the latter test, a graph may be printed in the test booklet which you are asked to use as the basis for answering questions.

4. Observation

A popular test for law-enforcement positions is the observation test. A picture is shown to you for several minutes, then taken away. Questions about the picture test your ability to observe both details and larger elements.

5. Following Directions

In many positions in the public service, the employee must be able to carry out written instructions dependably and accurately. You may be given a chart with several columns, each column listing a variety of information. The questions require you to carry out directions involving the information given in the chart.

6. Skills and Aptitudes

Performance tests effectively measure some manual skills and aptitudes. When the skill is one in which you are trained, such as typing or shorthand, you can practice. These tests are often very much like those given in business school or high school courses. For many of the other skills and aptitudes, however, no short-time preparation can be made. Skills and abilities natural to you or that you have developed throughout your lifetime are being tested.

Many of the general questions just described provide all the data needed to answer the questions and ask you to use your reasoning ability to find the answers. Your best preparation for these tests, as well as for tests of facts and ideas, is to be at your physical and mental best. You, no doubt, have your own methods of getting into an exam-taking mood and keeping "in shape." The next section lists some ideas on this subject.

IV. KINDS OF QUESTIONS

Only rarely is the "essay" question, which you answer in narrative form, used in civil service tests. Civil service tests are usually of the short-answer type. Full instructions for answering these questions will be given to you at the examination. But in case this is your first experience with short-answer questions and separate answer sheets, here is what you need to know.

1. Multiple-Choice Questions

Most popular of the short-answer questions is the "multiple-choice" or "best-answer" question. It can be used, for example, to test for factual knowledge, ability to solve problems, or judgment in meeting situations found at work.

A multiple-choice question is normally one of three types:

(1) It can begin with an incomplete statement followed by several possible endings. You are to find the one ending which *best* completes the statement, although some of the others may not be entirely wrong.

(2) It can also be a complete statement in the form of a question which is answered by choosing one of the statements listed.

(3) It can be in the form of a problem -- again you select the best answer.

Here is an example of a multiple-choice question with a discussion which should give you some clues as to the method for choosing the right answer:

SAMPLE QUESTION:

When an employee has a complaint about his assignment, the action which will *best* help him overcome his difficulty is

    (A) to discuss his difficulty with his co-workers
    (B) to take the problem to the head of the organization
    (C) to take the problem to the person who gave him the assignment
    (D) to say nothing to anyone about his complaint

In answering this question you should study each of the choices to find which is best. Consider choice (A). Certainly an employee may discuss his complaint with fellow employees, but no change or improvement can result, and the complaint remains unsolved. Choice (B) is a poor choice since the head of the organization probably does not know what assignment you have been given, and taking your problem to him is known as "going over the head" of the supervisor. The supervisor, or person who made the assignment, is the person who can clarify it or correct any injustice. Choice (C) is, therefore, correct. To say nothing, as in choice (D), is unwise. Supervisors have an interest in knowing the problems employees are facing, and the employee is seeking a solution to his problem.

2. True-False Questions

The "true-false" or "right-wrong" form of question is sometimes used. Here a complete statement is given. Your problem is to decide whether the statement is right or wrong.

SAMPLE QUESTION:

A person-to-person long distance telephone call costs less than a station-to-station call to the same city.

This question is wrong, or "false," since person-to-person calls are more expensive.

This is not a complete list of all possible question forms, although most of the others are variations of these common types. You will always get complete directions for answering questions. Be sure you understand *how* to mark your answers -- ask questions until you do.

V. RECORDING YOUR ANSWERS

For an examination with very few applicants, you may be told to record your answers in the test booklet itself. Separate answer sheets are much more common. If this separate answer sheet is to be scored by machine -- and this is often the case -- it is highly important that you mark your answers correctly in order to get credit.

An electric test-scoring machine is often used in civil service offices because of the speed with which papers can be scored. Machine-scored answer sheets must be marked with a special pencil, which will be given to you. This pencil has a high graphite content which responds to the electrical scoring machine. As a matter of fact, stray dots may register as answers, so do not let your pencil rest on the answer sheet while you are pondering the correct answer. Also, if your pencil lead breaks or is otherwise defective, ask for another.

Since the answer sheet will be dropped in a slot in the scoring machine, be careful not to bend the corners or get the paper crumpled.

The answer sheet normally has five vertical columns of numbers, with 30 numbers to a column. These numbers correspond to the question numbers in your test booklet. After each number, going across the page, are four or five pairs of dotted lines. These short dotted lines have small letters or numbers above them. The first two pairs may also have a "T" and "F" above the letters. This indicates that the first two pairs only are to be used if the questions are of the true-false type. If the questions are multiple-choice, disregard this "T" and "F" completely, and pay attention only to the small number or letters.

Answer your questions in the manner of the sample that follows. Proceed in the sequential steps outlined below.

Assume that you are answering question 32, which is:

    32. The largest city in the United States is:
        A. Washington, D.C.   B. New York City   C. Chicago
        D. Detroit   E. San Francisco

1. Choose the answer you think is best.
   New York City is the largest, so choice B is correct.
2. Find the row of dotted lines numbered the same as the question you are answering.
   This is question number 32, so find row number 32.
3. Find the pair of dotted lines corresponding to the answer you have chosen.
   You have chosen answer B, so find the pair of dotted lines marked "B".
4. Make a solid black mark between the dotted lines.
   Go up and down two or three times with your pencil so plenty of graphite rubs off, but do not let the mark get outside or above the dots.

VI. BEFORE THE TEST

Common sense will help you find procedures to follow to get ready for an examination. Too many of us, however, overlook these sensible measures. Indeed, nervousness and fatigue have been found to be the most serious reasons why applicants fail to do their best on civil service tests. Here is a list of reminders.

1. Begin Your Preparation Early

    Don't wait until the last minute to go scurrying around for books and materials or to find out what the position is all about.

2. Prepare Continuously

    An hour a night for a week is better than an all-night cram session. This has been definitely established. What is more, a night a week for a month will return better dividends than crowding your study into a shorter period of time.

3. Locate the Place of the Examination

    You have been sent a notice telling you when and where to report for the examination. If the location is in a different town or otherwise unfamiliar to you, it would be well to inquire the best route and learn something about the building.

4. Relax the Night Before the Test

    Allow your mind to rest. Do not study at all that night. Plan some mild recreation or diversion; then go to bed early and get a good night's sleep.

5. Get Up Early Enough to Make a Leisurely Trip to the Place for the Test

    Then unforeseen events, traffic snarls, unfamiliar buildings, will not upset you.

6. Dress Comfortably

    A written test is not a fashion show. You will be known by number and not by name, so wear something comfortable.

7. Leave Excess Paraphernalia at Home

    Shopping bags and odd bundles will get in your way. You need bring only the items mentioned in the official notice sent to you; usually everything you need is provided. Do not bring reference books to the examination. They will only confuse those last minutes and be taken away from you when in the test room.

8. Arrive Somewhat Ahead of Time

    If because of transportation schedules you must get there very early, bring a newspaper or magazine to take your mind off yourself while waiting.

9. Locate the Examination Room

    When you have found the proper room, you will be directed to the seat or part of the room where you will sit. Sometimes you are given a sheet of instructions to read while you are waiting. Do not fill out any forms until you are told to do so; just read them and be ready.

10. Relax and Prepare to Listen to the Instructions

11. If you have any physical problem that may keep you from doing your best, be sure to tell the test administrator. If you are sick, or in poor health, you really cannot do your best on the test. You can come back and take the test some other time.

II. AT THE TEST

    The day of the test is here and you have the test booklet in your hand. The temptation to get going is very strong. Caution! There is more to success than knowing the right answers. You must know how to identify your papers and understand variations in the type of short-answer question used in this particular examination. Follow these suggestions for maximum results from your efforts:

1. Cooperate with the Monitor

The test administrator has a duty to create a situation in which you can be as much at ease as possible. He will give instructions, tell you when to begin, check to see that you are marking your answer sheet correctly. He is not there to guard you, although he will see that your competitors do not take unfair advantage. He wants to help you do your best.

2. Listen to All Instructions

Don't jump the gun! Wait until you understand all directions. In most civil service tests you get more time than you need to answer the questions. So don't get in a hurry. Read each word of instructions until you clearly understand the meaning. Study the examples. Listen to all announcements. Follow directions. Ask questions if you do not understand what to do.

3. Identify Your Papers

Civil service examinations are usually identified by number only. You will be assigned a number; you must not put your name on your test papers. Be sure to copy your number correctly. Since more than one examination may be given, copy your exact examination title.

4. Plan Your Time

Unless you are told that a test is a "speed" or "rate-of-work" test, speed itself is not usually important. Time enough to answer all the questions will be provided. But this does not mean that you have all day. An overall time limit has been set. Divide the total time (in minutes) by the number of questions to get the approximate time you have for each question.

5. Do Not Linger Over Difficult Questions

If you come across a difficult question, mark it with a paper clip (useful to have along) and come back to it when you have been through the booklet. One caution if you do this -- be sure to skip a number on your answer sheet too. Check often to be sure that you have not lost your place and that you are marking in the row numbered the same as the question you are answering.

6. Read the Questions

Be sure you know what the question asks! Many capable people are unsuccessful because they failed to *read* the questions correctly.

7. Answer All Questions

Unless you have been instructed that a penalty will be deducted for incorrect answers, it is better to guess than to omit a question.

8. Speed Tests

It is often better *not* to guess on speed tests. It has been found that on timed tests people are tempted to spend the last few seconds before time is called in marking answers at random -- without even reading them -- in the hope of picking up a few extra points. To discourage this practice, the instructions may warn you that your score will be "corrected" for guessing. That is, a penalty will be applied. The incorrect answers will be deducted from the correct ones, or some other penalty formula will be used.

9. Review Your Answers

If you finish before time is called, go back to the questions you guessed or omitted to give further thought to them. Review other answers if you have time.

10. Return Your Test Materials

If you are ready to leave before others have finished or time is called, take *all* your materials to the monitor and leave quietly. Never take any test material with you. The monitor can discover whose papers are not complete, and taking a test booklet may be grounds for disqualification.

VIII. EXAMINATION TECHNIQUES

1. Read the *general* instructions carefully. These are usually printed on the first page of the examination booklet. As a rule, these instructions refer to the timing of the examination; the fact that you should not start work until the signal and must stop work at a signal, etc. If there are any *special* instructions, such as a choice of questions to be answered, make sure that you note this instruction carefully.

2. When you are ready to start work on the examination, that is as soon as the signal has been given, read the instructions to each question booklet, underline any key words or phrases, such as *least*, *best, outline, describe*, and the like. In this way you will tend to answer as requested rather than discover on reviewing your paper that you *listed without describing*, that you selected the *worst* choice rather than the *best* choice, etc.

3. If the examination is of the objective or so-called multiple-choice type, that is, each question will also give a series of possible answers: A, B, C, or D, and you are called upon to select the best answer and write the letter next to that answer on your answer paper, it is advisable to start answering each question in turn. There may be anywhere from 50 to 100 such questions in the three or four hours allotted and you can see how much time would be taken if you read through all the questions before beginning to answer any. Furthermore, if you come across a question or a group of questions which you know would be difficult to answer, it would undoubtedly affect your handling of all the other questions.

4. If the examination is of the esssay-type and contains but a few questions, it is a moot point as to whether you should read all the questions before starting to answer any one. Of course if you are given a choice, say five out of seven and the like, then it is essential to read all the questions so you can eliminate the two which are most difficult. If, however, you are asked to answer all the questions, there may be danger in trying to answer the easiest one first because you may find that you will spend too much time on it. The best technique is to answer the first question, then proceed to the second, etc.

5. Time your answers. Before the examination begins, write down the time it started, then add the time allowed for the examination and write down the time it must be completed, then divide the time available somewhat as follows:

(a) If 3½ hours are allowed, that would be 210 minutes. If you have 80 objective-type questions, that would be an average of 2½ minutes per question. Allow yourself no more than 2 minutes per question, or a total of 160 minutes, which will permit about 50 minutes to review.

(b) If for the time allotment of 210 minutes, there are 7 essay questions to answer, that would average about 30 minutes a question. Give yourself only 25 minutes per question so that you have about 35 minutes to review.

6. The most important instruction is *to read each question* and make sure you know what is wanted. The second most important instruction is to *time yourself properly* so that you answer every question. The third most important instruction is to *answer every question*. Guess if you have to but include something for each question. Remember that you will receive no credit for a blank and will probably receive some credit if you write something in answer to an essay question. If you guess a letter, say "B" for a multiple-choice question, you may have guessed right. If you leave a blank as the answer to a multiple-choice question, the examiners may respect your feelings but it will not add a point to your score.

7. Suggestions
   a. Objective-Type Questions
   (1) Examine the question booklet for proper sequence of pages and questions.
   (2) Read all instructions carefully.
   (3) Skip any question which seems too difficult; return to it after all other questions have been answered.
   (4) Apportion your time properly; do not spend too much time on any single question or group of questions.
   (5) Note and underline key words -- *all, most, fewest, least, best, worst, same, opposite*.
   (6) Pay particular attention to negatives.
   (7) Note unusual option, e.g., unduly long, short, complex, different or similar in content to the body of the question.
   (8) Observe the use of "hedging" words -- *probably, may, most likely, etc.*
   (9) Make sure that your answer is put next to the same number as the question.
   (10) Do not second-guess unless you have good reason to believe the second answer is definitely more correct.
   (11) Cross out original answer if you decide another answer is more accurate; do not erase.
   (12) Answer all questions; guess unless instructed otherwise.
   (13) Leave time for review.
   b. Essay-Type Questions
   (1) Read each question carefully.
   (2) Determine exactly what is wanted. Underline key words or phrases.
   (3) Decide on outline or paragraph answer.
   (4) Include many different points and elements unless asked to develop any one or two points or elements.
   (5) Show impartiality by giving pros and cons unless directed to select one side only.
   (6) Make and write down any assumptions you find necessary to answer the question.
   (7) Watch your English, grammar, punctuation, choice of words.
   (8) Time your answers; don't crowd material.

8. Answering the Essay Question
   Most essay questions can be answered by framing the specific response around several key words or ideas. Here are a few such key words or ideas:

M's: manpower, materials, methods, money, management;
P's: purpose, program, policy, plan, procedure, practice, problems, pitfalls, personnel, public relations.

a. Six Basic Steps in Handling Problems:
 (1) Preliminary plan and background development
 (2) Collect information, data and facts
 (3) Analyze and interpret information, data and facts
 (4) Analyze and develop solutions as well as make recommendations
 (5) Prepare report and sell recommendations
 (6) Install recommendations and follow up effectiveness

b. Pitfalls to Avoid
 (1) *Taking things for granted*
   A statement of the situation does not necessarily imply that each of the elements is necessarily true; for example, a complaint may be invalid and biased so that all that can be taken for granted is that a complaint has been registered.
 (2) *Considering only one side of a situation*
   Wherever possible, indicate several alternatives and then point out the reasons you selected the best one.
 (3) *Failing to indicate follow-up*
   Whenever your answer indicates action on your part, make certain that you will take proper follow-up action to see how successful your recommendations, procedures, or actions turn out to be.
 (4) *Taking too long in answering any single question*
   Remember to time your answers properly.

IX. AFTER THE TEST

Scoring procedures differ in detail among civil service jurisdictions although the general principles are the same. Whether the papers are hand-scored or graded by the electric scoring machine we have described, they are nearly always graded by number. That is, the person who marks the paper knows only the number -- never the name -- of the applicant. Not until all the papers have been graded will they be matched with names. If other tests, such as training and experience or oral interview ratings have been given, scores will be combined. Different parts of the examination usually have different weights. For example, the written test might count 60 percent of the final grade, and a rating of training and experience 40 percent. In many jurisdictions, veterans will have a certain number of points added to their grades.

After the final grade has been determined, the names are placed in grade order and an eligible list is established. There are various methods for resolving ties between those who get the same final grade: probably the most common is to place first the name of the person whose application was received first. Job offers are made from the eligible list in the order the names appear on it.

You will be notified of your grade and your rank order as soon as all these computations have been made. This will be done as rapidly as possible.

People who are found to meet the requirements in the announcement are called "eligibles." Their names are put on a list of eligibles. An eligible's chances of getting a job depend on how high he stands on this list and how fast agencies are filling jobs from the list.

When a job is to be filled from a list of eligibles, the agency asks for the names of people on the list of eligibles for that job.

When the civil service commission receives this request, it sends to the agency the names of the three people highest on the list. Or, if the job to be filled has specialized requirements, the office sends the agency, from the general list, the names of the top three persons who meet those requirements.

The appointing officer makes a choice from among the three people whose names were sent to him. If the selected person accepts the appointment, the names of the others are put back on the list to be considered for future openings.

That is the rule in hiring from all kinds of eligible lists, whether they are for typist, carpenter, chemist, or something else. For every vacancy, the appointing officer has his choice of any one of the top three eligibles on the list. This explains why the person whose name is on top of the list sometimes does not get an appointment when some of the persons lower on the list do. If the appointing officer chooses the No.2 or No.3 eligible, the No.1 eligible does not get a job at once, but stays on the list until he is appointed or the list is terminated.

X. HOW TO PASS THE INTERVIEW TEST

The examination for which you applied requires an oral interview test. You have already taken the written test and you are now being called for the interview test -- the final part of the formal examination.

You may think that it is not possible to prepare for an interview test and that there are no procedures to follow during an interview.

Our purpose is to point out some things you can do in advance that will help you and some good rules to follow and pitfalls to avoid while you are being interviewed.

A. WHAT IS AN INTERVIEW SUPPOSED TO TEST?

The written examination is designed to test the technical knowledge and competence of the candidate; the oral is designed to evaluate intangible qualities, not readily measured otherwise, and to establish a list showing the relative fitness of each candidate, *as measured against his competitors*, for the position sought. Scoring is not on the basis of "right" or "wrong," but on a sliding scale of values ranging from "not passable" to "outstanding." As a matter of fact, it is possible to achieve a relatively low score without a single "incorrect" answer because of evident weakness in the qualities being measured,

Occasionally, an examination may consist entirely of an oral test -- either an individual or a group oral. In such cases, information is sought concerning the technical knowledges and abilities of the candidate, since there has been no written examination for this purpose. More commonly, however, an oral test is used to supplement a written examination.

B. WHO CONDUCTS INTERVIEWS?

The composition of oral boards varies among different jurisdictions. In nearly all, a representative of the personnel department serves as chairman. One of the members of the board may be a representative of the department in which the candidate would work. In some cases, "outside experts" are used, and, frequently, a business man or some other representative of the general public is asked to serve. Labor and management or other special groups may be represented. The aim is to secure the services of experts in the appropriate field.

However the board is composed, it is a good idea (and not at all improper or unethical) to ascertain in advance of the interview who the members are and what groups they represent. When you are introduced to them, you will have some idea of their backgrounds and interests, and at least you will not stutter and stammer over their names.

C. WHAT TO DO BEFORE THE INTERVIEW

While knowledge about the board members is useful and takes some of the surprise element out of the interview, there is other preparation which is more substantive. It *is* possible to prepare for an oral -- in several ways:

1. Keep a Copy of Your Application and Review it Carefully Before the Interview

    This may be the only document before the oral board, and the starting point of the interview. Know what experience and education you have listed there, and the sequence and dates of it. Sometimes the board will ask *you* to review the highlights of your experience for them; you should not have to hem and haw doing it.

2. Study the Class Specification and the Examination Announcement

    Usually, the oral board has one or both of these to guide them. The qualities, characteristics, or knowledges required by the position sought are stated in these documents. They offer valuable clues as to the nature of the oral interview. For example, if the job involves supervisory responsibilities, the announcement will usually indicate that knowledge of modern supervisory methods and the qualifications of the candidate as a supervisor will be tested. If so, you can expect such questions, frequently in the form of a hypothetical situation which you are expected to solve. *Never* go into an oral without knowledge of the duties and responsibilities of the job you seek.

3. Think Through Each Qualification Required

    Try to visualize the kind of questions *you* would ask if you were a board member. How well could you answer them? Try especially to appraise your own knowledge and background in each area, *measured against the job sought,* and identify any areas in which you are weak. Be critical and realistic -- do not flatter yourself.

4. Do Some General Reading in Areas in Which You Feel You May be Weak

    For example, if the job involves supervision and your past experience has *not,* some general reading in supervisory methods and practices, particularly in the field of human relations, might be useful. *Do not* study agency procedures or detailed manuals. The oral board will be testing your understanding and capacity, *not* your memory.

5. Get a Good Night's Sleep and Watch Your General Health and Mental Attitude

    You will want a clear head at the interview. Take care of a cold or other minor ailment, and, of course, *no hangovers.*

13

D. *WHAT TO DO THE DAY OF THE INTERVIEW*

Now comes the day of the interview itself. Give yourself plenty of time to get there. Plan to arrive somewhat ahead of the scheduled time, particularly if your appointment is in the fore part of the day. If a previous candidate fails to appear, the board might be ready for you a bit early. By early afternoon an oral board is almost invariably behind schedule if there are many candidates, and you may have to wait. Take along a book or magazine to read, or your application to review. But leave any extraneous material in the waiting room when you go in for your interview. In any event, relax and compose yourself.

The matter of dress is important. The board is forming impressions about you -- from your experience, your manners, your attitudes, and from your appearance. Give your personal appearance careful attention. Dress your *best*, but not your flashiest. Choose conservative, appropriate clothing, and be sure it and you are immaculate. This is a business interview, and your appearance should indicate that you regard it as such. Besides, being well-groomed and properly dressed will help boost your confidence.

Sooner or later, someone will call your name and escort you into the interview room. *This is it.* From here on you are on your own. It is too late for any more preparation. But, remember, you asked for this opportunity to prove your fitness, and you are here because your request was granted.

E. *WHAT HAPPENS WHEN YOU GO IN?*

The usual sequence of events will be as follows: The clerk (who is often the board stenographer) will introduce you to the chairman of the oral board, who will introduce you to each other member of the board. Acknowledge the introductions before you sit down. Do not be surprised if you find a microphone facing you or a stenotypist sitting by. Oral interviews are usually recorded, in the event of an appeal or other review.

Usually the chairman of the board will open the interview by reviewing the highlights of your education and work experience from your application -- primarily for the benefit of the other members of the board, as well as to get the material into the record. Do not interrupt or comment unless there is an error or significant misinterpretation; if so, do not hesitate. But do not quibble about insignificant matters. Usually, also, he will ask you some question about your education, your experience, or your present job -- partly to get you started talking, to establish the interviewing "rapport." He may start the actual questioning, or turn it over to one of the other members. Frequently each member undertakes the questioning on a particular area, one in which he is perhaps most competent. So you can expect each member to participate in the examination. And because the time is limited, you may expect some rather abrupt switches in the direction the questioning takes. Do not be upset by it. Normally, a board member will not pursue a single line of questioning unless he discovers a particular strength or weakness.

After each member has participated, the chairman will usually ask whether any member has any further questions, then will ask you if you have anything you wish to add. Unless you are expecting this question, it may floor you. Or worse, it may start you off on an extended, extemporaneous speech. The board is not usually seeking more information. The question is principally to offer you a last opportunity to present further qualifications or to indicate that you have nothing to add. So, if you feel that a significant qualification or characteristic has been overlooked, it is proper to point it out in a sentence or so. Do not compliment the board on the thoroughness of their examination -- they have been sketchy, and you know it. If you wish, merely say, "No thank you, I have nothing further to add." This is a point where you can "talk yourself out" of a good impression or fail to present an important bit of information. *Remember, you close the interview yourself.*

The chairman will then say, "That is all, Mr. Smith, thank you." Do not be startled; the interview is over, and quicker than you think. Say, "Thank you and good morning," gather up your belongings and take your leave. Save your sigh of relief for the other side of the door.

F. *HOW TO PUT YOUR BEST FOOT FORWARD*

Throughout all this process, you may feel that the board individually and collectively is trying to pierce your defenses, to seek out your hidden weaknesses, and to embarrass and confuse you. Actually, this is not true. They are obliged to make an appraisal of your qualifications for the job you are seeking, and they *want to see you in your best light*. Remember, they must interview all candidates and a noncooperative candidate may become a failure in spite of their best efforts to bring out his qualifications. Here are fifteen(15) suggestions that will help you:

1. Be Natural. Keep Your Attitude Confident, But Not Cocky

If *you* are not confident that you can do the job, do not ex- expect the *board* to be. Do not apologize for your weaknesses, try to bring out your strong points. The board is interested in a positive, not a negative presentation. Cockiness will antagonize any board member, and make him wonder if you are covering up a weakness by a false show of strength.

2. Get Comfortable, But Don't Lounge or Sprawl

Sit erectly but not stiffly. A careless posture may lead the board to conclude you are careless in other things, or at least that you are not impressed by the importance of the occasion to you. Either conclusion is natural, even if incorrect. Do not fuss with your clothing, or with a pencil or an ashtray. Your hands may occasionally be useful to emphasize a point; do not let them become a point of distraction.

3. Do Not Wisecrack or Make Small Talk

This is a serious situation, and your attitude should show that you consider it as such. Further, the time of the board is limited; they do not want to waste it, and neither should you.

4. Do Not Exaggerate Your Experience or Abilities

In the first place, from information in the application, from other interviews and other sources, the board may know more about you than you think; in the second place, you probably will not get away with it in the first place. An experienced board is rather adept at spotting such a situation. Do not take the chance.

5. If You Know a Member of the Board, Do Not Make a Point of It, Yet Do Not Hide It.

Certainly you are not fooling him, and probably not the other members of the board. Do not try to take advantage of your acquaintanceship -- it will probably do you little good.

6. Do Not Dominate the Interview

Let the board do that. They will give you the clues -- do not assume that you have to do all the talking. Realize that the board has a number of questions to ask you, and do not try to take up all the interview time by showing off your extensive knowledge of the answer to the first one.

7. Be Attentive

You only have twenty minutes or so, and you should keep your attention at its sharpest throughout. When a member is addressing a problem or a question to you, give him your undivided attention. Address your reply principally to him, but do not exclude the other members of the board.

8. Do Not Interrupt

A board member may be stating a problem for you to analyze. He will ask you a question when the time comes. Let him state the problem, and wait for the question.

9. Make Sure You Understand the Question

Do not try to answer until you are sure what the question is. If it is not clear, restate it in your own words or ask the board member to clarify it for you. But do not haggle about minor elements.

10. Reply Promptly But Not Hastily

A common entry on oral board rating sheets is "candidate responded readily," or "candidate hesitated in replies." Respond as promptly and quickly as you can, but do not jump to a hasty, ill-considered answer.

11. Do Not Be Peremptory in Your Answers

A brief answer is proper -- but do not fire your answer back. That is a losing game from your point of view. The board member can probably ask questions much faster than you can answer them.

12. Do Not Try To Create the Answer You Think the Board Member Wants

He is interested in what kind of mind you have and how it works -- not in playing games. Furthermore, he can usually spot this practice and will usually grade you down on it.

13. Do Not Switch Sides in Your Reply Merely to Agree With a Board Member

Frequently, a member will take a contrary position merely to draw you out and to see if you are willing and able to defend your point of view. Do not start a debate, yet do not surrender a good position. If a position is worth taking, it is worth defending.

] Do Not Be Afraid to Admit an Error in Judgment if You Are Shown to Be Wrong

The board knows that you are forced to reply without any opportunity for careful consideration. Your answer may be demonstrably wrong. If so, admit it and get on with the interview.

15. Do Not Dwell at Length on Your Present Job

The opening question may relate to your present assignment. Answer the question but do not go into an extended discussion. You are being examined for a *new* job, not your present one. As a matter of fact, try to phrase *all* your answers in terms of the job for which you are being examined.

G. BASIS OF RATING

Probably you will forget most of these "do's" and "don'ts" when you walk into the oral interview room. Even remembering them all will not insure you a passing grade. Perhaps you did not have the qualifications in the first place. But remembering them *will* help you to put your best foot forward, without treading on the toes of the board members.

Rumor and popular opinion to the contrary notwithstanding, an oral board wants you to make the best appearance possible. They know you are under pressure -- but they also want to see how you respond to it as a guide to what your reaction would be under the pressures of the job you seek. They will be influenced by the degree of poise you display, the personal traits you show, and the manner in which you respond.

EXAMINATION SECTION

EXAMINATION SECTION

TEST 1

DIRECTIONS: Each question or incomplete statement is followed by several suggested answers or completions. Select the one that BEST answers the question or completes the statement. *PRINT THE LETTER OF THE CORRECT ANSWER IN THE SPACE AT THE RIGHT.*

1. Which of the following basic listening skills is pre-requisite to the others?
    A. Identifying stated main ideas
    B. Making generalizations
    C. Drawing conclusions
    D. Comparing different points of view

1. __A__

2. Which of the following factors is the MOST important indication of a child's readiness for reading?
    A. Motor development   B. Maturational age
    C. Physical development   D. Chronological age

2. __B__

Questions 3-4.

DIRECTIONS: Read the passage below from MYTHOLOGY, and then answer Questions 3 and 4.

The first written record of Greece is the ILIAD. Greek mythology begins with Homer, generally believed to be not earlier than a thousand years before Christ. The ILIAD is, or contains, the oldest Greek literature; and it is written in a rich and subtle and beautiful language which must have had behind it centuries when men were striving to express themselves with clarity and beauty, an indisputable proof of civilization. The tales of Greek mythology do not throw any clear light upon what early mankind was like - a matter, it would seem, of more importance to us, who are their descendants intellectually, artistically, and politically, too. Nothing we learn about them is alien to ourselves.

3. Which line from the passage is a statement of fact?
    A. The tales of Greek mythology do not throw any clear light upon what early mankind was like.
    B. Nothing we learn about them is alien to ourselves.
    C. It is written in a rich and subtle and beautiful language which must have had behind it centuries when men were striving to express themselves with clarity and beauty.
    D. The ILIAD is, or contains, the oldest Greek literature.

3. __D__

4. The author's point of view toward the subject of this passage is one of
    A. humorous indulgence   B. respect and admiration
    C. tongue-in-cheek flattery   D. longing and nostalgia

4. __B__

5. Which of the following sentences is capitalized   5.
CORRECTLY?
   A. My aunt told Uncle Leon about the documentary she
      saw at the Biograph Theater.
   B. In the Southern Hemisphere, the first day of winter
      is in june.
   C. The Riveras plan to spend their vacation in California
      at Yosemite national Park.
   D. Gloria's room had an Eastern exposure, and the sun
      woke her up at dawn.

6. Which sentence demonstrates proper pronoun-antecedent   6. D
   agreement?
   A. The council of officials has announced his decision.
   B. All public parks will close its gates at 5:00 P.M.
   C. All wardens must report to her stations by 5:15 P.M.
   D. Workers in public parks must display their identifi-
      cation cards.

7. Which of the following is a compound sentence?   7. A
   A. Sonya painted the sign, and I did the lettering.
   B. Without a dictionary, I couldn't check my spelling.
   C. No one noticed the mistakes until this morning.
   D. Of twelve words on the sign, three were misspelled.

8.   8. B

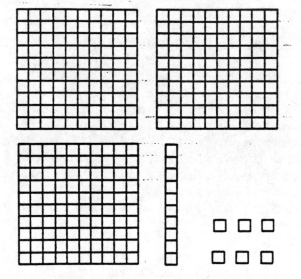

What number is represented above?
   A. 136   B. 316   C. 361   D. 631

9. Marcy is practicing for a track meet. Each day she runs   9. C
   around a quarter-mile track two and one-half times.
   How many miles does she run in five days?
   ____ miles.
   A. 5/8   B. 1¼   C. 3 1/8   D. 12½

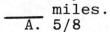

.20 x 12.95 + .20 x 23.95

10. Everything in a hardware store is being sold at 20 percent   10. B
    off the regular price. Mark bought a garden hose regularly
    priced at $12.95 and a wheelbarrow regularly priced at
    $23.95.
    What operations are needed to calculate how much Mark had
    to pay?
       A. Divide 0.20 by $23.95 and add $12.95
       B. Add $12.95 and $23.95 and multiply the sum by 0.8
       C. Multiply $23.95 by 0.20 and add $12.95
       D. Subtract $12.95 from $23.95 and multiply by 0.2

11. How many lines of symmetry does an equilateral triangle   11. C
    have?
       A. One   B. Two   C. Three   D. Four

12. Humans are responsible for the extinction of other   12. D
    species PRIMARILY through
       A. environmental pollution
       B. experimental hybridization
       C. hunting and poaching
       D. habitat destruction

13. Replacement of a cold air mass by a warm air mass is   13. A
    usually FIRST indicated by the formation of which cloud
    type?
       A. Cirrus   B. Cumulonimbus
       C. Cumulus   D. Stratus

Road Clouds

14. Edward is writing a brief report on specific examples   14. D
    of extreme weather conditions in the United States.
    Which of the following pieces of information would be
    MOST relevant to his report?
       A. A hurricane is defined as a storm in which winds
          blow at greater than 74 miles per hour near the
          storm center.
       B. The highest temperature ever recorded was in Libya
          in 1922; it was 136 degrees Fahrenheit.
       C. In the Texas panhandle, snowfall averages about
          2 feet each year.
       D. The greatest rainfall ever recorded in 1 minute was
          1.23 inches; it occurred in Unionville, Maryland.

15. In the United States, all citizens have the responsibility   15. C
    to
       A. petition the government
       B. exercise freedom of religion
       C. serve on juries
       D. determine the rate of income tax

16.

16. A

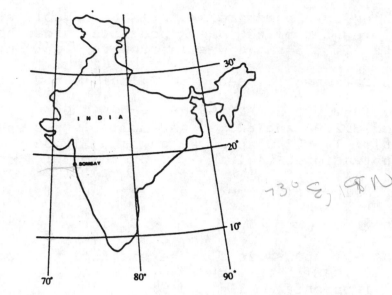

73°E, 19°N

According to the map above, Bombay, India, is located at
APPROXIMATELY which longitude and latitude?
Longitude ____; latitude ____.
  A. 73°E; 19°N   B. 21°N; 73°E
  C. 73°E; 21°N   D. 19°N; 73°E

17. The Monroe Doctrine was intended to   17. C
      A. promote commercial relations with the Concert of
         Europe
      B. protect American sailors from involuntary service
      C. prevent European expansion in Latin America
      D. open the southeastern United States to settlement

18. Which of the following activities would be MOST helpful   18. B
    for a sixth grader in developing his or her individual
    response to art?
      A. Matching artistic techniques to artworks
      B. Participating in a critique of various artworks
      C. Matching artists to their works
      D. Learning terminology associated with art criticism

KEY (CORRECT ANSWERS)

1.	A	10.	B
2.	B	11.	C
3.	D	12.	D
4.	B	13.	A
5.	A	14.	D
6.	D	15.	C
7.	A	16.	A
8.	B	17.	C
9.	C	18.	B

TEST 2

1. At the early elementary level, which of the following activities would be MOST appropriate for developing fine-motor skills?
   A. Tying shoelaces
   B. Pushing a swing
   C. Throwing a ball
   D. Skipping rope

1. A

2. When educationally disadvantaged students enter school, the problems they face are MOST often a function of
   A. traumatic childhood incidents
   B. an inability to think clearly in solving problems
   C. overemphasis on achievement
   D. a lack of exposure to positive, varied experiences

2. D

3. Which of the following criteria is MOST important in determining whether a given learning opportunity is appropriate for an elementary class?
   A. Levels of cognitive and psychomotor development among students
   B. Content of available textbooks
   C. Usefulness of the subject matter in life outside the classroom
   D. Testing programs in use at the school

3. A

4. Which of the following is MOST important for a teacher to consider when selecting materials for a specific lesson?
   A. Relationship to learner objectives
   B. Popularity of the material
   C. Relationship to the teacher's personal interests
   D. Publisher of the material

4. A

5. Recent data from nationwide standardized tests show that students in the Alpha school district scored below average in mathematics skills.
   Based on these data, which is the MOST appropriate short-term goal for this school district?
   A. Emphasize higher-level skills in mathematics
   B. Assess students' strengths and weaknesses in reading
   C. Improve Alpha's curriculum in reading and mathematics
   D. Compare the Alpha curriculum with those of other districts

5. A

6. A class has just read *Jack and the Beanstalk*.
Which of the following questions would be MOST appropriate
for a teacher to ask if the objective of the lesson is
to teach interpretive reading skills?
   A. How many times did Jack climb the beanstalk?
   B. Who planted the beanstalk?
   C. What did Jack do before he climbed the beanstalk?
   D. Why did Jack climb the beanstalk the third time?

6. _D_

7. In the scope and sequence of social studies skills, the
emphasis of objectives in the elementary grades tends to
follow a progression from
   A. history to politics
   B. self to family to community
   C. culture to economics
   D. world to nation to neighborhood

7. _B_

8. A teacher notes that on a particular multiple-choice test
item, about the same number of students chose each of the
four responses.
This MOST likely means that the
   A. item was too easy for the students
   B. students did not follow the directions
   C. item had two correct responses
   D. students were guessing at the answer

8. _D_

9. One advantage of essay tests as compared with multiple-
choice tests is that essay tests
   A. are more easily standardized
   B. allow for more creative responses
   C. can be completed in a shorter period of time
   D. are easier to score

9. _B_

10. When using a criterion-referenced test, student test
scores should be compared with
   A. average statewide scores
   B. scores of other students
   C. a preset standard of mastery
   D. national norms

10. _C_

11. Which of the following should be the FIRST step in
teaching material related to a new learning objective?
   A. Assign related readings
   B. Give a preview of new vocabulary
   C. Present the necessary information
   D. Explain the purpose of the lesson

11. _D_

12. A teacher plans to teach students how to locate resources
in the school library.
How could the teacher approach this objective using
didactic methodology?
   A. Encourage independent exploration to discover how
      library materials are organized
   B. Have students find materials through a process of
      trial and error

12. _C_

    C. Teach one skill at a time and provide frequent
       practice
    D. Give students a self-directed guide to using the
       library

13. A teacher has passed out reading material with a brief   13. C
    glossary of new words.
    The BEST way to ensure that students understand the new
    words is to assign the students to
        A. circle the new words where they occur in the text
        B. read the material aloud to each other
        C. write sentences using the new words
        D. arrange the new words in alphabetical order

14. Good rapport between students and teachers is MOST likely   14. D
    to occur in classrooms in which
        A. rules are permissive
        B. students determine the pace of instruction
        C. decisions are made democratically
        D. teacher expectations are clear and reasonable

15. Which of the following is the MOST effective way to   15. A
    manage instruction for an elementary class involving
    students with a wide range of ability?
        A. Divide the class into small groups according to level
        B. Use the same materials for all students to challenge
           the weaker ones
        C. Assign extra work to those students who are furthest
           behind
        D. Work directly with the weakest students and ask
           others to work on their own

16. When applying discipline in an elementary school class-   16. C
    room, it is MOST important for the teacher to be
        A. compassionate   B. firm and strong
        C. consistent   D. broad-minded

17. In the school system, a MAJOR function of setting long-   17. A
    range educational goals is to
        A. provide overall direction for the curriculum
        B. make sure parents know what their children are
           learning
        C. find out what students need to learn
        D. eliminate repetition from one grade to another

18. According to the Family Educational Rights and Privacy   18. B
    Act, also known as the Buckley Amendment, parents have
    the right to
        A. select the public schools their children will attend
        B. inspect and review their children's educational records
        C. withhold information about their children from school
           officials
        D. attend classes with their children to monitor progress

KEY (CORRECT ANSWERS)

1.	A	10.	C
2.	D	11.	D
3.	A	12.	C
4.	A	13.	C
5.	A	14.	D
6.	D	15.	A
7.	B	16.	C
8.	D	17.	A
9.	B	18.	B

———

EXAMINATION SECTION

DIRECTIONS: Each question or incomplete statement is followed by several suggested answers or completions. Select the one that BEST answers the question or completes the statement. *PRINT THE LETTER OF THE CORRECT ANSWER IN THE SPACE AT THE RIGHT.*

Questions 1-5.

DIRECTIONS: In the following word groups, the *italicized* word at the left is followed by four lettered words or expressions. In each group, select the word or expression that MOST NEARLY defines the italicized word. *PRINT THE LETTER OF THE CORRECT ANSWER IN THE SPACE AT THE RIGHT.*

1. *Reluctance*   1. B
   A. relief   B. unwillingness
   C. forgetfulness   D. measure of light

2. *Relevant*   2. C
   A. brotherly   B. disappearing
   C. appropriate   D. ascending

3. *Mediator*   3. B
   A. lawyer   B. intermediary
   C. expert   D. official

4. *Jovial*   4. D
   A. kingly   B. flattering
   C. stern   D. jolly

5. *Ominous*   5. A
   A. threatening   B. large
   C. in transit   D. inclusive

Questions 6-10.

DIRECTIONS: In each of the following groups, one sentence contains an *italicized* word which makes the sentence INCORRECT. Select this sentence and print the letter in the space at the right.

6. A. Congress *retrenched* its expenses by adding millions   6. A
to the harbor improvement bill.
  B. Thoreau found a way to *obviate* his dependence on money; he simplified his needs.
  C. Under feudalism, an accepted *hierarchy* of social obligations made for political stability.
  D. Long reflection, rather than sudden inspiration, is the *germinating* soil of great poetry.

7. A. The circus fat man is known as a man of *infinitesimal* bulk.
    B. The opening chapter of a mystery story contains *subtle* indications of the final outcome.
    C. A *tyro* sometimes surprises everyone by defeating the most experienced player.
    D. *Sporadic* outbursts of gunfire could be heard throughout the night.

    7. ___

8. A. His *infallibility* was the reason for his many errors and omissions.
    B. A soupy fog *encompassed* the huddled buildings of the big city.
    C. Efforts to *adjudicate* the disagreement were rejected by both parties.
    D. The development of his fortune was detailed in *chronological* order.

    8. ___

9. A. Atomic energy can be used effectively in the *desalinization* of ocean water.
    B. It was surprising that anyone should take *umbrage* at his joking remark.
    C. The conflicting points of view were at length *suffused* by the efforts of mediators.
    D. The guard's failure to appear was a *dereliction* of duty.

    9. ___

10. A. He *arrogated* to himself the privilege of selecting his successor.
    B. Many treaties provide for the *secession* of areas of land to one nation by another.
    C. His sweeping generalizations failed to *delineate* the problem.
    D. The legislature's failure to act on pollution was considered *deleterious* to the welfare of the people.

    10. ___

Questions 11-15.

DIRECTIONS: In each of the groups of four words, one is misspelled. Find the misspelled word in each group and print the letter of the CORRECT answer in the space at the right.

11. A. efficient   B. received
    C. incandescent   D. indefatigible

    11. ___

12. A. gossip   B. seige
    C. resistance   D. inoculate

    12. ___

13. A. orthadox   B. probably
    C. coarse   D. least

    13. ___

14. A. euphoria   B. felon
    C. vengence   D. morgue

    14. ___

15. A. oweing   B. cancel
    C. satisfactorily   D. communication

    15. ___

3

Questions 16-20.

DIRECTIONS: In each of the following groups of sentences, one of the four sentences is faulty in capitalization, punctuation, grammar, sentence structure, diction, etc. Select the INCORRECT sentence in each case and print the letter in the space at the right.

16. A. This list supersedes all previous notices.   16. _D_
    B. Unlike Susan, Frances has a calm disposition.
    C. The census report indicates that the village had fewer inhabitants in 1970 than in 1960.
    D. "Drive carefully," he warned. Speed is the cause of most accidents."

17. A. When I see John, I shall urge him to vote.   17. _D_
    B. The tyrant was hanged in effigy.
    C. The cinnamon bun tastes sweet.
    D. Turning the corner, the Leaning Tower came into view.

18. A. The reason for his illness is because he caught cold. 18. _A_
    B. Jack's brother said, "I don't think Jack will accept the nomination."
    C. Old people will feel the full effects of this ruling.
    D. Neither is a very competent secretary.

19. A. Get here at once - we need you!   19. _D_
    B. We gladly welcomed the Reverend John Baxter, D.D.
    C. We packed suits, dresses, coats, etc.
    D. He flouted the law, irregardless of its justice.

20. A. Football may be played in sunshine, snow, and when it rains. 20. _A_
    B. I'll be glad to enroll for that course, provided I get college credit for it.
    C. TALES OF A TRAVELER is among Washington Irving's best collections of short stories.
    D. Her manner, albeit disconcerting, is understandable.

Questions 21-75.

DIRECTIONS: In each of the following, select the one of the four lettered choices which will make the sentence *most nearly* CORRECT. Print the letter of the correct answer in the space at the right.

21. A ship's surgeon finds himself shipwrecked on the island   21. _B_
    of Lilliput in the novel
        A. THE PIRATE. . . . . Sir Walter Scott
        B. GULLIVER'S TRAVELS. . . . Jonathan Swift
        C. RODERICK RANDOM . . . . . Tobias Smollett
        D. BRIGHTON ROCK . . . . . . Graham Greene

22. The following musicals are all correctly matched with   22. _A_
    the work upon which they are based EXCEPT
        A. My Fair Lady . . . . . . CANDIDA
        B. Dear World . . . . THE MADWOMAN OF CHAILLOT
        C. Carousel. . . . . LILIOM
        D. Man of La Mancha . . . . DON QUIXOTE

23. "For fools rush in where angels fear to ____"
    The word omitted in the above line by Alexander Pope is
       A. walk   B. stride   C. tread   D. go
                                                          23. C

24. All of the following were famous collaborators EXCEPT
       A. Rodgers and Hart   B. Keats and Shelley
       C. Wordsworth and Coleridge D. Gilbert and Sullivan
                                                           24. B

25. "Hitch your wagon to a star" is a quotation from a work by
       A. Ralph W. Emerson   B. David Thoreau
       C. James R. Lowell   D. Horace Mann
                                              25. A

26. An American writer of sea stories that are set in the South Pacific is
       A. Joseph Conrad   B. Somerset Maugham
       C. William James   D. Herman Melville
                                              26. D

27. APOLOGY, CRITO, PHAEDO, and REPUBLIC are dialogues by
       A. Plato   B. Aristotle   C. Euripides   D. Menander
                                              27. A

28. THE SHOES OF THE FISHERMAN by Morris West is
       A. an account of St. Peter and the Early Church
       B. the story of a Russian who became Bishop of Rome
       C. a biography of Izaak Walton
       D. a tale about a Japanese spy in World War II
                                              28. B

29. The story in which a man is condemned to the Bastille
    because of his knowledge of the cruel treatment offered
    a peasant family is found in
       A. THE CRIME OF SYLVESTRE BONNARD. . . Anatole France
       B. THE PLAGUE . . . . Albert Camus
       C. A TALE OF TWO CITIES. . . . . . . Charles Dickens
       D. A LOST LADY . . . . Willa Cather
                                              29. C

30. All of the following deal mainly with the theme of war
    EXCEPT
       A. JOURNEY'S END . . . . Robert C. Sherriff
       B. IDIOT'S DELIGHT . . . . Robert E. Sherwood
       C. HEARTBREAK HOUSE . . . . George B. Shaw
       D. THE SKIN OF OUR TEETH . . . . . . Thornton Wilder
                                              30. D

31. Each of the following Black leaders is correctly matched
    with an activity for which he became famous EXCEPT
       A. Frederick Douglass . . . writer
       B. Thurgood Marshall . . . first Black Justice of the
                              Supreme Court
       C. Nat Turner . . . . leader of a slave insurrection
                              in Virginia in the 1830's
       D. Ralph Bunche . . . . . President of Tuskegee Institute
                                              31. D

32. Each of the following organizations was created by the
    United Nations EXCEPT the
       A. International Civil Aviation Organization
       B. International Labor Organization
       C. Food and Agricultural Organization
       D. World Health Organization
                                              32. B

5

33. All of the following are famous straits EXCEPT   33. A
    A. Voringfoss   B. Dardanelles
    C. Bosporus   D. Gibraltar

34. Each of the following men was, at one time, a Chief   34. A
    Justice of the United States Supreme Court EXCEPT
    A. George C. Marshall   B. William Howard Taft
    C. Salmon P. Chase   D. John Jay

35. When census officials refer to the *missing Americans*, they   35. B
    are speaking of
    A. prisoners of war
    B. the many Black citizens uncounted in the 1960 census
    C. middle-class people who refuse to fill out the census
       forms
    D. the silent majority

36. Each of the following present or former prime ministers   36. A
    is matched correctly with his country EXCEPT
    A. Jomo Kenyatta . . . . . Republic of South Africa
    B. Pierre Trudeau . . . . . Canada
    C. Ian Smith . . . . Rhodesia
    D. Edward Heath . . . . . Great Britain

37. The section of Nigeria which recently failed to gain its   37. D
    independence in a civil war is known as
    A. Basutoland B. Burundi   C. Mali   D. Biafra

38. The Mayor of New York has the power to   38. D
    A. fix the annual tax rate
    B. appoint the President of the City Council
    C. veto a budget adopted by the Board of Estimate and
       the City Council
    D. appoint the head of the Fire Department

39. Each of the following is a trend of our current economy   39. A
    EXCEPT
    A. a significant decrease in unemployment
    B. an increase in inflationary pressures
    C. high bank interest rates
    D. a decrease in the purchasing value of the dollar

40. The conduct of foreign affairs is entrusted by the   40. C
    American Constitution to the
    A. Secretary of State
    B. Senate's Committee on Foreign Affairs
    C. President
    D. House of Representatives

41. The rate of metabolism in the human body is MOST closely   41. D
    associated with the activity of the
    A. adrenal glands   B. stomach
    C. pancreas   D. thyroid

42. A planet that has the fastest orbital speed around the   42. B
    sun is
    A. Pluto   B. Mercury   C. Jupiter   D. Neptune

43. The nutrient that is MOST useful for growth and repair of body cells is
    A. fats   B. sugar   C. starch   D. protein

43. D

44. Each of the following instruments is correctly associated with what it measures EXCEPT
    A. anemometer . . . . precipitation
    B. hygrometer . . . . humidity
    C. barograph . . . . air pressure
    D. seismograph . . . . . . earthquakes

44. A

45. All of the following statements concerning magnetism are correct EXCEPT:
    A. Any object that is attracted by a magnet becomes a magnet itself while in contact with the real magnet
    B. Like poles repel each other
    C. When a bar magnet is bent into a horsehoe, its strength increases
    D. When a bar magnet is cut in two, it loses one of its poles

45. D

46. The term *shuttlecock* refers to the object the players hit or strike at in the game of
    A. badminton   B. golf   C. hockey   D. tennis

46. A

47. Of the following ways of viewing a solar eclipse, the SAFEST is
    A. through sunglasses
    B. by looking through clear plastic
    C. indirectly
    D. through smoked glass

47. C

48. In tennis, the MINIMUM number of games necessary to complete a regulation set is
    A. two   B. four   C. six   D. eight

48. C

49. In the human circulatory system, the blood vessels that carry the blood AWAY from the heart is called
    A. veins   B. capillaries
    C. valves   D. arteries

49. D

50. All of the dances indicated below are correctly paired with their country of origin EXCEPT
    A. Tarantella . . . . Spain
    B. Troika . . . . Russia
    C. La Raspa . . . . Mexico
    D. Circassian Circle . . . . United States

50. A

51. A song in a minor key *usually* ends on
    A. do   B. sol   C. la   D. re

51. C

52. The YOUNG PERSON'S GUIDE TO THE ORCHESTRA was composed by
    A. Bernstein   B. Britten
    C. Kleinsinger   D. Prokofiev

52. B

53. The following are all sung in the MIKADO EXCEPT
    A. Three Little Maids From School
    B. I've Got a Little List
    C. I'm Called Little Buttercup
    D. Tit-Willow

53. C

54. A dot following a note increases the note's value
    A. to twice its original value
    B. by an extra beat
    C. to three times its original value
    D. by half of its original value

54. D

55. All of the following composers are noted for their frequently produced operas EXCEPT
    A. Mozart   B. Haydn   C. Puccini   D. Wagner

55. B

56. Chichén Itzá, Monte Albán, and Mitla are Latin American sites renowned for
    A. displaying giant sculptural forms during the Olympic Games of recent years
    B. modern housing developments near Mexico City
    C. their ancient universities
    D. pre-Columbian (Hispanic) architecture

56. D

57. Of the following artists, the one known for his painting, BIRTH OF VENUS, depicting a beautiful maiden rising from a shell, is
    A. Fra Angelico   B. Cellini
    C. Botticelli   D. Raphael

57. C

58. Sargent, Lawrence, Stuart, and Van Dyke
    A. were Greenwich Village artists circa 1915
    B. are well known for their portraits
    C. were members of the Dutch School of artists
    D. are known for introducing distorted objects into their paintings

58. B

59. On the Acropolis in Athens stand the remains of a glorious Greek temple known as the
    A. Parthenon   B. Onias   C. Pantheon   D. Karnak

59. A

60. Claude Monet, Camille Pissarro, and Auguste Renoir are generally classified as
    A. Dadaists   B. Impressionists
    C. Abstractionists   D. pottery makers

60. B

61. A store ran a sale, marking everything at 75% of the original price. A dress was sold at the sale for $48.00. Its original price was
    A. $36.00   B. $60.00   C. $64.00   D. $75.00

61. C

62. A roast requires 20 minutes of cooking time per pound. If the roast weighs 6 pounds and 12 ounces and is placed in the oven at 4:30 P.M., it should be ready at ____ P.M.
    A. 6:10   B. 6:45   C. 6:52   D. 7:22

62. B

63. The group which contains a number that is NOT prime is   63. A
    A. 21, 23, 29, 31   B. 11, 13, 17, 19
    C. 2, 3, 5, 7   D. 37, 41, 43, 47

64. A recipe for syrup calls for 1½ cups of sugar to 3/4 cup   64. C
of boiling water. Mrs. Jones has only 1 cup of sugar.
She should use ____ cup of boiling water.
    A. 1/4   B. 1/3   C. 1/2   D. 5/6

65. If John is younger than 20 years of age and Mary is   65. B
younger than 10 years of age, we may conclude that
    A. John is younger than Mary
    B. the combined ages of John and Mary cannot exceed 30
    C. John is twice as old as Mary
    D. John is older than Mary

66. A man drives 90 miles at an average of 30 miles per hour   66.
and returns to his starting point at an average of 45 miles
per hour.
His average rate for the round trip is ____ m.p.h.
    A. 40   B. 37½   C. 36   D. 34

67. A baseball team has won 50 of the 75 games played thus   67. C
far. There are 120 games in the entire season.
How many more games must the team win to end with an
average of 80% won?
    A. 40   B. 45   C. 46   D. 50

68. A bank customer borrowed $600 for one month. He paid   68. B
$3.00 interest.
What is the rate of interest for the month?
    A. .05%   B. .5%   C. 5%   D. 50%

69. The number missing in the series 3, 4, 7, 12, ____, 28 is   69. B
    A. 17   B. 19   C. 21   D. 22

70. A man left an estate of $24,000. According to his will,   70. C
10% went to a college, 15% to a hospital, with the remainder
to be shared equally by four nieces.
Each niece received
    A. $2,000   B. 3,600   C. $4,500   D. $6,000

71. A teacher wishes to show 30% of the circle on a circular   71. D
graph.
The central angle of that sector must be
    A. 50°   B. 54°   C. 90°   D. 108°

72. Of the packaged cereals listed below, all of equal quality,   72.
the MOST economical is
    A. 6 oz. for 15¢   B. 14 oz. for 34¢
    C. 1 lb. 3 oz. for 48¢   D. 2 lbs. for 75¢

73. The MOST common explanation given by the young addict for   73. C
drug usage is
    A. an unstable family life
    B. that the problems of life fade away
    C. that it leads to acceptance by peers
    D. the thrill of committing an illegal act

74. The glue sniffer may *usually* be recognized by   74. D
    A. the way he picks sores constantly
    B. the way he licks his lips frequently
    C. his animated behavior with rapid, loud talking
    D. the odor of the substance inhaled on his breath or the clothes

75. The odor of marijuana smoke is frequently described as   75. B
    A. sour   B. sweetish   C. pungent   D. irritating

KEY (CORRECT ANSWERS)

1. B	16. D	31. D	46. A	61. C
2. C	17. D	32. B	47. C	62. B
3. B	18. A	33. A	48. C	63. A
4. D	19. D	34. A	49. D	64. C
5. A	20. A	35. B	50. A	65. B
6. A	21. B	36. A	51. C	66. C
7. A	22. A	37. D	52. B	67. C
8. A	23. C	38. D	53. C	68. B
9. C	24. B	39. A	54. D	69. B
10. B	25. A	40. C	55. B	70. C
11. D	26. D	41. D	56. D	71. D
12. B	27. A	42. B	57. C	72. D
13. A	28. B	43. D	58. B	73. C
14. C	29. C	44. A	59. A	74. D
15. A	30. D	45. D	60. B	75. B

EXAMINATION SECTION
LANGUAGE USAGE

TEST 1
SPELLING

DIRECTIONS

This test is composed of a series of words. Some of them are correctly spelled; some are incorrectly spelled. You are to indicate whether each word is spelled right or wrong by blackening the proper space on the separate Answer Sheet. If the spelling of the word is **right,** fill in the space under RIGHT. If it is spelled **wrong,** fill in the space under WRONG. Use C for correct; W for wrong.

EXAMPLES   SAMPLE OF ANSWER SHEET

W. man

X. gurl

Y. catt

Z. dog

If you finish Part I before time is called, check your work. Do not go on to Part II until you are told to do so.

mostly rushing

1. apointed
2. commission
3. limited
4. arival
5. comunity
6. variety
7. agentcy
8. distrubute
9. hereafter
10. conference
11. salery
12. preveous
13. colusion
14. director
15. essential
16. cilinder
17. astablish
18. quarrel
19. premeum
20. relize
21. gratitude
22. sugestion
23. consinment
24. revenue
25. inferier
26. condem
27. absolutely
28. cancel
29. carreer
30. bullitin
31. oposition
32. ammunition
33. survay
34. energey
35. sundery
36. visinity
37. sheriff
38. pamflet
39. conserning
40. securety
41. necessity
42. expences
43. testomony
44. avalable
45. stating
46. courtesy
47. naturaly
48. apoligy
49. invilid
50. construction

2

51. secratary w

duh ✗52. duplacate r

53. gosple w

54. traffic r

55. captian w

56. sanatary w

57. specimen r

58. accommodate r

59. Sabbath r

60. consious w

61. athority w

62. owing r

63. emergancy w

64. opperation w

65. sylable w

66. talant w

67. nourish r

68. ignorence w

69. behavor w

70. exceedingly r

71. murmer w

duh ✗72. signiture r signature

73. guardian r

74. interrupt r

75. congradulate w

76. deploma w

duh ✗77. abundent r abundant

78. tedious r

79. dilegent w

✗80. aquainted r acquainted

81. resonable w

82. customery w

? — 83. muslin r

muslum 84. investagation w

85. temperary w

86. indignant r

87. wretched r

88. unusal w

89. definate w

✗90. garrulous ⇐ right

91. allowence w

92. appropriate r

93. rememberance w

94. presense w

? ✗95. caisson right

96. appendicitis r

97. convienient w

98. occured w

99. intuition intuit

100. greatful w

Spelling
KEY (CORRECT ANSWERS)

1. W	41. C	81. W
2. C	42. W	82. W
3. C	43. W	83. C
4. W	44. W	84. W
5. W	45. C	85. W
6. C	46. C	86. C
7. W	47. W	87. C
8. W	48. W	88. W
9. C	49. W	89. W
10. C	50. C	90. C
11. W	51. W	91. W
12. W	52. W	92. C
13. W	53. W	93. W
14. C	54. C	94. W
15. C	55. W	95. C
16. W	56. W	96. C
17. W	57. C	97. W
18. C	58. C	98. W
19. W	59. C	99. C
20. W	60. W	100. W
21. C	61. W	
22. W	62. C	
23. W	63. W	
24. C	64. W	
25. W	65. W	
26. W	66. W	
27. C	67. C	
28. C	68. W	
29. W	69. W	
30. W	70. C	
31. W	71. W	
32. C	72. W	
33. W	73. C	
34. W	74. C	
35. W	75. W	
36. W	76. W	
37. C	77. W	
38. W	78. C	
39. W	79. W	
40. W	80. W	

4

LANGUAGE USAGE

TEST 2
SENTENCES

DIRECTIONS

This test consists of a series of sentences, each divided into five parts lettered A, B, C, D, and E. You are to look at each and decide which of the lettered parts have errors in grammar, punctuation or spelling. When you have decided which parts are wrong, fill in the space under those letters after that item number on the separate Answer Sheet.

EXAMPLE   SAMPLE OF ANSWER SHEET

Ain't we / going to the / office / next week / at all.
  A   B   C   D   E

A	B	C	D	E
▌	⋮	⋮	⋮	▌

The space under A has been filled in because "ain't" is wrong; the space under E has been blackened because "at all" should be followed by a question mark. There is nothing wrong in Parts B, C and D, so the spaces under those letters have been left blank.

Some of the sentences are entirely correct. Others may have from **one** to **five** parts wrong. For each part of each sentence which you think is wrong, blacken the space under that letter on the separate Answer Sheet.

1. Where / did you / stop at / on your trip / to Chicago.
   A   B   C   D   E

2. Was it / him / who / got burned / when the boiler bursted?
   A   B   C   D   E

3. The dog laid / sleeping / after chasing John and I / with hardly no / time out.
   A   B   C   D   E

4. I doubt / if Jack / has fewer / than sixteen / baseball bats.
   A   B   C   D   E

5. "It is me," / said Will, / as his mother / answered / his knock.
   A   B   C   D   E

6. If I were / he, / I'd be / sure / of myself.
   A   B   C   D   E

7. I could / of won / if I had stood / in the game / a little longer.
   A   B   C   D   E

8. If John were here / he'd sure / have done / faster work / than Fred.
   A   B   C   D   E

9. I can't hardly / raise my hand / more than / three foot / above the board.
   A   B   C   D   E

10. I sung / until / I was hoarse, / and then drunk / a quart of water.
    A   B   C   D   E

11. Neither money / or fame / would of been / alright as payment / for such a job.
    A   B   C   D   E

12. I don't understand / how anyone / could admire / a person as careless / as her.
    A   B   C   D   E

13. Is it / I / whom / they / are calling?
    A   B   C   D   E

14. I didn't feel / good enough / to attend / the conference / last tuesday.
    A   B   C   D   E

15. I did / pretty good / in history / on last / week's quizzes.
    A   B   C   D   E

16. Her father replied / "I feel / that Carol / is some better / than Mary."
    A   B   C   D   E

17. The rivers raised / ten feet / after the rains, / overflowing / their banks.
    A   B   C   D   E

18. I thought / you was through / doing / your work / all ready.
    A   B   C   D   E

19. We O.K.'d / there proposal / that we cooperate / for our / mutual profit.
    A   B   C   D   E

20. The writer / made / an illusion / to his hero's / earlier exploits.
    A   B   C   D   E

21. I don't like / those kind / of peaches; / give me some / of the ripe ones.
    A   B   C   D   E

22. Leave / me go / with John / and she / to the show.
    A   B   C   D   E

23. He is / one of those men / who works / well / and long.   correct
    A   B   C   D   E

24. James said, / "Work, / not words, / is what / is needed."
    A   B   C   D   E

25. None of the books / were / worth reading / more then / once or twice.
    A   B   C   D   E

6

26. They / nearly were / starved / before they landed / somewheres in Florida.
    A   B   C   D   E

27. She / got hurt / when the dish / busted / in her hands.
    A   B   C   D   E

28. I thought it / was him, / and it sure / looked like him / from this distance.
    A   B   C   D   E

29. Who / do you / think / your / talking about?
    A   B   C   D   E

30. The number / of volunteers / were / seldom ever / enough.
    A   B   C   D   E

31. One issue of bonds / were / distributed / between / three banks.
    A   B   C   D   E

32. There goes / John and Bill, / fighting / like / always.
    A   B   C   D   E

33. Is it / me / who / you wanted / to see?
    A   B   C   D   E

34. I don't see / as good / as Tom, / my friend / can.
    A   B   C   D   E

35. Paul had / promised / to return / the book / in two weeks.
    A   B   C   D   E

36. The man who / everybody likes / is one / who / they can trust.
    A   B   C   D   E

37. He asked / we three, / "where / is the folks / which lived here?"
    A   B   C   D   E

38. I've had / less headaches / since I / went to sleep / earlier.
    A   B   C   D   E

39. The books / laid / in the grass / all day / and got wet.
    A   B   C   D   E

40. You can / leave the house / in an hour / if you feel / good.
    A   B   C   D   E

41. I will / be real glad / to visit you / whenever / you would prefer.
    A   B   C   D   E

42. The bible / is one / of the best books / their / are for serious study.
    A   B   C   D   E

43. Each of / these flowers / look best / in a different / sort of a plot.
    A   B   C   D   E

44. We allways turn / to who / we use to / know. the old friend / is best.
    A   B   C   D   E

45. Being that / a pipe bust, / we hadn't / hardly / any water.
    A   B   C   D   E

46. He had smoked / their tobacco, / drank their wine / and heard / their tales.
    A   B   C   D   E

47. A man, / who beats his wife, / is considered depraved / by people / nowadays.
    A   B   C   D   E

48. We seldom ever / have to / watch close / in our kind / of a job.
    A   B   C   D   E

49. If it was possible, / we would of / gave him / the workers / which he wanted.
    A   B   C   D   E

50. Neither Jones / nor Smith / are / the men / for that sort of a job.
    A   B   C   D   E

7

Language Usage
KEY (CORRECT ANSWERS)

1. C		41. BE	
2. BDE		42. DE — wrong	
3. ACDE		43. CE	
4. B		44. ABD	
5. A		45. ABCD	
6. Correct		46. Correct	
7. BC		47. AE wrong	
8. BD		48. ACE	
9. AD		49. ABCE	
10. AD		50. E wrong	

11. BCD
12. E
13. C
14. BE
15. B

16. AD
17. A
18. BE
19. AB
20. C

21. B
22. AD
23. Correct
24. Correct
25. BD

26. BE
27. BD
28. BC
29. D
30. CD

31. BD
32. AD
33. B
34. BC
35. Correct

36. A
37. BDE ← wrong
38. B
39. B
40. E

EXAMINATION SECTION
LANGUAGE USAGE

TEST 1
SPELLING

DIRECTIONS

This test is composed of a series of words. Some of them are correctly spelled; some are incorrectly spelled. You are to indicate whether each word is spelled right or wrong by blackening the proper space on the separate Answer Sheet. If the spelling of the word is **right,** fill in the space under RIGHT. If it is spelled **wrong,** fill in the space under WRONG. Use C for correct; W for wrong.

EXAMPLES

W. man

X. gurl

Y. catt

Z. dog

SAMPLE OF ANSWER SHEET

	RIGHT	WRONG
W	▌	⦙
X	⦙	▌
Y	⦙	▌
Z	▌	⦙

1. instrement W
2. administration C
3. expedition C
4. abilaty W
5. coperate W
6. attitude C
7. distinguish C
8. liable C
9. conected W
10. charety W
11. corespond W
12. defieance W
13. secureing W
14. gallant C
15. voluntery W
16. misary W
17. completely C
18. intensity C
19. corperation W
20. imitation W
21. genius C
22. oppertunity W
23. styleish W
24. afection W
25. nonsense C

26. consequence C
27. merit C
28. usualy W
29. decloration W
30. seinor W
31. insurence W
32. regestration W
33. athletic C
34. distant C
35. shepard W
36. compond W
37. comercial W
38. campain W
39. insolent C
40. capeable W
41. contence W
42. obsticle W
43. recipe C
44. vertue W
45. compansate W
46. sufficient C
47. discourge W
48. delecate W
49. curculation W
50. prior C

2

51. legeslature W
52. cristal W
53. imortal W
54. advertiseing W
55. accompany C
56. executive C
57. posibility W
58. civilazation W
59. atractive W
60. criticism C
61. simester W
62. scarlit W
63. memorandum C
64. lovable C
65. document C
66. referance W
67. asure W
68. garantee W
69. conclued W
70. curcumstance W
71. vulgar C
72. uttmost W
73. readly W
74. inquirey W
75. sacrafice W

76. remedy C
77. reciept W
78. employement W
79. prelimanary W
80. sarcastic C
81. antisipate W
82. underware W
83. sensable W
84. patent C
85. indulgence C
86. representitive W
87. herewith C
88. warrent W
89. responsability W
90. forfeit C
91. preperation W
92. morgage C
93. ordinarally W
94. heretofore C
95. recomendation W
96. duely W
97. similar Simila
98. intellegence W
99. accelerate C
100. dilemma C

3

KEY (CORRECT ANSWERS)

1. W		41. W		81. W	
2. C		42. W		82. W	
3. C		43. C		83. W	
4. W		44. W		84. C	
5. W		45. W		85. C	
6. C		46. C		86. W	
7. C		47. W		87. C	
8. C		48. W		88. W	
9. W		49. W		89. W	
10. W		50. C		90. C	
11. W		51. W		91. W	
12. W		52. W		92. W	
13. W		53. W		93. W	
14. C		54. W		94. C	
15. W		55. C		95. W	
16. W		56. C		96. W	
17. C		57. W		97. C	
18. C		58. W		98. W	
19. W		59. W		99. C	
20. C		60. C		100. C	
21. C		61. W			
22. W		62. W			
23. W		63. C			
24. W		64. C			
25. C		65. C			
26. C		66. W			
27. C		67. W			
28. W		68. W			
29. W		69. W			
30. W		70. W			
31. W		71. C			
32. W		72. W			
33. C		73. W			
34. C		74. W			
35. W		75. W			
36. W		76. C			
37. W		77. W			
38. W		78. W			
39. C		79. W			
40. W		80. C			

LANGUAGE USAGE

TEST 2
SENTENCES

DIRECTIONS

This test consists of a series of sentences, each divided into five parts lettered A, B, C, D, and E. You are to look at each and decide which of the lettered parts have errors in grammar, punctuation or spelling. When you have decided which parts are wrong, fill in the space under those letters after that item number on the separate Answer Sheet.

EXAMPLE   SAMPLE OF ANSWER SHEET

Ain't we / going to the / office / next week / at all.

A   B   C   D   E

A	B	C	D	E
▮	᠁	᠁	᠁	▮

The space under A has been filled in because "ain't" is wrong; the space under E has been blackened because "at all" should be followed by a question mark. There is nothing wrong in Parts B, C and D, so the spaces under those letters have been left blank.

Some of the sentences are entirely correct. Others may have from **one** to **five** parts wrong. For each part of each sentence which you think is wrong, blacken the space under that letter on the separate Answer Sheet.

1. I looked / everywheres, / but couldn't / find / but six pencils.
      A   B   C   D   E

2. If the ball team / don't listen / to the coach, / they will / lose the game.
      A   B   C   D   E

3. No one / never / told me / who / the winner was.
      A   B   C   D   E

4. Sit / the saucepan / on the fire, / but don't / let it burn.
      A   B   C   D   E

5. The money was / divided / equally / among / John and Frank.
      A   B   C   D   E

6. Neither / the coat / nor the hat / is / yours.
      A   B   C   D   E

7. Each of us / has / their own burdens / to bear / in this world.
      A   B   C   D   E

8. I generally always / go to church / on Sunday / in my neighbor's / sedan.
      A   B   C   D   E

9. A book / or a radio / provide a good / evening's entertainment / for anyone.
      A   B   C   D   E

10. Tony had / already / made a few / pictures with his / candid camera.
      A   B   C   D   E

11. I shall / learn / him not / to steal / off me.
      A   B   C   D   E

12. Mary rang / all the water / from the towel / before she hanged / it up.
      A   B   C   D   E

13. Do you / agree / with the plan / their proposing / for the office?
      A   B   C   D   E

14. I won't do / the work without / he leaves me / do it / my own way.
      A   B   C   D   E

15. There / are people / which think / entirely too well / of theirselves.
      A   B   C   D   E

16. I'll let / you in / on a secret, just / between you, I, / and the lamppost.
      A   B   C   D   E

17. If you were / he, / could / you drink / that liquid?
      A   B   C   D   E

18. Each mother / thinks / their / own child is / most pretty.
      A   B   C   D   E

19. I shall / excuse / whoever / is successful / in the examination.
      A   B   C   D   E

20. Speaking serious, / do you think / Bill is / getting along / good?
      A   B   C   D   E

21. I don't want / no lunch, / on account of / I just / ate.
      A   B   C   D   E

22. "Mary is / the best cook / of the two," / said Jane / to her father.
      A   B   C   D   E

23. I come / near guessing / whom / he thought / had phoned.
      A   B   C   D   E

24. There's / the boys / who / I saw / talking.
      A   B   C   D   E

25. Neither Frances nor Betty / is willing / to leave / the book / alone.
           A   B   C   D   E

26. He don't care / whether / or not / he sells / his merchandise.
    A   B   C   D   E

27. They lay / the carpet / on the floor / yesterday / about 2 P M.
    A   B   C   D   E

28. "Look," he said / after a while, / why don't you / start a / sort of scrapbook"?
    A   B   C   D   E

29. Us people / could of / set / their / for allways.
    A   B   C   D   E

30. John and me / worked until / we couldn't hardly / stand / at all.
    A   B   C   D   E

31. I am sure / it was her / who they expected / would win / the race.
    A   B   C   D   E

32. I was / real sorry / to hear / she acted / different.
    A   B   C   D   E

33. We didn't like / him working / only / when the boss / was there.
    A   B   C   D   E

34. "For goodness' sake," / said Mary / "Is that / the Times's / leading article?"
    A   B   C   D   E

35. He saw a man / whom / he thought / was me, / but it wasn't.
    A   B   C   D   E

36. An increase in the sale / of radios and irons / are expected / by them / and I.
    A   B   C   D   E

37. Mary is / the tallest / of the twins, / and the prettiest / as well.
    A   B   C   D   E

38. If you want / to learn / watch / real / close.
    A   B   C   D   E

39. The meeting / looked like / it would / end up / in a fight.
    A   B   C   D   E

40. If she / was older, / she could do / the work / easier.
    A   B   C   D   E

41. Every boy and girl / thought they / done better / then / anyone else.
    A   B   C   D   E

42. I had swam / in most every pool / around here / both large / and small ones.
    A   B   C   D   E

43. It / was them / we set / with / on the lawn.
    A   B   C   D   E

44. Are / either of you / the owner / of a set of books which / give the facts?
    A   B   C   D   E

45. I don't / expect as / either of you / are the / best man.
    A   B   C   D   E

46. Can / John / and me / borrow / them tools?
    A   B   C   D   E

47. Your / easy / as good as / them at / busting records.
    A   B   C   D   E

48. There's / less / good roads / in Mexico / than New York.
    A   B   C   D   E

49. When a jury / hand in a verdict, / they / are dismissed / immediately.
    A   B   C   D   E

50. Your / liable / to get hurt / if your careless / around machinery.
    A   B   C   D   E

7

KEY (CORRECT ANSWERS)

1. BE
2. ABD
3. B
4. A
5. D

6. Correct
7. C
8. A
9. C
10. C

11. BE
12. AD
13. D
14. BC
15. CDE

16. D
17. Correct
18. CE
19. C
20. AE

21. BCDE
22. B
23. AB
24. A
25. C

26. A
27. Correct
28. ABE wrong
29. ABCDE
30. ACE

31. B
32. BE
33. B
34. BC
35. D

36. CE
37. BD
38. BDE
39. BD
40. BE

41. BCD
42. ABCDE
43. ABC
44. A
45. BDE

46. CE
47. ABDE
48. B
49. BCD
50. D

SPELLING
EXAMINATION SECTION
TEST 1

DIRECTIONS: In each of the following tests in this part, select the letter of the one MISSPELLED word in each of the following groups of words. *PRINT THE LETTER OF THE CORRECT ANSWER IN THE SPACE AT THE RIGHT.*

-1" correct

1. A. grateful   B. fundimental   1. B
   C. census   D. analysis

2. A. installment   B. retrieve   2. D
   C. concede   D. dissapear

3. A. accidentaly   B. dismissal   3. A
   C. conscientious   D. indelible

4. A. perceive   B. carreer   C. anticipate   D. acquire   4. B

5. A. facillity   B. reimburse   C. assortment   D. guidance   5. A

6. A. plentiful   B. across   6. C
   C. advantagous   D. similar

7. A. omission   B. pamphlet   C. guarrantee   D. repel   7. C

8. A. maintenance   B. always   8. D
   C. liable   D. anouncement

9. A. exaggerate   B. sieze   C. condemn   D. commit   9. B

10. A. pospone   B. altogether   C. grievance   D. excessive   10. A

11. A. banana   B. trafic   C. spectacle   D. boundary   11. B

12. A. commentator   B. abbreviation   12. C
    C. battaries   D. monastery

13. A. practically   B. advise   13. C
    C. pursuade   D. laboratory

14. A. fatigueing   B. invincible   14. A
    C. strenuous   D. ceiling

15. A. propeller   B. reverence   C. piecemeal   D. underneth   15. D

16. A. annonymous   B. envelope   C. transit   D. variable   16. A

17. A. petroleum   B. bigoted   C. meager   D. resistence   17. D -
    resistance

18. A. permissible   B. indictment   18. C
    C. fundemental   D. nowadays

19. A. thief   B. bargin   C. nuisance   D. vacant   X19. A
20. A. technique   B. vengeance   C. aquatic   D. heighth   C 20. D

TEST 2

1. A. apparent   B. superintendent   1 C
   C. releive   D. calendar
2. A. foreign   B. negotiate   C. typical   D. disipline   2. D
3. A. posponed   B. argument   3. A
   C. susceptible   D. deficit
4. A. preferred   B. column   C. peculiar   D. equiped   4. D
5. A. exaggerate   B. disatisfied   5. B
   C. repetition   D. already
6. A. livelihood   B. physician   C. obsticle   D. strategy   6 C
7. A. courageous   B. ommission   C. ridiculous   D. awkward   7. B
8. A. sincerely   B. abundance   C. negligable   D. elementary   8 C
9. A. obsolete   B. mischievous   9. D
   C. enumerate   D. atheletic
10. A. fiscel   B. beneficiary   10. A
    C. concede   D. translate
11. A. segregate   B. excessivly   C. territory   D. obstacle   11. B
12. A. unnecessary   B. monopolys   12. B
    C. harmonious   D. privilege
13. A. sinthetic   B. intellectual   13. A
    C. gracious   D. archaic
14. A. beneficial   B. fulfill   C. sarcastic   D. disolve   14. D
15. A. umbrella   B. sentimental   15. C
    C. inefficent   D. psychiatrist
16. A. noticable   B. knapsack   C. librarian   D. meant   16. A
17. A. conference   B. upheaval   C. vulger   D. odor   17 C
18. A. surmount   B. pentagon   C. calorie   D. inumerable   18. D
19. A. classifiable   B. moisturize   19. D
    C. monitor   D. assesment
20. A. thermastat   B. corrupting   C. approach   D. thinness   20 A

2

TEST 3

1. A. typical   B. descend   C. summarize   D. continuel   1. _D_

2. A. courageous   B. recomend   C. omission   D. eliminate   2. _B_

3. A. compliment   B. illuminate   3. _C_
    C. auxilary   D. installation

4. A. preliminary   B. aquainted   4. _B_
    C. syllable   D. analysis
                                      analysis

5. A. accustomed   B. negligible C. interupted   D. bulletin   5. _C_

6. A. summoned   B. managment   C. mechanism   D. sequence   6. _B_

7. A. commitee   B. surprise   C. noticeable   D. emphasize   7. _A_

8. A. occurrance   B. likely   C. accumulate   D. grievance   8. _A_

9. A. obstacle   B. particuliar   9. _B_
    C. baggage   D. fascinating

10. A. innumerable   B. seize   10. _D_
    C. applicant   D. dictionery

11. A. monkeys   B. rigid   C. unnatural   D. roomate   11. _D_

12. A. surveying   B. figurative C. famous   D. curiosety   12. _D_

13. A. rodeo   B. inconcievable   13. _B_
    C. calendar   D. magnificence

14. A. handicaped   B. glacier   C. defiance   D. emperor   14. _A_

15. A. schedule   B. scrawl   C. seclusion   D. sissors   15. _D_

16. A. tissues   B. tomatos   C. tyrants   D. tragedies   16. _B_

17. A. casette   B. graceful   C. penicillin   D. probably   17. _A_

18. A. gnawed   B. microphone C. clinicle   D. batch   18. _C_

19. A. amateur   B. altitude   C. laborer   D. expence   19. _D_

20. A. mandate   B. flexable   C. despise   D. verify   20. _B_

TEST 4

1. A. primery   B. mechanic   C. referred   D. admissible   1. _A_

2. A. cessation   B. beleif   C. aggressive   D. allowance   2. _B_

3. A. leisure   B. authentic   3. _C_
    C. familiar   D. contemptable

familiar
familar

3

4. A. volume   B. forty   C. dilemma   D. seldum   4. D

5. A. discrepancy   B. aquisition   5. B
    C. exorbitant   *discrepancy*   D. lenient

6. A. simultanous   B. penetrate   6. A
    C. revision   D. conspicuous

7. A. ilegible   B. gracious   C. profitable   D. obedience   7. A

8. A. manufacturer   B. authorize   8. D
    C. compelling   D. pecular

9. A. anxious   B. rehearsal   C. handicaped   D. tendency   9. C

10. A. meticulous   B. accompaning   10. B
    C. initiative   D. shelves

11. A. hammaring   B. insecticide   11. A
    C. capacity   D. illogical

12. A. budget   B. luminous   C. aviation   D. lunchon   12. D

13. A. moniter   B. bachelor   13. A
    C. pleasurable   D. omitted

14. A. monstrous   B. transistor C. narrative   D. anziety   14. D

15. A. engagement B. judical   C. pasteurize   D. tried   15. B

16. A. fundimental   B. innovation   16. A
    C. perpendicular   D. extravagant

17. A. bookkeeper B. brutality   C. gymnaseum   D. cemetery   17. C

18. A. sturdily   B. pretentious   18. D
    C. gourmet   D. enterance

19. A. resturant   B. tyranny   19. A
    C. kindergarten   D. ancestry

20. A. benefit   B. possess   C. speciman   D. noticing   20. C

TEST 5

1. A. arguing   B. correspondance   1. B
    C. forfeit   D. dissension

2. A. occasion   B. description   2. D
    C. prejudice   D. elegible

3. A. accomodate B. initiative C. changeable   D. enroll   3. A
    accommodate

4

4. A. temporary   B. insistent   C. benificial   D. separate   4. C

5. A. achieve   B. dissappoint   *disappoint*   5. B
    C. unanimous   D. judgment

6. A. procede   B. publicly   C. sincerity   D. successful   6. A

7. A. deceive   B. goverment   C. preferable   D. repetitive   7. B

8. A. emphasis   B. skillful   C. advisible   D. optimistic   8. C

9. A. tendency   B. rescind   C. crucial   D. noticable   9. D

10. A. privelege   B. abbreviate   C. simplify   D. divisible   10. A

11. A. irresistible   B. varius   11. B
    C. mutual   D. refrigerator

12. A. amateur   B. distinguish   12. D
    C. rehearsal   D. poision

13. A. biased   B. ommission   C. precious   D. coordinate X13. A

14. A. calculated   B. enthusiasm   C. sincerely   D. parashute   14. D

15. A. sentry   B. materials   C. incredable   D. budget   15. C

16. A. chocolate   B. instrument   C. volcanoe   D. shoulder   16. C

17. A. ancestry   B. obscure   C. intention   D. ninty   17. D

18. A. artical   B. bracelet   C. beggar   D. hopeful   18. A

19. A. tournament   B. sponsor   19. C
    C. perpendiclar   D. dissolve

20. A. yeild   B. physician   C. greasiest   D. admitting   20. A

TEST 6

1. A. achievment   B. maintenance   C 1. A
    C. questionnaire   D. all are correct

2. A. prevelant   *prewelen*   B. pronunciation   X 2. D
    C. separate   *separ* *prewelant*   D. all are correct

3. A. permissible   B. relevant   X 3. A
    C. seize   D. all are correct

4. A. corroborate   B. desparate   4. B
    C. eighth   D. all are correct

5

5. A. exceed   B. feasibility   5. C
    C. psycological   D. all are correct

6. A. parallel   B. aluminum   C. calendar   D. eigty   6. D

7. A. microbe   B. ancient   C. autograph   D. existance   7. D

8. A. plentiful   B. skillful   C. amoung   D. capsule   8. C

9. A. erupt   B. quanity   C. opinion   D. competent   9. B

10. A. excitement   B. discipline   C. luncheon   D. regreting   10. D

11. A. magazine   B. expository   C. imitation   D. permenent   11. D

12. A. ferosious   B. machinery   12. A
    C. precise   D. magnificent

13. A. conceive   B. narritive   C. separation   D. management   13. B

14. A. muscular   B. witholding   C. pickle   D. glacier   14. B

15. A. vehicel   B. mismanage   15. A
    C. correspondence   D. dissatisfy

16. A. sentince   B. bulletin   C. notice   D. definition   16. A

17. A. appointment   B. exactly   17. C
    C. typest   D. light

18. A. penalty   B. suparvise   C. consider   D. division   18. B

19. A. schedule   B. accurate   C. corect   D. simple   19. C

20. A. suggestion   B. installed   C. proper   D. agincy   20. D

TEST 7

1. A. symtom   B. serum   C. antiseptic   D. aromatic   1. A

2. A. register   B. registrar   C. purser   D. burser   2. D C

3. A. athletic   B. tragedy   C. batallion   D. sophomore   3. B

4. A. latent   B. godess   C. aisle   D. whose   4. B

5. A. rhyme   B. rhythm   C. thime   D. thine   5. A
                                        rhyme

6. A. eighth   B. exaggerate   C. electorial   D. villain   6. D
                                                        villian

7. A. statute   B. superintendent   7. C
    C. iresistible   D. colleague

6

8. A. sieze   B. therefor   C. auxiliary   D. changeable   8. B

9. A. siege   B. knowledge   C. lieutenent   D. weird   9. D

10. A. acquitted   B. polititian   C. professor   D. conqueror   10. B

11. A. changeable   B. chargeable   C. salable   D. useable   11. D

12. A. promissory   B. prisoner   C. excellent   D. tyrrany   12. D

13. A. conspicuous   B. essance   13. B
    C. comparative   D. brilliant

14. A. notefying   B. accentuate   C. adhesive   D. primarily   14. A

15. A. exercise   B. sublime   C. stuborn   D. shameful   15. C

16. A. presume   B. transcript   C. strech   D. wizard   16. C

17. A. specify   B. regional   17. D
    C. arbitrary   D. segragation

18. A. requirement   B. happiness   18. D
    C. achievement   D. gentlely

19. A. endurance   B. fusion   C. balloon   D. enormus   19. P

20. A. luckily   B. schedule   C. simplicity   D. sanwich   20. D

TEST 8

1. A. maintain   B. maintainance   1. B
   C. sustain   D. sustenance

2. A. portend   B. portentious   ? × 2. ___
   C. pretend   D. pretentious

3. A. prophesize   B. prophesies   D × 3. A
   C. farinaceous   D. spaceous

4. A. choose   B. chose   C. choosen   D. chasten   4. C

5. A. censure   B. censorious   5. D
   C. pleasure   D. pleasurible

6. A. cover   B. coverage   C. adder   D. adege   6. D

7. A. balloon   B. diregible   C. direct   D. descent   7. B

8. A. whemsy   B. crazy   C. flimsy   D. lazy   8. A

9. A. derision   B. pretention   C. sustention   D. contention   9. C

7

10. A. question   B. questionaire   ? 10.___
     C. legion   D. legionary

11. A. chattle   B. cattle   C. dismantle   D. kindle   11. A

12. A. canal   B. cannel   C. chanel   D. colonel   12. B
                                  channel

13. A. hemorrage B. storage   C. manage   D. foliage   13. A

14. A. surgeon   B. sturgeon   C. luncheon   D. stancheon ? 14. D

15. A. diploma   B. commission C. dependent   D. luminious ? 15. D

16. A. likelihood B. blizzard   C. machanical D. suppress   16. C

17. A. commercial B. releif   C. disposal   D. endeavor   17. B

18. A. operate   B. bronco   C. excaping   D. grammar   18. C

19. A. orchard   B. collar   C. embarass   D. distant   19. C

20. A. sincerly   B. possessive C. weighed   D. waist   20. A

TEST 9

1.   A. statute   B. stationary   ? 1. C
     C. staturesque   D. stature

2.   A. practicible   B. practical   ? 2. A
     C. particle   D. reticule

3.   A. plague   B. plaque   C. ague   D. aigrete   3. C

4.   A. theology B. idealogy   C. psychology D. philology   4. D

5.   A. dilema   B. stamina   C. feminine   D. strychnine 5. A

6.   A. deceit   B. benefit   C. grieve   D. hienous   6. D

7.   A. commensurable   B. measurable   7. C
     C. duteable   D. salable

8.   A. homogeneous   B. heterogeneous   8. D
     C. advantageous   D. religeous

9.   A. criticize B. dramatise   C. exorcise   D. exercise   9. B

10. A. ridiculous B. comparable C. merciful   D. cotten   10. D

11. A. antebiotic B. stitches   C. pitiful   D. sneaky   11. A

12. A. amendment   B. candadate   12. B
     C. accountable   D. recommendation

13. A. avocado   B. recruit   C. tripping   D. probally   13. D

14. A. calendar   B. desirable   C. familar   D. vacuum   14. C

15. A. deteriorate   B. elligible   15. B
     C. liable   D. missile

16. A. amateur   B. competent   16. D
     C. mischeivous   OCCASSKN   D. occasion

17. A. friendliness   B. saleries   17. B
     C. cruelty   D. ammunition

18. A. wholesome   B. cieling   C. stupidity   D. eligible   18. B

19. A. comptroller   B. traveled   ~ 19. D
     C. accede   D. procede

20. A. Britain   B. Brittainica   20. B
     C. conductor   D. vendor

TEST 10

1.   A. lengthen   B. region   C. gases   D. inspecter   1. D

2.   A. imediately   B. forbidden   2. A
     C. complimentary   D. aeronautics

3.   A. continuous   B. paralel   C. opposite   D. definite   3. B

4.   A. Antarctic   B. Wednesday   C. Febuary   D. Hungary   4. C

5.   A. transmission   B. exposure   5. D
     C. pistol   D. customery

6.   A. juvinile   B. martyr   6. A
     C. deceive   D. collaborate

7.   A. unnecessary   B. repetitive   7. D
     C. cancellation   D. airey

8.   A. transit   B. availible   C. objection   D. galaxy   8. B

9.   A. ineffective   B. believeable   9. B
     C. arrangement   D. aggravate

10. A. possession   B. progress   C. reception   D. predjudice   10. D

11. A. congradulate   B. percolate   11. A
     C. major   D. leisure

12. A. convenience   B. privilige   12. B
     C. emerge   D. immerse

9

13. A. erasable   B. inflammable   X13. A
     C. audable   *audible*   D. laudable

14. A. final   B. fines   C. finis   D. Finish *Finnish*   X14. C

15. A. emitted   B. representative   15. D
     C. discipline   D. insistance

16. A. diphthong   B. rarified *rarefied*   C. library   D. recommend   X16. A
                          rar

17. A. compel   B. belligerent   17. D
     C. successful   D. sargeant *sto sargeant*

18. A. dispatch B. dispise C. dispose D. dispute 18. B

19. A. administrator   B. adviser   19. D
     C. diner   D. celluler

20. A. ignite B. ignision C. igneous D. ignited 20. B

TEST 11

saxophone

1. A. repellent B. secession C. sebaceous D. saxaphone X 1 B

2. A. navel   B. counteresolution   2. B
    C. marginalia   D. perceptible

3. A. Hammerskjold   B. Nehru   ? 3. D
    C. U Thamt *UThant*   D. Khrushchev
                           krush

4. A. perculate   B. periwinkle   A   4. C
    C. perigee *bucanoer* D. retrogression

5. A. buccaneer B. tobacco C. Buffalo D. oscilate *oscillate* ? X5. A

6. A. siege B. wierd *Weird* C. seize D. cemetery X6. A

7. A. equaled   B. bigoted *kaleidoscope cemetery*   7. C
    C. benefited *benefitted* D. kaleideoscope
                equalle

8. A. blamable   B. bullrush *bullrush seige*   ? 8. C
    C. questionnaire   D. irascible *blami*

9. A. tobagganed   B. acquiline *aquiline*   X9. A
    C. capillary   D. cretonne

10. A. daguerrotype   B. elegiacal   10. A
    C. iridescent   D. inchoate

11. A. bayonet   B. braggadocio *connoisseur* ? X11. B
    C. corollary   D. connoiseur

10

12.   A. equinoctial   B. fusillade   ?D   12. _A_
        C. fricassee   D. potpouri   *pot pouri*

13.   A. octameter   B. impressario   B   13. _A_
        C. hyetology   D. hieroglyphics

14.   A. innanity   B. idyllic   C. fylfot   D. inimical   14. _A_

15.   A. liquefy   B. rarefy   C. putrify   D. sapphire   C   15. _A_
       liquify

16.   A. canonical   B. stupified   B   16. _A_
        C. millennium   D. memorabilia

17.   A. paraphenalia   B. odyssey   A   17. _D_
        C. onomatopoeia   D. osseous

18.   A. peregrinate   B. pecadillo   B   18. _C_
        C. reptilian   D. uxorious

19.   A. pharisaical   B. vicissitude   D   19. _A_
        C. puissance   D. wainright

20.   A. holocaust   B. tesselate   C. scintilla   D. staccato   ?20. _B_

TEST 12

1.   A. questionnaire   B. gondoleer   1. _B_
       C. chandelier   D. acquiescence

2.   A. surveillence   B. surfeit   D   2. _D_
       C. vaccinate   D. belligerent   *belligerent*

3.   A. occassionally   *occasionally*   B. recurrence   3. _A_
       C. silhouette   D. incessant

4.   A. transferral   B. benefical   *beneficial*   4. _B_
       C. descendent   D. dependent

5.   A. separately   B. flouresence   *fluorescence*   5. _B_
       C. deterrent   *deterrant*   D. parallel

6.   A. acquittal   B. enforceable   *enforable*   D   6. _B_
       C. counterfeit   D. indispensible

7.   A. susceptible   B. accelarate   *accelerate*   7. _B_
       C. exhilarate   D. accommodation

8.   A. impedimenta   B. collateral   *maison*   8. _D_
       C. liason   D. epistolary

9.   A. inveigle   B. panegyric   C. reservoir   D. manuver   D   ?9. _A_
             manuver   *maneuver*

10. A. synopsis   B. parephernalia   10.B
     C. affidavit   D. subpoena

11. A. grosgrain   B. vermilion   C. abbatoir   D. connoiseur   11.B

12. A. gabardine   B. camoflage   Ç. hemorrhage   D. contraband   12.C
                  vermillion
                  Camoflauge

13. A. opprobrious   B. defalcate   ? 13.C
     C. fiduciery   D. recommendations
           hemorrage
           fiduciary

14. A. nebulous   B. necessitate *neces* ?14.C
     C. impricate   D. discrepancy *discrepency*

15. A. discrete   B. condesension   15.B
     C. condign   D. condiment *condescen*

16. A. cavalier   B. effigy   16.C
     C. legitimatly   D. misalliance

17. A. rheumatism   B. vaporous   17.B
     C. cannister   D. hallucinations

18. A. paleonthology   B. octogenarian   18.A
     C. gradient   D. impingement

19. A. fusilade   B. fusilage   C. ensilage   D. desiccate   *desic* 19.D

20. A. rationale   B. raspberry   C. reprobate   D. varigated   20.?
                  vari

KEY (CORRECT ANSWERS)

Tests 1-6

TEST 1

1. B. fundamental
2. D. disappear
3. A. accidentally
4. B. career
5. A. facility

6. C. advantageous
7. C. guarantee
8. D. announcement
9. B. seize
10. A. postpone

11. B. traffic
12. C. batteries
13. C. persuade
14. A. fatiguing
15. D. underneath

16. A. anonymous
17. D. resistance
18. C. fundamental
19. B. bargain
20. D. height

TEST 2

1. C. relieve
2. D. discipline
3. A. postponed
4. D. equipped
5. B. dissatisfied

6. C. obstacle
7. B. omission
8. C. negligible
9. D. athletic
10. A. fiscal

11. B. excessively
12. B. monopolies
13. A. synthetic
14. D. dissolve
15. C. inefficient

16. A. noticeable
17. C. vulgar
18. D. innumerable
19. D. assessment
20. A. thermostat

TEST 3

1. D. continual
2. B. recommend
3. C. auxiliary
4. B. acquainted
5. C. interrupted

6. B. management
7. A. committee
8. A. occurrence
9. B. particular
10. D. dictionary

11. D. roommate
12. D. curiosity
13. B. inconceivable
14. A. handicapped
15. D. scissors

16. B. tomatoes
17. A. cassette
18. C. clinical
19. D. expense
20. B. flexible

TEST 4

1. A. primary
2. B. belief
3. D. contemptible
4. D. seldom
5. B. acquisition

6. A. simultaneous
7. A. illegible
8. D. peculiar
9. C. handicapped
10. B. accompanying

11. A. hammering
12. D. luncheon
13. A. monitor
14. D. anxiety
15. B. judicial

16. A. fundamental
17. C. gymnasium
18. D. entrance
19. A. restaurant
20. C. specimen

TEST 5

1. B. correspondence
2. D. eligible
3. A. accommodate
4. C. beneficial
5. B. disappoint

6. A. proceed
7. B. government
8. C. advisable
9. D. noticeable
10. A. privilege

11. B. various
12. D. poison
13. B. omission
14. D. parachute
15. C. incredible

16. C. volcano
17. D. ninety
18. A. article
19. C. perpendicular
20. A. yield

TEST 6

1. A. achievement
2. A. prevalent
3. D all are correct
4. B. desperate
5. C. psychological

6. D. eighty
7. D. existence
8. C. among
9. B. quantity
10. D. regretting

11. D. permanent
12. A. ferocious
13. B. narrative
14. B. withholding
15. A. vehicle

16. A. sentence
17. C. typist
18. B. supervise
19. C. correct
20. D. agency

13

3

TEST 7

1. A. symptom
2. D. bursar
3. C. battalion
4. B. goddess
5. C. thyme
6. C. electoral
7. C. irresistible
8. A. seize
9. C. lieutenant
10. B. politician
11. D. usable
12. D. tyrany
13. B. essence
14. A. notifying
15. C. stubborn
16. C. stretch
17. D. segregation
18. D. gently
19. D. enormous
20. D. sandwich

TEST 8

1. B. maintenance
2. B. portentous
3. D. spacious
4. C. chosen
5. D. pleasurable
6. D. adage
7. B. dirigible
8. A. whimsy
9. B. pretension
10. B. questionnaire
11. A. chattel
12. C. channel
13. A. hemorrhage
14. D. stanchion
15. D. luminous
16. C. mechanical
17. B. relief
18. C. escaping
19. C. embarrass
20. A. sincerely

-14

TEST 9

1. C. statuesque
2. A. practicable
3. D. aigrette
4. B. ideology
5. A. dilemma
6. D. heinous
7. C. dutiable
8. D. religious
9. B. dramatize
10. D. cotton
11. A. antibiotic
12. B. candidate
13. D. probably
14. C. familiar
15. B. eligible
16. C. mischievous
17. B. salaries
18. B. ceiling
19. D. proceed
20. B. Brittanica

TEST 10

1. D. inspector
2. A. immediately
3. B. parallel
4. C. February
5. D. customary
6. A. juvenile
7. D. airy
8. B. available
9. B. believable
10. D. prejudice
11. A. congratulate
12. B. privilege
13. C. audible
14. D. Finnish
15. D. insistence
16. B. rarefied
17. D. sergeant
18. B. despise
19. D. cellular
20. B. ignition

TEST 11

1. D. saxophone
2. B. counterresolution
3. C. U Thant
4. A. percolate
5. D. oscillate
6. B. weird
7. D. kaleidoscope
8. B. bulrush
9. B. aquiline
10. A. daguerreotype
11. D. connoisseur
12. D. potpourri
13. B. impresario
14. A. inanity
15. C. putrefy
16. B. stupefied
17. A. paraphernalia
18. B. peccadillo
19. D. wainwright
20. B. tessellate

TEST 12

8

1. B. gondolier
2. A. surveillance
3. A. occasionally
4. B. beneficial
5. B. fluorescence
6. D. indispensable
7. B. accelerate
8. C. liaison
9. D. maneuver
10. B. paraphernalia
11. D. connoisseur
12. B. camouflage
13. C. fiduciary
14. C. imprecate
15. B. condescension
16. C. legitimately
17. C. canister
18. A. paleontology
19. A. fusillade
20. D. variegated

EXAMINATION SECTION

DIRECTIONS: Each question or incomplete statement is followed by several suggested answers or completions. Select the one that BEST answers the question or completes the statement. *PRINT THE LETTER OF THE CORRECT ANSWER IN THE SPACE AT THE RIGHT.*

- 5 out of 35
T = The Book was wrong

Questions 1-10.

DIRECTIONS: Some of the following groups of words make correct, complete sentences. Others contain errors or are not complete sentences. If the group of words makes a correct, complete sentence, indicate 0 (ZERO). If the group of words does not make a correct, complete sentence, indicate the letter of the part which contains the error or which should be changed to make a complete sentence.

1. (A) No one   (B) knows   (C) why he came   (D) or where he went.   1. _0_

2. (A) What do you   (B) think   (C) is the answer   (D) to the problem?   2. _0_

3. (A) What   (B) fun to be   (C) on the   (D) relay team!   3. _B_

4. (A) Hope   (B) to win   (C) the next set   (D) of races.   4. _A_

5. (A) The class giving   (B) a play   (C) for parents   (D) and friends.   5. _A_

6. (A) How   (B) exciting   (C) winning   (D) would be!   6. _0_

7. (A) Richard   (B) likes   (C) swimming and to water ski   (D) in the summer.   7. _C_

8. Charles   (A) has played   (B) football for   (C) three years and   (D) will again next year.   8. _D_

9. He likes   (A) all sports the coach   (B) says Charles is the best   (C) all-round athlete   (D) the school has ever had.   9. _A_

10. (A) Although the weather   (B) is cold,   (C) we can see (D) signs of nature's reawakening.   10. _0_

Questions 11-25.

DIRECTIONS: In each sentence below, one or more letters are
               underlined. Indicate C (CORRECT) or W (WRONG) in
               the space at the right of each sentence in which
               the letter or letters underlined are CORRECTLY
               capitalized.

11. Tom learned much about the sea from captain Jones.   11. W

12. Dear sir: 12. W

13. Will you please send us information about tours through   13. W
     the east? I am especially interested in seeing

14. india and the   14. W

15. Taj Mahal.   15. C

16. Yours very sincerely,   16. C
     John Brown

17. Jeffrey calls his dog Frisker.   17. C

18. He bought the dog from a neighbor who lives a block   18. C
     north of Jeffrey.

19. He got the dog last Summer.   19. W

20. Once we visited the United States senate.   20. W

21. Washington Irving wrote "The legend of Sleepy Hollow."   21. W

22. My uncle says that story is one of his favorites.   22. C

23. I shall always remember my drive through the Cumberland   23. C
     Mountains.

24. "It is early," the guide said, "but we shall be ready to 24. C
     start the tour soon."

25. "I am glad," Jane replied. "we are very eager to go."   25. W

Questions 26-50.

DIRECTIONS: From the list of choices below, select the punctuation
               mark which should be used where the parenthesis appear
               in each sentence. Indicate the letter of the correct
               answer in the space at the right.

A. Colon   G. Question mark
B. Comma   H. Period
C. Dash   I. Semicolon
D. Double quotation marks   J. Single quotation marks
E. Exclamation point   K. No punctuation
F. Hyphen

26. Last night we heard a bird call from the woods near   26. H
    our home()

27. We wondered what it could be()   27. H

28. Because we had not heard the call before() we did not   28. B
    recognize it as the song of a whippoorwill.

29. Are you ready for school now() Nancy?   29. B

30. School does not begin until 8()30.   30. A

31. I want to arrive in time to see Miss Smith() the music   31. B
    teacher.

32. I should like to join the chorus() but tryouts come   32. B
    during the time when I have band practice.

33. It is possible() of course() that band practice will be   33. B B
    over before the tryouts are.

34. The snow() covered bushes looked like ghosts huddled   34. F
    together.

35. On the farm were the following()   35. A

36. cows() pigs() chickens() and geese.   36. B B B

37. The farm is near Lincoln() Nebraska.   37. B

38. On our vacation, we traveled in Minnesota() and   duh k X 38. B B k
    Wisconsin() and Michigan.   no pencel

39. What interesting experiences we had()   39. E

40. Someone said the world would end on August 7() 1987.   40. B

41. Sammy's bright() happy smile made him popular with   41. B
    everyone.

42. We appreciate your help; however() it is too late to   42. B
    continue.

43. Da Vinci() who was famous as a painter() was also a   43. B B
    scientist and an inventor.

44. Please mail the package to 412 Park Avenue() Denver.   44. B

45. Mother said the border was three and three() fourths   45. F
    inches wide.

46. Miss Swanson() our home economics teacher() has taught   46. B B
    us to bake bread.

47. The Home Economics Club is for everyone() who enjoys
    cooking or sewing.   47. K

48. The path was steep and rough() nevertheless, we did
    not turn back.   48. I

49. "Father likes to quote the lines, ()He prayeth best
    who loveth best,()" said Joanne.   49. J

50. "Do you like poetry()" asked James.   50. G

Questions 51-60.

DIRECTIONS: In Questions 51 through 60, indicate the CORRECT answer.

51. Perhaps the jewelry is   51. A
    A. hers   B. her's   C. hers'

52. ____ the best musician in our group.   52. A
    A. You're   B. Your

53. ____ painting did you think was most pleasing?   53. B
    A. Who's   B. Whose

54. The children gave ____ pennies to buy a gift for the   54. B
    sick child.
    A. there   B. their   C. they're

55. It is ____ too warm for ice fishing.   55. B
    A. all together   B. altogether

56. ____ going to rain soon.   56. B
    A. Its   B. It's

57. The speaker used so many ____ that we found it tiresome   57. C
    to listen to him.
    A. wells   B. wells'   C. well's

58. ____ eyes were sparkling happily.   58. D
    A. Agneses   B. Agne's   D. Agnes's

59. We faced the mountain and called, but only our ____   59. B
    answered us.
    A. echos   B. echoes

60. Alice likes skiing and skating —   60. C
    A. to   B. two   C. too

Questions 61-75.

DIRECTIONS: In Questions 61 through 75, indicate which choice **makes the sentence CORRECT.**

61. Paul ____ hardly started to wade when his foot slipped, and he fell into the water.　　61. _A_
    A. had   B. had not

62. ____ across a chair was a beautiful Spanish shawl.　　62. _A_
    A. Lying   B. Laying

63. The book had been ____ by some careless child.　　63. C
    A. teared   B. tore   C. torn

64. The clown ____ a tattered hat.　　64. B
    A. weared   B. wore   C. worn

65. Someone had ____ all of the orange juice.　　65. C
    A. drinked   B. drank   C. drunk

66. Our dog ____ like music.　　66. B
    A. don't   B. doesn't

67. The child had ____ so softly that we were not sure that we had heard him correctly.　　67. C
    A. speaked   B. spoke   C. spoken

68. Jim had ____ across the pool twice before I even got started.　　68. C
    A. swimmed   B. swam   C. swum

69. The ____ milk　　69. B
    A. freezed   B. frozen   C. froze

70. ____ the bottle.　　correct? 70. C
    A. busted   B. bursted   C. burst

71. ____ are always teasing each other.　　71. A
    A. She and Joanne   B. Her and Joanne

72. Where had you ____ the drawings?　　correct? 72. B
    A. lay   B. laid   C. lain

73. Children were ____ on the stairway.　　73. A
    A. sitting   B. setting

74. I have ____ most of the invitations.　　74. C
    A. writed   B. wrote   C. written

75. Holding onto a flimsy thread of its web,　　75. A
    A. a spider swayed back and forth.
    B. we saw a spider swaying back and forth.

6

Questions 76-115.

DIRECTIONS: Indicate from the even-numbered items that which makes the sentence correct. Select from the odd-numbered choices that rule which makes the sentence incorrect.

76.   John is wittier than   76. _A_
      A. I   B. me   C. myself
                                                                       _A_
77.   A. Nominative case, predicate pronoun   Is the   77. _D_
      B. Objective case, object of a preposition   Book
      C. Reflexive pronoun, to refer to the speaker correct?
      D. Nominative case, subject of a verb understood

78.   No one could catch Jack and   78. _B_
      A. I   B. me   C. myself

79.   A. Nominative case, predicate pronoun   79. _B_
      B. Objective case, object of a verb
      C. Objective case, object of a preposition
      D. Reflexive pronoun, to refer to the speaker

80.   One of the children ____ an excellent violinist.   80. _A_
      A. is   B. are

81.   A. Singular verb, to agree with One   81. _A_
      B. Singular verb, to agree with violinist
      C. Plural verb, to agree with children

82.   Neither Tom nor his brothers ____ able to play yesterday.   82. _B_
      A. was   B. were

83.   A. Singular verb, to agree with Tom   83. _C_
      B. Singular verb, to agree with Neither
      C. Plural verb, to agree with brothers
      D. Plural verb, to agree with a compound subject

84.   Either the team members or the coach ____ asked to pick   84. _A_
      up the trophy.
      A. was   B. were

85.   A. Singular verb, to agree with coach   85. _A_
      B. Singular verb, to agree with team
      C. Plural verb, to agree with members
      D. Plural verb, to agree with a compound subject

86.   Both of the boys ____ excellent students.   86. _B_
      A. is   B. are

87.   A. Singular verb, to agree with Both   87. _B_
      B. Plural verb, to agree with Both
      C. Plural verb, to agree with boys

88. Everybody at the party ____ having a good time.   88. A
    A. was   B. were

89. A. Singular verb, to agree with Everybody   89. A
    B. Singular verb, to agree with party
    C. Singular verb, to agree with time
    D. Plural verb, to agree with Everybody

90. Which of the two dresses do you think is the   90. A
    A. prettier   B. prettiest

91. A. Comparative degree of an adjective   91. A
    B. Superlative degree of an adjective
    C. Comparative degree of the adverb

Accident — I knew this one

92. Miss Brown sent Bob and ____ postcards from France. 92. B
    A. I   B. me   C. myself

to

93. A. Nominative case, predicate pronoun   93. C
    B. Objective case, direct object of the verb
    C. Objective case, indirect object of the verb
    D. Reflexive pronoun, to refer to the speaker

Book is wrong! X Correct

94. Because the gift came from Jerry and ____, we appreciated 94. B
    it very much.
    A. he   B. him

95. A. Nominative case, predicate pronoun   95. C
    B. Objective case, object of the verb
    C. Objective case, object of a preposition

96. Everyone present had ____ own opinion about the problem. 96. A
    A. his   B. their

97. A. Singular pronoun, to refer to Everyone   97. A
    B. Singular pronoun, to refer to problem
    C. Plural pronoun, to refer to Everyone

98. It is ____ too late to call now.   98. B
    A. sure   B. surely

99. A. Adjective, to modify It   99. B
    B. Adverb, to modify is
    C. Adverb, to modify to call

100. The sunset was ____ beautiful.   100. B
    A. real   B. very

101. A. Adjective, to modify sunset   101. C
    B. Adverb, to modify was
    C. Adverb, to modify beautiful

102. Velvet feels   102. A
        A. soft   B. softly

103. A. Adjective, to modify Velvet   103. A
        B. Adverb, to modify feels
        C. Adjective, to modify feels

104. Jane asked ____ rang the doorbell.   104. A
        A. who   B. whom

105. A. Objective case, object of asked   105. C
        B. Objective case, object of rang
        C. Nominative case, subject of rang

106. For ____ did you ask when you telephoned the office?   106. B
        A. who   B. whom

107. A. Nominative case, subject of did ask   107. C
        B. Objective case, object of the verb
        C. Objective case, object of a preposition

108. ____ can laugh at himself will probably make an   108. A
      agreeable companion.
        A. Whoever   B. Whomever

109. A. Nominative case, subject of will make   109. B
        B. Nominative case, subject of can laugh
        C. Objective case, object of can laugh
        D. Objective case, object of will make

110. Father thinks that ____ tries can succeed.   110. A
        A. whoever   B. whomever

111. A. Nominative case, subject of can succeed   X   111. A/B
        B. Nominative case, subject of tries
        C. Objective case, object of thinks

112. Our government is run by ____ the people elect.   112. B
        A. whoever   B. whomever

113. A. Objective case, object of a preposition   113. A
        B. Objective case, object of elect
        C. Nominative case, predicate nominative

114. The child speaks   114. B
        A. distinct   B. distinctly

115. A. Adverb, to modify speaks   115. A
        B. Adjective, to modify child
        C. Adjective, to modify speaks

Questions 115-125.

DIRECTIONS: Indicate the letter of the part of speech which
correctly describes the use of the word, phrase,
or clause in the sentences below. Choose the
parts of speech from the column on the right.

Early one May morning, we headed our car toward the Great
Plains. The sun was just rising, in a burst of rosy splendor,
above the horizon. To be alive and free to travel on a day
such as that one was pure joy.

Parts of Speech

116.	Early	A. Adjective	*Book is wrong→*	116. ~~B~~ A
117.	May	B. Adverb		117. A
118.	Plains	C. Conjunction		118. E
119.	was rising	D. Interjection		119. H
120.	of rosy splendor	E. Noun	*prep phrase used as adj*	120. F
121.	above	F. Preposition	*Book wrong*	121. F
122.	to be alive and free	G. Pronoun	*Book wrong*	122. E
123.	and	H. Verb		123. C
124.	the			124. A
125.	we			125. G

Questions 126-135.

DIRECTIONS: Indicate the title of the book which would be
alphabetized FIRST among the choices that follow.

126.	A. WIND IN THE PINES	B. NIGHT WIND		126.	C
	C. IVANHOE	D. KIDNAPED			
127.	A. VELVET SHOES	B. USES OF COAL		127.	B
	C. WONDER LAND	D. YOUNG HEROES			
128.	A. BUFFALO BILL	B. CARAVAN		128.	A
	C. DAYS TO REMEMBER	D. FROM DAWN TO DUSK			
129.	A. TELEPHONE TALES	B. TELEGRAPHIC CODES		129.	B
	C. TEMPEST IN A TEAPOT	D. TELLING SEA TALES			
130.	A. LEARNING TO SWIM	B. THE LAST LEAF		130.	B
	C. THE SPIDER	D. THE MAN WITHOUT A COUNTRY			

9
0

131. A. FOG   B. THE GYPSY   131. A
      C. HOBBIES   D. A PECK OF GOLD

132. A. SKATING   B. SILVER SHIPS   132. C
      C. THE MAN WITH THE MASK   D. TIMBER COUNTRY

133. A. WILD ANIMALS I HAVE KNOWN   133. B
      B. FOOL'S GOLD
      C. THE JESTER
      D. UNCLE JAKE'S ADVENTURES WITH A WILDCAT

134. A. PAUL REVERE'S RIDE   B. PRIVATE ZOO   134. C
      C. LOCHINVAR   D. TOP SECRET

135. A. ONCE UPON A STORYTIME   135. C
      B. HEROES OF PROGRESS
      C. HEART, HEALTH, AND HAPPINESS
      D. HENRIETTA HARVEY'S HAVEN

KEY (CORRECT ANSWERS)

1. O	31. B	61. A	91. A	121. A
2. O	32. B	62. A	92. B	122. F
3. B	33. B	63. C	93. B	123. C
4. A	34. F	64. B	94. B	124. A
5. A	35. A	65. C	95. C	125. G
6. O	36. B	66. B	96. A	126. C
7. C	37. B	67. C	97. A	127. B
8. D	38. K	68. C	98. B	128. A
9. A	39. E	69. B	99. B	129. B
10. O	40. B	70. C	100. B	130. B
11. W	41. B	71. A	101. C	131. A
12. W	42. B	72. B	102. A	132. C
13. W	43. B	73. A	103. A	133. B
14. W	44. B	74. C	104. A	134. C
15. C	45. F	75. A	105. C	135. C
16. C	46. B	76. A	106. B	
17. C	47. K	77. A	107. C	
18. C	48. I	78. B	108. A	
19. W	49. J	79. B	109. B	
20. W	50. G	80. A	110. A	
21. W	51. A	81. A	111. A	
22. C	52. A	82. B	112. B	
23. C	53. B	83. C	113. A	
24. C	54. B	84. A	114. B	
25. W	55. B	85. A	115. A	
26. H	56. B	86. B	116. A	
27. H	57. A	87. B	117. E	
28. B	58. C	88. A	118. E	
29. B	59. B	89. A	119. H	
30. A	60. C	90. A	120. F	

EXAMINATION SECTION

DIRECTIONS: Each question or incomplete statement is followed by
several suggested answers or completions. Select the
one that BEST answers the question or completes the
statement. *PRINT THE LETTER OF THE CORRECT ANSWER IN
THE SPACE AT THE RIGHT.*

Questions 1-30.

DIRECTIONS: In each of the following sentences, one or more of
the punctuation marks are enclosed in brackets.
If the punctuation enclosed in brackets is CORRECT,
mark C in the space at the right. If any punctuation mark in brackets is NOT the CORRECT mark for
the place, mark W in the space at the right.

1. Why was Frederick , the Great[,] called *great*?   1. ___

2. A distant whistle sounded[,] and there was a shuffling   2. C
   of feet on the platform.

3. George turned to the banker[;] the only one of the group   3. W
   he knew.

4. The road wound[,] along the river[,] and under the long   4. W
   lines of poplars.

5. The group of men behind Edward hesitated[;] glanced   5. W
   questioningly at one another[;] and awkwardly followed
   his example.

6. Hoping to find his friend at home[,] Joe knocked on the   6. C
   door.

7. Dear Sir[,]   7. W
   Please send the books by express.

8. My address has been 1342 State Street, Kansas City,   8. C
   Missouri[,] since Christmas.

9. "You are going with us[?]" asked Jane, as soon as she   9. C
   saw me.

10. Mrs. Green and her daughter, Miss[.] Eva Green, are   10. W
    members of our party.

11. On their way they passed a weather[-]beaten, stone house.   11. C

12. Senator Martin, if elected in[,] November, 1988, will be   12. W
    in Washington for the next six years.

13. The freshman had many things to do[;] such as enrolling for classes, unpacking his trunk, and writing home.   13. W

14. Mrs. Carter is a leader in several of the women[']s organizations.   14. C

15. We did not tell Clarke[,] who the man was.   15. W

16. Steavens, the young stranger[,] noticed the card on the door.   16. C

17. "No, they have not come yet[;] the family is scattered," was the reply.   17. C

18. There were one hundred[-]twelve people at the lecture.   *wrong*   (18. 3C

19. James asked his brother ["]where he had left the car.["]   19. W

20. "Who is the congressman from this district," asked Charles, "if it is not Mr. James[?]"   20. C

21. The sailor had a three months['] *correct* leave of absence.   3/ 21. C

22. "It's a long walk," said Jones. "You ought to take a taxi.["] ["]Our car is not running."   22. W

23. It has been three hours['] since the train left.   23. W

24. There were not more than forty[-]two boys in the class.   24. C

25. The woman was beautifully[-]dressed in a light blue velvet gown.   25. W

26. He answered the question[;] then he rose and left the room.   26. C

27. The boy[,] that delivers the Gazette[,] has come to collect his money.   27. W

28. "If Roberts is captain," said James[,] "we shall be happy."   28. C

29. A fast train from Chicago[,] to New York[,] makes the distance in eighteen hours.   29. W

30. My mother[,] who has been in Kansas City for a week[,] returned home yesterday.   30. C

Questions 31-40.

DIRECTIONS: Questions 31 through 40 refer to capitalization.
If the sentence is correct, indicate C (CORRECT).
If the sentence is incorrect, indicate W (WRONG).

31. A new junior high school was built in our city.   31. C

32. Ten seniors in Lincoln High School will attend college   32. C
next fall.

33. Vermont was the native state of ex-President Coolidge.   33. C

34. The highway we took going north was no. 75.   34. W

35. A good road in the middle west is between Tulsa and   35. W
Winnipeg.

36. Five nations were represented in a Disarmament   36. C
Conference in London in January, 1930.

37. For a number of years Father subscribed to Harper's   37. C
Magazine.

38. Yours Sincerely,   38. W
Mary Orr

39. James Smith from Portland County was elected to the   39. C
United States Senate.

40. The president of Lawrence College attended the N.E.A.   40. C
meeting at Columbus.

Questions 41-70.

DIRECTIONS: In each of the following sentences, one of the
lettered words is INCORRECTLY used. Indicate the
letter of this word in the space at the right.
If you think that a sentence has more than one
error, indicate only the one that you think is
the WORST.

41. Success (A) is   (B) when one   (C) accomplishes the task   41. B
(D) that he undertakes.

42. Paul has (A) eaten one of the apples which   (B) were   42. B
given to him and has distributed the   (C) balance
(D) among his friends.

43. Since the (A) taking of the 1980 census, it has been   43. D
announced   (B) that New York City has a million more
inhabitants   (C) than   (D) any city in the United
States.

44. As (A) most all the students were studying in the   44. A
    library   (B) because it was   (C) quiet there, only a
    (D) few heard the fire alarm.

45. (A) Due to a mistake of   (B) only a   (C) few cents,   45. A
    John had (D) already refused to pay the bill.   B

46. Had we not been (A) present and   (B) seen the accident,   46. C
    we could not   (C) of explained why the car   (D) had
    turned over.

47. Anyone (A) who has had good training in high school   47. D
    (B) can do   (C) well in college if   (D) they study
    sufficiently.

48. After (A) ringing the bell for   (B) only a few seconds, 48. B
    the door opened   (C) slowly.   (D) Who do you think   A
    entered?

49. Upon (A) entering the class, the first words heard were, 49. A/B
    "If (B) your absence was   (C) due to illness,   (D) all
    right. You may be excused."

50. The reason there is a junior college in (A) almost every 50. B
    city of fifteen thousand is   (B) because there is
    economy in a   (C) student's living at home while he is
    (D) attending college.

51. The boys seemed (A) real   (B) sure that   (C) their   51. A
    school would   (D) lose only one game.

52. There can (A) not but one of   (B) us girls go; therefore, 52. A
    he must make a (C) choice between you and (D) me.

53. Their reason for (A) feeling certain   (B) of victory was 53. D
    (C) that they had a center, dependable in every way,
    (D) and who had been on a winning team for three years.

54. Soon after (A) enrolling in the class, John learned he   54. C
    (B) would not pass   (C) without he studied three hours
    (D) a day.

55. A (A) dark-complected youth entered the office and left   55. D
    (B) without   (C) my asking   (D) who he was.   A

56. The (A) principal in our school is   (B) quite different 56. D
    (C) than the one   (D) whom we met at the Walnut School.   C

57. The men (A) effected a settlement and ended   (B) all   57. D
    the disputes   (C) without calling an officer,
    (D) which was gratifying to every one.

58. Neither the debaters (A) or   (B) their coach   (C) was   present at last   (D) night's meeting.

58. A

59. People of Asia have such different (A) customs   (B) from (C) those we in America have that   (D) it is a great curiosity.

59. C

60. We agreed (A) with the plan   (B) that the committee (C) was offering   (D) us.

60. C

61. The rope became (A) loose and   (B) laid on the ground in curved lines   (C) as if some one had   (D) laid it there.

61. B

62. The principal (A) ought to have known better   (B) than to   (C) let   (D) them boys go.

62. D

63. Our radio has (A) two knobs, the   (B) turning of one of (C) which very much   (D) effects the tone.

63.

64. The (A) principal reason for our country's   (B) demanding passports is   (C) that the country may keep out undesirable (D) immigrants.

64. B

65. The children were (A) so quiet that   (B) some one remarked how   (C) like   (D) statues they looked.

65. B

66. If Miss James (A) accepts the position in Kansas City, the superintendent   (B) will   (C) leave her have charge (D) of the sixth grade.

66. C

67. After (A) examining my surroundings   (B) thoroughly, I could not remember   (C) of   (D) having been there before.

67. C

68. Mr. Roe is a teacher, (A) well-liked by his students, (B) and whom   (C) his co-workers appreciate,   (D) too.

68. B

69. Years (A) ago   (B) most men thought a great event in (C) their lives was   (D) when they rode in an airplane.

69. D

70. (A) Because thousands of   (B) persons   (C) travel by air today is a sign   (D) that great progress has been made in the scientific world.

70. B

6

Questions 71-85.

DIRECTIONS: Here are fifteen numbered groups of words. Some of these groups make complete sentences; others do not. Indicate C (CORRECT) if the sentence is complete; indicate W (WRONG) if the sentence is incomplete.

71. Last night read in a magazine a story of some children being lost in the mountains.   71. W

72. A boy, seven years old, and a girl, nine.   72. W

73. They having strolled away from camp where a party of tourists had stopped for the night.   73. W

74. There was great excitement among the other members of the party.   74. C

75. Especially was the mother of the children wild with anxiety.   75. C

76. As she knew of many dangers that surrounded her dear ones.   76. W

77. She also imagined many others.   77. C

78. If only for a minute, put yourself in her place.   78. C

79. Everyone out to find the children, both those who were of their party and those from other camps who heard of the trouble.   79. W

80. What a great commotion there was!   80. C

81. Some calling, others whistling, and the mother crying.   81. W

82. When finally the report came that the children had been found playing beside a brook which they had followed, up a narrow valley.   82. W

83. Then was everyone greatly relieved.   83. C

84. Why should anyone have thought them lost?   84. C

85. Knew all the time where they were and how to get back.   85. W

Questions 86-100.

DIRECTIONS: In each of the following sentences, a word is
               enclosed in brackets. If this word is the correct
               word for the place, indicate C (CORRECT). If the
               word is NOT the correct one, indicate W (WRONG).

86.   Had the coach [knew] the rules better, we might have   86. W
      won the game.

87.   Not a voice [raised] in our behalf.   87. W

88.   I am certain James would have [spoke] to us.   88. W

89.   The man had [shaken] his head in protest.   89. C

90.   The boat had tipped over and had [sank] to the bottom.   90. W

91.   All night long they had [ridden] on the train.   91. C

92.   Many beautiful blankets are [woven] by the Indians.   92. C

93.   Have the new strawberry plants [grown] as fast as last   93. C
      year's plants?

94.   Long before frost came, the apples were [shook] from the   94. W
      tree.

95.   Was the first prize in the contests [took] by John or   95. W
      Mary?

96.   For a day or two the ships had [lain] there in the   96. C
      harbor.

97.   How many miles had they [driven] that day?   97. C

98.   No one knows why he [choose] to attend that college.   98. W

99.   George hopes to get the work all [done] before he leaves.   99. C

100. The plank bent low, then [sprang] back quickly.   100. C

Questions 101-150.

DIRECTIONS: Each of the following sentences marked *a* has a word in
               brackets. If the word is the correct grammatical form
               to be used in that place, indicate C (CORRECT). If
               the form is incorrect, indicate W (WRONG).

               Under *b* is a reason for the form of the word to be used
               in the brackets in *a*. If the reason is the correct one
               to be applied in this case, indicate C (CORRECT). If
               the reason is NOT the correct one, indicate W (WRONG).

101. *a.* Anyone who [likes] to read will enjoy this book.   101. C

102. *b.* Singular number should be used, to agree with *who*. 102.

103. *a.* [Has] either of the girls been in to see you? 103.

104. *b.* Plural number should be used, to agree with *girls*. 104.

105. *a.* There [have] been many a dollar spent on the new road. 105. W

106. *b.* Plural number should be used, to agree with *many*. 106. W

107. *a.* The doctor asked me, who [am] still in high school, if I were going to college. 107. WP

108. *b.* First person should be used, to agree with *who*. 108. C

109. *a.* A large flock of geese [was] shown in the picture last night. 109. C

110. *b.* Singular number should be used, to agree with subject *flock*. 110. C

111. *a.* The banker looked [sharp] at the stranger. 111. W

112. *b.* Adverb should be used, to modify *looked*. 112. C

113. *a.* The table feels [roughly], as I run my hand over it. 113. W

114. *b.* Predicate adjective should be used with *feels*. 114. C

115. *a.* I can [easily] feel the rough board underneath the cloth. 115. C

116. *b.* Adverb should be used, to modify verb *feel*. 116. C

117. *a.* The superintendent left word for John and [I] to report the next day. 117. W

118. *b.* Nominative case should be used, subject of *report*. 118. W

119. *a.* It could not have been [them] whom we saw yesterday. 119. W

120. *b.* Objective case should be used, object of *could have been*. 120. W

121. *a.* My aunt wishes that you and [she] could go to Europe. 121. C

122. *b.* Nominative case should be used, subject of verb *could go*. 122. C

123. *a.* It was announced that James and [myself] ranked high in the music contest. 123. W

124. *b.* Reflexive pronoun should be used, to refer to speaker. 124. W

125.   *a.* Did you know all [we] four had our names in last   125. C
               night's paper?

126.   *b.* Nominative case should be used, subject of *had*.   126. C

127.   *a.* The teacher had heard of [our] being late.   127. C

128.   *b.* Objective case should be used, object of *of*.   128. W

129.   *a.* It might have been [I] whom you saw.   129 C

130.   *b.* Nominative case should be used, predicate nominative.   130. C

131.   *a.* I supposed the girl who was telephoning to be [her].   131. W

132.   *b.* Objective case should be used, to agree with *girl*.   132. W

133.   *a.* It seems to be [us] who are wrong.   133. W

134.   *b.* Nominative case should be used, after *seems to be*.   134. C

135.   *a.* Two boys, Mark and [me], were detailed to carry   135. W
               water to the camp kitchen.

136.   *b.* Nominative case should be used, to agree with *boys*.   136. C

137.   *a.* No one realized how the coach hoped [to have won]   137. W
               that game.

138.   *b.* Perfect infinitive should be used, to indicate past   138. ?
               time.

139.   *a.* I wish I [were] in Boston today.   139. C

140.   *b.* Present tense should be used, to agree with *today*.   140. W

141.   *a.* [Having delivered] his oration, the boy left the   141. C
               stage.

142.   *b.* Present participle should be used, to indicate same   142. C
               time as verb *left*.

143.   *a.* The librarian gave the book to [whoever] she   143. W
               thought would appreciate it.

144.   *b.* Objective case should be used, object of *to*.   144. C

145.   *a.* The students did not know [whom] the principal   145. C
               would appoint to fill the vacancy.

146.   *b.* Objective case should be used, object of verb *know*.   146. C

147.   *a.* Boys especially admire Colonel Johnson, [whom] they   147. W
               consider their ideal.

148.   *b.* Objective case should be used, object of *consider*.   148. ___

10

149. *a.* We are going faster now than [they].   149. C

150. *b.* Objective case should be used, object of *than*.   150. W

KEY (CORRECT ANSWERS)

1. W	31. C	61. B	91. C	121. C
2. C	32. C	62. D	92. C	122. C
3. W	33. C	63. D	93. C	123. W
4. W	34. W	64. D	94. W	124. W
5. W	35. W	65. B	95. W	125. C
6. C	36. C	66. C	96. C	126. C
7. W	37. C	67. C	97. C	127. C
8. C	38. C	68. A	98. W	128. W
9. C	39. C	69. D	99. C	129. C
10. W	40. W	70. C	100. C	130. C
11. C	41. B	71. W	101. C	131. W
12. W	42. C	72. W	102. C	132. W
13. W	43. D	73. W	103. C	133. W
14. C	44. A	74. C	104. W	134. C
15. W	45. A	75. W	105. C	135. W
16. C	46. C	76. W	106. C	136. C
17. C	47. D	77. C	107. C	137. C
18. W	48. A	78. C	108. C	138. C
19. W	49. A	79. W	109. C	139. C
20. C	50. B	80. C	110. C	140. W
21. C	51. A	81. W	111. W	141. C
22. W	52. A	82. W	112. C	142. W
23. W	53. D	83. C	113. W	143. W
24. C	54. C	84. C	114. C	144. C
25. W	55. A	85. W	115. C	145. C
26. C	56. C	86. W	116. C	146. C
27. W	57. D	87. W	117. W	147. C
28. C	58. A	88. W	118. W	148. C
29. W	59. D	89. C	119. W	149. C
30. C	60. A	90. W	120. W	150. W

SENTENCE COMPLETION

EXAMINATION SECTION

TEST 1

DIRECTIONS: Each question in this part consists of a sentence in which one word is missing; a blank line indicates where the word has been removed from the sentence. Beneath each sentence are five words, one of which is the missing word. You are to select the number of the missing word by deciding which one of the five words BEST fits in with the meaning of the sentence. *PRINT THE LETTER OF THE CORRECT ANSWER IN THE SPACE AT THE RIGHT.*

1. Although they had little interest in the game they were playing, rather than be _____, they played it through to the end.
   A. inactive   B. inimical   C. busy
   D. complacent   E. vapid

   1. D

2. That he was unworried and at peace with the world could be, perhaps, observed from his _____ brow.
   A. unwrinkled   B. wrinkled   C. furrowed
   D. twisted   E. askew

   2. A

3. Among the hundreds of workers in the assembly plant of the factory, one was _____ because of his skill and speed.
   A. steadfast   B. condemned   C. consistent
   D. outstanding   E. eager

   3. D

4. The story of the invention of many of our best known machines is a consistent one: they are the result of a long series of experiments by many people; thus, the Wright Brothers in 1903 _____ the airplane rather than invented it.
   A. popularized   B. regulated   C. perfected
   D. contrived   E. developed

   4. C

5. As soon as the former political exile returned to his native country, he looked up old supporters, particularly those whom he knew to be _____ and whose help he might need.
   A. potent   B. pusillanimous C. attentive
   D. free   E. retired

   5. C

6. A recent study of the New Deal shows that no other man than the President could have brought together so many _____ interests and combined them into so effective a political organization.
   A. secret   B. interior   C. predatory
   D. harmonious   E. conflicting

   6. E

7. A study of tides presents an interesting ____ in that, while the forces that set them in motion are universal in application, presumably affecting all parts of our world without distinction, the action of tides in particular areas is completely local in nature.
    A. phenomenon   B. maneuver   C. paradox
    D. quality   E. spontaneity

8. Many of the facts that are found in the ancient archives constitute ____ that help shed light upon human activities in the past.
    A. facts   B. reminders   C. particles
    D. sources   E. indications

9. It is a regrettable fact that in a caste society which deems manual toil a mark of ____, rarely does the laborer improve his social position or gain political power.
    A. inferiority   B. consolation   C. fortitude
    D. hardship   E. brilliance

10. As a generalization, one can correctly say that crises in history are caused by the re-opening of questions which have been safely ____ for long periods of time.
    A. debated   B. joined   C. recondite
    D. settled   E. unanswered

TEST 2

1. We can see in retrospect that the high hopes for lasting peace conceived at Versailles in 1919 were ____.
    A. ingenuous   B. transient   C. nostalgic
    D. ingenious   E. species

2. One of the constructive effects of Nazism was the passage by the U.N. of a resolution to combat ____.
    A. armaments   B. nationalism   C. colonialism
    D. genocide   E. geriatrics

3. In our prisons, the role of ____ often gains for certain inmates a powerful position among their fellow prisoners.
    A. informer   B. clerk   C. warden
    D. trusty   E. turnkey

4. It is the ____ liar, experienced in the ways of the world, who finally trips upon some incongruous detail.
    A. consummate   B. incorrigible   C. congenital
    D. flagrant   E. contemptible

5. Anyone who is called a misogynist can hardly be expected to look upon women with ____ contemptuous eyes.
    A. more than   B. nothing less than C. decidedly
    D. other than   E. always

6. Demagogues such as Hitler and Mussolini aroused the masses   6. A
   by appealing to their ____ rather than to their intellect.
      A. emotions   B. reason   C. nationalism
      D. conquests   E. duty

7. He was in great demand as an entertainer for his ____   7. A
   abilities: he could sing, dance, tell a joke, or relate
   a story with equally great skill and facility.
      A. versatile   B. logical   C. culinary
      D. histrionic   E. creative

8. The wise politician is aware that, next to knowing when   8. E
   to seize an opportunity, it is also important to know when
   to ____ an advantage.
      A. develop B. seek   C. revise   D. proclaim E. forego

9. Books on psychology inform us that the best way to break   9. B
   a bad habit is to ____ a new habit in its place.
      A. expel   B. substitute   C. conceal
      D. curtail   E. supplant

10. The author who uses one word where another uses a whole   ?   10. C
    paragraph, should be considered a ____ writer.
       A. successful   B. grandiloquent   C. succinct
       D. prolix   E. experienced

____

TEST 3

1. The prime minister, fleeing from the rebels who had   x 1. B (E)
   seized the government, sought ____ in the church.
      A. revenge   B. mercy   C. relief
      D. salvation   E. sanctuary

2. It does not take us long to conclude that it is foolish   2. A
   to fight the ____, and that it is far wiser to accept it.
      A. inevitable   B. inconsequential C. impossible
      D. choice   E. invasion

3. ____ is usually defined as an excessively high rate of   3. E
   interest.
      A. Injustice   B. Perjury   C. Exorbitant
      D. Embezzlement   E. Usury

4. "I ask you, gentlemen of the jury, to find this man guilty   4. A
   since I have ____ the charges brought against him."
      A. documented   B. questioned   C. revised
      D. selected   E. confused

5. Although the critic was a close friend of the producer,   5. D
   he told him that he could not ____ his play.
      A. condemn   B. prefer   C. congratulate
      D. endorse   E. revile

6. Knowledge of human nature and motivation is an important ____ in all areas of endeavor.
   A. object   B. incentive   C. opportunity
   D. asset   E. goal

6. D

7. Numbered among the audience were kings, princes, dukes, and even a maharajah, all attempting to ____ one another in the glitter of their habiliments and the number of their escorts.
   A. supersede   B. outdo   C. guide
   D. vanquish   E. equal

7. B

8. There seems to be a widespread feeling that peoples who are located below us in respect to latitude are ____ also in respect to intellect and ability.
   A. superior   B. melodramatic   C. inferior
   D. ulterior   E. contemptible

8. C

9. This should be considered a(n) ____ rather than the usual occurrence.
   A. coincidence   B. specialty   C. development
   D. outgrowth   E. mirage

9. A

10. Those who were considered states' rights aherents in the early part of our history espoused the diminution of the powers of the national government because they had always been ____ of these powers.
    A. solicitous   B. advocates   C. apprehensive
    D. mindful   E. respectful

10. C

TEST 4

1. The life of the mining camps as portrayed by Bret Harte - boisterous, material, brawling - was in direct ____ to the contemporary Eastern world of conventional morals and staid deportment depicted by other men of letters.
   A. model   B. parallel   C. antithesis
   D. relationship   E. response

1. C

2. The agreements were to remain in force for three years and were subject to automatic ____ unless terminated by the parties concerned on one month's notice.
   A. renewal   B. abrogation   C. amendment
   D. confiscation   E. option

2. A

3. In a democracy, people are recognized for what they do rather than for their ____.
   A. alacrity   B. ability   C. reputation
   D. skill   E. pedigree

3. E

4. Although he had often loudly proclaimed his ____ concerning world affairs, he actually read widely and was usually the best informed person in his circle.
   A. weariness   B. complacency   C. condolence
   D. indifference   E. worry

4. D

5. This student holds the ____ record of being the sole failure in his class.   5. D
   A. flagrant   B. unhappy   C. egregious
   D. dubious   E. unusual

6. She became enamored ____ the acrobat when she witnessed his act.   6. B or D
   enamored of
   A. of   B. with   C. for   D. by   E. about

7. This will ____ all previous wills.   7. C
   A. abrogates   B. denies   C. supersedes
   D. prevents   E. continues

8. In the recent terrible Chicago ____, over ninety children were found dead as a result of the fire.   8. E
   A. hurricane   B. destruction   C. panic
   D. holocaust   E. accident

9. I can ascribe no better reason why he shunned society than that he was a ____.   9. D
   A. mentor   B. Centaur   C. aristocrat
   D. misanthrope   E. failure

10. One who attempts to learn all the known facts before he comes to a conclusion may most aptly be described as a ____.   10. A
   A. realist   B. philosopher   C. cynic
   D. pessimist   E. skeptic

TEST 5

1. The judge exercised commendable ____ in dismissing the charge against the prisoner. In spite of the clamor that surrounded the trial, and the heinousness of the offense, the judge could not be swayed to overlook the lack of facts in the case.   1. D
   A. avidity   B. meticulousness   C. clemency
   D. balance   E. querulousness

2. The pianist played the concerto ____, displaying such facility and skill as has rarely been matched in this old auditorium.   2. E
   A. strenuously   B. deftly   C. passionately
   D. casually   E. spiritedly

3. The Tanglewood Symphony Orchestra holds its outdoor concerts far from city turmoil in a ____, bucolic setting.   3. C
   A. spectacular   B. atavistic   C. serene
   D. chaotic   E. catholic

4. Honest satire gives true joy to the thinking man. Thus, the satirist is most ____ when he points out the hypocrisy in human actions.   4. A
   A. elated   B. humiliated   C. ungainly
   D. repressed   E. disdainful

5. She was a(n) ____ who preferred the company of her books   5. _E_
   to the pleasures of cafe society.
      A. philanthropist   B. stoic   C. exhibitionist
      D. extrovert   E. introvert

6. So many people are so convinced that people are driven by   6. _B_
   ____ motives that they cannot believe that anybody is
   unselfish!
      A. interior   B. ulterior   C. unworthy
      D. selfish   E. destructive

7. These ____ results were brought about by a chain of   7. ____
   fortuitous events.
      A. unfortunate   B. odd   C. harmful
      D. haphazard   E. propitious

8. The bank teller's ____ of the funds was discovered the   8. _A_
   following month when the auditors examined the books.
      A. embezzlement   B. burglary   C. borrowing
      D. assignment   E. theft

9. The monks gathered in the ____ for their evening meal.   9. _D_
      A. lounge   B. auditorium   C. refectory
      D. rectory   E. solarium

10. Local officials usually have the responsibility in each   10. _E_
    area of determining when the need is sufficiently great
    to ____ withdrawals from the community water supply.
       A. encourage   B. justify   C. discontinue
       D. advocate   E. forbid

KEYS (CORRECT ANSWERS)

TEST 1	TEST 2	TEST 3	TEST 4	TEST 5
1. A	1. A	1. E	1. C	1. D
2. A	2. D	2. A	2. A	2. B
3. D	3. A	3. E	3. E	3. C
4. C	4. A	4. A	4. D	4. A
5. A	5. D	5. D	5. D	5. E
6. E	6. A	6. D	6. A	6. B
7. C	7. A	7. B	7. C	7. D
8. D	8. E	8. C	8. D	8. A
9. A	9. B	9. A	9. D	9. C
10. A	10. C	10. C	10. E	10. B

PREPARING WRITTEN MATERIALS

EXAMINATION SECTION

DIRECTIONS: Each question or incomplete statement is followed by several suggested answers or completions. Select the one that BEST answers the question or completes the statement. *PRINT THE LETTER OF THE CORRECT ANSWER IN THE SPACE AT THE RIGHT.*

Questions 1-21.　　　　**TEST 1**

DIRECTIONS: In each of the following sentences, which were taken from students' transcripts, there may be an error. Indicate the appropriate correction in the space at the right. If the sentence is correct as is, indicate this choice. Unnecessary changes will be considered incorrect.

1. In that building there seemed to be representatives of Teachers College, the Veterans Bureau, and the Businessmen's Association.
    A. Teacher's College   B. Veterans' Bureau
    C. Businessmens Association   D. Correct as is

1.B

2. In his travels, he visited St. Paul, San Francisco, Springfield, Ohio, and Washington, D.C..
    A. Ohio and   B. Saint Paul
    C. Washington, D.C.   D. Correct as is

2.C

3. As a result of their purchasing a controlling interest in the syndicate, it was well-known that the Bureau of Labor Statistics' calculations would be unimportant.
    A. of them purchasing   B. well known
    C. Statistics   D. Correct as is

3.D

4. Walter Scott, Jr.'s, attempt to emulate his father's success was doomed to failure.
    A. Junior's,   B. Scott's, Jr.
    C. Scott, Jr.'s attempt D. Correct as is

4.C

5. About B.C. 250 the Romans invaded Great Britain, and remains of their highly developed civilization can still be seen.
    A. 250 B.C.   B. Britain and
    C. highly-developed   D. Correct as is

5.A

6. The two boss's sons visited the children's department.
    A. bosses   B. bosses'
    C. childrens'   D. Correct as is

6.B

7. Miss Amex not only approved the report, but also decided that it needed no revision.
    A. report; but   B. report but
    C. report. But   D. Correct as is

7.B

8. Here's brain food in a jiffy--economical, too!   8. _D_
   A. economical too!   B. 'brain food'
   C. jiffy-economical   D. Correct as is

9. She said, "He likes the "Gatsby Look" very much."   9. _C_
   A. said "He   B. "he
   C. 'Gatsby Look'   D. Correct as is

10. We anticipate that we will be able to   10. _C_
    visit them briefly in Los Angeles on Wed-
    nesday after a five-day visit.
    A. Wednes-   B. 5 day
    C. five day   D. Correct as is

11. She passed all her tests, and, she now has a good 11. _A_
    position.
    A. tests, and she   B. past
    C. tests;   D. Correct as is

Check

12. The billing clerk said, "I will send the bill today";   12. _A_
    however, that was a week ago, and it hasn't arrived yet!
    A. today;"   B. today,"
    C. ago and   D. Correct as is

13. "She types at more-than-average speed," Miss Smith said, 13. _A_
    "but I feel that it is a result of marvelous concentra-
    tion and self control on her part."
    A. more than average   B. "But
    C. self-control   D. Correct as is

14. The state of Alaska, the largest state in the union, is 14. _A_
    also the northernmost state.
    A. Union   B. Northernmost State
    C. State of Alaska   D. Correct as is

15. The memoirs of Ex-President Nixon, it is rumored, will 15. _B_
    sell more copies than Six Crises, the book he wrote in
    the 60's.
    A. Six Crises   B. ex-President
    C. 60s   D. Correct as is

16. "There are three principal elements, determining the 16. _A_
    hazard of buildings: the contents hazard, the fire
    resistance of the structure, and the character of the
    interior finish," concluded the speaker.
    The one of the following statements that is MOST
    acceptable is that, in the above passage,
    A. the comma following the word *elements* is incorrect
    B. the colon following the word *buildings* is incorrect
    C. the comma following the word *finish* is incorrect
    D. there is no error in the punctuation of the sentence

17. He spoke on his favorite topic, "Why We Will Win." (How 17. D
    could I stop him?)
    A. Win".   B. him?).
    C. him)?   D. Correct as is

18. "All any insurance policy is, is a contract for services," 18. D
    said my insurance agent, Mr. Newton.
    A. Insurance Policy   B. Insurance Agent
    C. policy is is a   D. Correct as is

19. Inasmuch as the price list has now been up dated, we   19. B
    should send it to the printer.
    A. In as much   B. updated
    C. pricelist   D. Correct as is

20. We feel that "Our know-how" is responsible for the   20. A
    improvement in technical developments.
    A. "our   B. know how
    C. that,   D. Correct as is

21. Did Cortez conquer the Incas? the Aztecs? the South   21. A
    American Indians?
    A. Incas, the Aztecs, the South American Indians?
    B. Incas; the Aztecs; the South American Indians?
    C. south American Indians?
    D. Correct as is

22. Which one of the following forms for the typed name of   22. C
    the dictator in the closing lines of a letter is
    generally MOST acceptable in the United States?
    A. (Dr.) James F. Farley
    B. Dr. James F. Farley
    C. Mr. James F. Farley, Ph.D.
    D. James F. Farley

23. The plural of   23. B
    A. turkey is turkies
    B. cargo is cargoes
    C. bankruptcy is bankruptcys
    D. son-in-law is son-in-laws

24. The abbreviation *viz.* means MOST NEARLY   24. A
    A. namely   B. for example
    C. the following   D. see

25. In the sentence, *A man in a light-gray suit waited*   25. C
    thirty-five minutes in the ante-room for the all-
    important document, the word IMPROPERLY hyphenated is
    A. light-gray   B. thirty-five
    C. ante-room   D. all-important

KEY (CORRECT ANSWERS)

1.	D	11.	A
2.	C	12.	D
3.	B	13.	D
4.	D	14.	A
5.	A	15.	B
6.	B	16.	A
7.	B	17.	D
8.	D	18.	D
9.	C	19.	B
10.	C	20.	A

21. D
22. D
23. B
24. A
25. C

TEST 2

DIRECTIONS: Each question or incomplete statement is followed by several suggested answers or completions. Select the one that BEST answers the question or completes the statement. *PRINT THE LETTER OF THE CORRECT ANSWER IN THE SPACE AT THE RIGHT.*

Questions 1-10.

DIRECTIONS: In each of the following groups of four sentences, one sentence contains an error in sentence structure, grammar, usage, diction, or punctuation. Indicate the INCORRECT sentence.

1. A. The lecture finished, the audience began asking questions.
    B. Any man who could accomplish that task the world would regard as a hero.
    C. Our respect and admiration are mutual.
    D. George did like his mother told him, despite the importunities of his playmates.

2. A. I cannot but help admiring you for your dedication to your job.
    B. Because they had insisted upon showing us films of their travels, we have lost many friends whom we once cherished.
    C. I am constrained to admit that your remarks made me feel bad.
    D. My brother having been notified of his acceptance by the university of his choice, my father immediately made plans for a vacation.

3. A. In no other country is freedom of speech and assembly so jealously guarded.
    B. Being a beatnik, he felt that it would be a betrayal of his cause to wear shoes and socks at the same time.
    C. Riding over the Brooklyn Bridge gave us an opportunity to see the Manhattan skyline.
    D. In 1961, flaunting SEATO, the North Vietnamese crossed the line of demarcation.

4. A. I have enjoyed the study of the Spanish language not only because of its beauty and the opportunity it offers to understand the Hispanic culture but also to make use of it in the business associations I have in South America.
    B. The opinions he expressed were decidedly different from those he had held in his youth.
    C. Had he actually studied, he certainly would have passed.
    D. A supervisor should be patient, tactful, and firm.

5. A. At this point we were faced with only three alterna-
       tives: to push on, to remain where we were, or to
       return to the village.
    B. We had no choice but to forgive so venial a sin.
    C. In their new picture, the Warners are flouting tradi-
       tion.
    D. Photographs taken revealed that 2.5 square miles had
       been burned.

5. __

6. A. He asked whether he might write to his friends.
    B. There are many problems which must be solved before
       we can be assured of world peace.
    C. Each person with whom I talked expressed his opinion
       freely.
    D. Holding on to my saddle with all my strength the horse
       galloped down the road at a terrifying pace.

6. D

7. A. After graduating high school, he obtained a position
       as a runner in Wall Street.
    B. Last night, in a radio address, the President urged
       us to subscribe to the Red Cross.
    C. In the evening, light spring rain cooled the streets.
    D. "Un-American" is a word which has been used even by
       those whose sympathies may well have been pro-Nazi.

7. A

8. A. It is hard to conceive of their not doing good work.
    B. Who won - you or I?
    C. He having read the speech caused much comment.
    D. Their finishing the work proves that it can be done.

8. C

9. A. Our course of study should not be different now than
       it was five years ago.
    B. I cannot deny myself the pleasure of publicly thanking
       the mayor for his actions.
    C. The article on "Morale" has appeared in the Times
       Literary Supplement.
    D. He died of tuberculosis contracted during service with
       the Allied Forces.

9. C

10. A. If it wasn't for a lucky accident, he would still be
       an office-clerk.
    B. It is evident that teachers need help.
    C. Rolls of postage stamps may be bought at stationery
       stores.
    D. Addressing machines are used by firms that publish
       magazines.

10. A

11. The one of the following sentences which contains NO
    error in usage is:
    A. After the robbers left, the proprietor stood tied in
       his chair for about two hours before help arrived.
    B. In the cellar I found the watchmans' hat and coat.
    C. The persons living in adjacent apartments stated
       that they had heard no unusual noises.
    D. Neither a knife or any firearms were found in the room.

11. C

12. The one of the following sentences which contains NO
    error in usage is:
    A. The policeman lay a firm hand on the suspect's
       shoulder.
    B. It is true that neither strength nor agility are the
       most important requirement for a good patrolman.
    C. Good citizens constantly strive to do more than merely
       comply the restraints imposed by society.
    D. Twenty years is considered a severe sentence for a
       felony.

    12.___

13. Select the sentence containing an adverbial objective.
    A. Concepts can only acquire content when they are
       connected, however indirectly, with sensible experi-
       ence.
    B. The cloth was several shades too light to match the
       skirt which she had discarded.
    C. The Gargantuan Hall of Commons became a tri-daily
       horror to Kurt, because two youths discerned that
       he had a beard and courageously told the world about
       it.
    D. Brooding morbidly over the event, Elsie found herself
       incapable of engaging in normal activity.

    13.___

14. Select the sentence containing a verb in the subjunctive
    mood.
    A. Had he known of the new experiments with penicillin
       dust for the cure of colds, he might have been
       tempted to try them in his own office.
    B. I should be very much honored by your visit.
    C. Though he has one of the highest intelligence quo-
       tients in his group, he seems far below the average
       in actual achievement.
    D. Long had I known that he would be the man finally
       selected for such signal honors.

    14.___

15. Select the sentence containing one (or more) passive
    perfect participle(s).
    A. Having been apprised of the consequences of his
       refusal to answer, the witness finally revealed the
       source of his information.
    B. To have been placed in such an uncomfortable posi-
       tion was perhaps unfair to a journalist of his
       reputation.
    C. When deprived of special immunity he had, of course,
       no alternative but to speak.
    D. Having been obdurate until now, he was reluctant to
       surrender under this final pressure exerted upon him.

    15.___

16. Select the sentence containing a predicate nominative.
    A. His dying wish, which he expressed almost with his
       last breath, was to see that justice was done toward
       his estranged wife.
    B. So long as we continue to elect our officials in truly
       democratic fashion, we shall have the power to pre-
       serve our liberties.

    16.___

C. We could do nothing, at this juncture, but walk the five miles back to camp.
D. There was the spaniel, wet and cold and miserable, waiting silently at the door.

17. Select the sentence containing exactly TWO adverbs.   17. C
    A. The gentlemen advanced with exasperating deliberate-ness, while his lonely partner waited.
    B. If you are well, will you come early?
    C. I think you have guessed right, though you were rather slow, I must say.
    D. The last hundred years have seen more change than a thousand years of the Roman Empire, than a hundred thousand years of the stone age.

Questions 18-24.

DIRECTIONS: Select the choice describing the error in the sentence.

18. If us seniors do not support school functions, who will?   18. C
    A. Unnecessary shift in tense
    B. Incomplete sentence
    C. Improper case of pronoun
    D. Lack of parallelism

19. The principal has issued regulations which, in my opinion,   19. D
    I think are too harsh.
    A. Incorrect punctuation   B. Faulty sentence structure
    C. Misspelling   D. Redundant expression

20. The freshmens' and sophomores' performances equaled those   20. B
    of the juniors and seniors.
    A. Ambiguous reference
    B. Incorrect placement of punctuation
    C. Misspelling of past tense
    D. Incomplete comparison

21. Each of them, Anne and her, is an outstanding pianist;   21. B
    I can't tell you which one is best.
    A. Lack of agreement
    B. Improper degree of comparison
    C. Incorrect case of pronoun
    D. Run-on sentence

22. She wears clothes that are more expensive than my other   22. D
    friends.
    A. Misuse of *than*   B. Incorrect relative pronoun
    C. Shift in tense   D. Faulty comparison

23. At the very end of the story it implies that the   23. B
    children's father died tragically.
    A. Misuse of *implies*   B. Indefinite use of pronoun
    C. Incorrect spelling   D. Incorrect possessive

24. At the end of the game both of us, John and me, couldn't   24. D
    scarcely walk because we were so tired.
    A. Incorrect punctuation
    B. Run-on sentence
    C. Incorrect case of pronoun
    D. Double negative

Questions 25-30.

DIRECTIONS: Questions 25 through 30 consist of a sentence lacking
              certain needed punctuation. Pick as your answer the
              description of punctuation which will CORRECTLY complete
              the sentence.

25. If you take the time to keep up your daily correspondence   25. B
    you will no doubt be most efficient.
    A. Comma only after *doubt*
    B. Comma only after *correspondence*
    C. Commas after *correspondence, will,* and *be*
    D. Commas after *if, correspondence,* and *will*

26. Because he did not send the application soon enough he   26. C
    did not receive the up to date copy of the book.
    A. Commas after *application* and *enough,* and quotation
       marks before *up* and after *date*
    B. Commas after *application* and *enough,* and hyphens
       between *to* and *date*
    C. Comma after *enough,* and hyphens between *up* and *to*
       and between *to* and *date*
    D. Comma after *application,* and quotation marks before
       up and after *date*

27. The coordinator requested from the department the follow-   27. C
    ing items a letter each week summarizing progress personal
    forms and completed applications for tests.
    A. Commas after *items* and *completed*
    B. Semi-colon after *items* and *progress,* comma after *forms*
    C. Colon after *items,* commas after *progress* and *forms*
    D. Colon after *items,* commas after *forms* and *applications*

28. The supervisor asked Who will attend the conference next   28. D
    month.
    A. Comma after *asked,* period after *month*
    B. Period after *asked,* question mark after *month*
    C. Comma after *asked,* quotation marks before *Who,*
       quotation marks after *month,* and question mark after
       the quotation marks
    D. Comma after *asked,* quotation marks before *Who,*
       question mark after *month,* and quotation marks after
       the question mark

29. When the statistics are collected, we will forward the   29. D
    results to you as soon as possible.
    A. Comma after *you*
    B. Commas after *forward* and *you*
    C. Commas after *collected, results,* and *you*
    D. Comma after *collected*

30. The ecology of our environment is concerned with man's   30. B
     pollution of the atmosphere.
        A. Comma after *ecology*
        B. Apostrophe after *n* and before *s* in *mans*
        C. Commas after *ecology* and *environment*
        D. Apostrophe after *s* in *mans*

KEY (CORRECT ANSWERS)

1. D	11. C	21. B
2. A	12. D	22. D
3. D	13. B	23. B
4. A	14. A	24. D
5. B	15. A	25. B
6. D	16. A	26. C
7. A	17. C	27. C
8. C	18. C	28. D
9. A	19. D	29. D
10. A	20. B	30. B

TEST 3

DIRECTIONS: Each question or incorrect statement is followed by several suggested answers or completions. Select the one that BEST answers the question or completes the statement. *PRINT THE LETTER OF THE CORRECT ANSWER IN THE SPACE AT THE RIGHT.*

Questions 1-6.

DIRECTIONS: From the four choices offered in Questions 1 through 6, select the one which is INCORRECT.

1. A. Before we try to extricate ourselves from this struggle   1. A
       in which we are now engaged in, we must be sure that we
       are not severing ties of honor and duty.
    B. Besides being an outstanding student, he is also a
       leader in school government and a trophy-winner in
       school sports.
    C. If the framers of the Constitution were to return to
       life for a day, their opinion of our amendments would
       be interesting.
    D. Since there are three m's in the word, it is frequently
       misspelled.

2. A. It was a college with an excellance beyond question.   2. A
    B. The coach will accompany the winners, whomever they
       may be.
    C. The dean, together with some other faculty members,
       is planning a conference.
    D. The jury are arguing among themselves.

3. A. This box is less nearly square than that one.   3. C
    B. Wagner is many persons' choice as the world's greatest
       composer.
    C. The habits of Copperheads are different from Diamond
       Backs.
    D. The teacher maintains that the child was insolent.

4. A. There was a time when the Far North was unknown terri-   4. B
       tory. Now American soldiers manning radar stations
       there wave to Boeing jet planes zooming by overhead.
    B. Exodus, the psalms, and Deuteronomy are all books of
       the Old Testament.
    C. Linda identified her china dishes by marking their
       bottoms with india ink.
    D. Harry S. Truman, former president of the United States,
       served as a captain in the American army during World
       War I.

5. A. The sequel of their marriage was a divorce.   5. A
    B. We bought our car secondhand.
    C. His whereabouts is unknown.
    D. Jones offered to use his own car, providing the company
       would pay for gasoline, oil, and repairs.

6.   A. I read Golding's "Lord of the Flies".   6. _A_
      B. The orator at the civil rights rally thrilled the
         audience when he said, "I quote Robert Burns's line,
         'A man's a man for a' that.'"
      C. The phrase "producer to consumer" is commonly used by
         market analysts.
      D. The lawyer shouted, "Is not this evidence illegal?"

Questions 7-9.

DIRECTIONS: In answering Questions 7 through 9, mark the letter A
              if faulty because of incorrect grammar, mark the letter
              B if faulty because of incorrect punctuation, mark the
              letter C if correct.

7.   Mr. Brown our accountant, will audit the accounts next   7. _B_
     week.

8.   Give the assignment to whomever is able to do it most   8. _A_
     efficiently.

9.   The supervisor expected either your or I to file these   9. _A_
     reports.

Questions 10-14.

DIRECTIONS: In each of the following groups of four sentences, one
              sentence contains an error in sentence structure, grammar,
              usage, diction, or punctuation. Indicate the INCORRECT
              sentence.

10. A. The agent asked, "Did you say, 'Never again?'"   10. _A_
      B. Kindly let me know whether you can visit us on the
         17th.
      C. "I cannot accept that!" he exploded. "Please show me
         something else."
      D. Ed, will you please lend me your grass shears for an
         hour or so.

11. A. Recalcitrant though he may have been, Alexander was   11. _B_
        wilfully destructive.
      B. Everybody should look out for himself.
      C. John is one of those students who usually spends most
        of his time in the principal's office.
      D. She seems to feel that what is theirs is hers.

12. A. Be he ever so much in the wrong, I'll support the man   12. _B_
        while deploring his actions.
      B. The schools' lack of interest in consumer education
        is shortsighted.
      C. I think that Fitzgerald's finest stanza is one which
        includes the reference to youth's "sweet-scented
        manuscript."
      D. I never would agree to Anderson having full control of
        the company's policies.

13. A. We had to walk about five miles before finding a gas   13. B
        station.
     B. The willful sending of a false alarm has, and may,
        result in homicide.
     C. Please bring that book to me at once!
     D. Neither my sister nor I am interested in bowling.

14. A. He is one of the very few football players who doesn't   14. A
        wear a helmet with a face guard.
     B. But three volunteers appeared at the recruiting office.
     C. Such consideration as you can give us will be appre-
        ciated.
     D. When I left them, the group were disagreeing about the
        proposed legislation.

Question 15.

DIRECTIONS: Question 15 contains two sentences concerning criminal
              law. The sentences could contain errors in English
              grammar or usage. A sentence does not contain an error
              simply because it could be written in a different
              manner. In answering this question, choose answer
                A. if only sentence I is correct
                B. if only sentence II is correct
                C. if both sentences are correct
                D. if neither sentence is correct

15.   I. The use of fire or explosives to destroy tangible   15. A
         property is proscribed by the criminal mischief
         provisions of the Revised Penal Law.
     II. The defendant's taking of a taxicab for the immediate
         purpose of affecting his escape did not constitute
         grand larceny.

———————

KEY (CORRECT ANSWERS)

1. A	6. A	11. C
2. B	7. B	12. D
3. C	8. A	13. B
4. B	9. A	14. A
5. D	10. A	15. A

WRITTEN ENGLISH EXPRESSION
EXAMINATION SECTION

TEST 1

DIRECTIONS: In each of the sentences below, four portions are
underlined and lettered. Read each sentence and
decide whether any of the UNDERLINED parts contains
an error in spelling, punctuation, or capitalization,
or employs grammatical usage which would be inappro-
priate for carefully written English. If so, note
the letter printed under the unacceptable form and
indicate this choice in the space at the right. If
all four of the underlined portions are acceptable
as they stand, select the answer E.
(No sentence contains more than ONE unacceptable form.)

1. The revised procedure was quite different than the one
          A   B   C
which was employed up to that time. No error
     D   E   1. C

2. Blinded by the storm that surrounded him, his plane
     A   B
kept going in circles. No error
     C   D   E   2. A

3. They should give the book to whoever they think deserves
          A   B   C
it. No error
 D   E   3. B

4. The government will not consent to your firm sending that
        A   B   C
package as second class matter. No error
            D   E   4.

5. She would have avoided all the trouble that followed if
       A   B
she would have waited ten minutes longer. No error
        C   D   E   5.

6. His poetry, when it was carefully examined, showed
   A   B
characteristics not unlike Wordsworth. No error
        C   D   E   6. D

7. <u>In my opinion</u>, based upon long years of research, <u>I think</u>
     A   B
the plan offered by my opponent is <u>unsound</u>, because it is
                                  C
not <u>founded</u> on true facts. <u>No error</u>
     D   E

7. _____

8. The soldiers of <u>Washington's</u> army at Valley Forge <u>were</u> men
                  A   B
ragged in <u>appearance</u> but <u>who were</u> noble in character.
             C   D
<u>No error</u>
  E

8. _____

9. Rabbits <u>have a distrust</u> of man <u>due to</u> the fact <u>that</u> they
               A   B   C
are <u>so often</u> shot. <u>No error</u>
     D   E

9. _____

10. <u>This</u> is the man <u>who</u> I believe <u>is</u> best <u>qualified</u> for the
     A   B   C   D
position. <u>No error</u>
           E

10. _____

11. Her voice was <u>not only</u> good, but <u>she</u> also very clearly
               A   B   C
<u>enunciated</u>. <u>No error</u>
   D   E

11. _____

12. <u>Today he</u> is wearing a <u>different</u> suit <u>than</u> the <u>one</u> he wore
     A   B   C   D
yesterday. <u>No error</u>
            E

12. _____

13. Our work <u>is</u> to improve the club; if anybody <u>must</u> resign,
          A   B
let it <u>not</u> be you or <u>I</u>. <u>No error</u>
       C   D   E

13. _____

14. There was so much talking <u>in back of</u> me <u>as</u> I <u>could</u> not
                          A   B   C
<u>enjoy</u> the music. <u>No error</u>
   D   E

14. _____

15. <u>Being that</u> he is that <u>kind of</u> boy, he cannot be blamed
       A   B   C
<u>for</u> the mistake. <u>No error</u>
 D   E

15. _____

16. The king, having read the speech, he and the queen
    _____A_____   __B__   __C__
    departed.   No error
    ___D____   __E__   16. [handwritten] A

17. I am so tired I can't scarcely stand.   No error
      _A _so_tired_ _C_ ___D___   __E__   17. [handwritten] D

18. We are mailing bills to our customers in Canada, and,
             ____A____   ____B____
    being eager to clear our books before the new season opens,
    __C__
    it is to be hoped they will send their remittances promptly.
          ___D_____
    No error
    __E__   18. [handwritten] B

19. I reluctantly acquiesced to the proposal.   No error
    _A ____B____ ___C____   ___D___   __E__   19. [handwritten] E

20. It had lain out in the rain all night.   No error
    _A _B___ __C_   __D_____   __E__   20. [handwritten] A

21. If he would have gone there, he would have seen a
    _____A_____ _B__   ___C_____
    marvelous sight.   No error
    ___D____   __E__   21. [handwritten] A

22. The climate of Asia Minor is somewhat like Utah.   No error
                __A_   _B_   __C__ _D_   __E__   22. [handwritten] D

23. If everybody did unto others as they would wish others to
       ___A___ _B_ ___C____   _____D____
    do unto them, this world would be a paradise.   No error
                                                     __E__   23. [handwritten] B

24. This was the jockey whom I saw was most likely to win the
    __A__   __B__   _C_   ___D__
    race.   No error
            __E__   24. [handwritten] B

25. The only food the general demanded was potatoes.   No error
        __A__   __B___   _C_ __D___   __E__   25. [handwritten] A

KEY (CORRECT ANSWERS)

1.	C	11.	C
2.	A	12.	C
3.	E	13.	D
4.	B	14.	B
5.	C	15.	A
6.	D	16.	A
7.	B	17.	C
8.	D	18.	C
9.	B	19.	E
10.	E	20.	E

21.	A
22.	D
23.	D
24.	B
25.	E

TEST 2

DIRECTIONS: In each of the sentences below, four portions are
underlined and lettered. Read each sentence and
decide whether any of the UNDERLINED parts contains
an error in spelling, punctuation, or capitalization,
or employs grammatical usage which would be inappro-
priate for carefully written English. If so, note
the letter printed under the unacceptable form and
indicate this choice in the space at the right. If
all four of the underlined portions are acceptable
as they stand, select the answer E.
(No sentence contains more than ONE unacceptable form.)

1. A party like that only comes once a year. No error
            A   B   C   D   E

2. Our's is a swift moving age. No error
    A   B C   D   E

3. The healthy climate soon restored him to his accustomed
        A   B   C   D
    vigor. No error
            E

4. They needed six typists and hoped that only that many
    A   B   C
    would apply for the position. No error
    D   E

5. He interviewed people whom he thought had something
       A   B   C
    to impart. No error
    D   E

6. Neither of his three sisters is older than he. No error
    A   B   C D   E

7. Since he is that kind of a boy, he cannot be expected to
    A   B   C   D
    cooperate with us. No error
                        E

8. When passing through the tunnel, the air pressure affected
         A   B   C
    our ears. No error
    D   E

9. The story having a sad ending, it never achieved popularity   9. A
   ⎯⎯⎯⎯⎯⎯⎯⎯⎯⎯⎯⎯   ⎯⎯   ⎯⎯⎯⎯⎯⎯⎯⎯
         A   B   C
   among the students.   No error
   ⎯⎯⎯⎯⎯   ⎯⎯⎯⎯⎯⎯⎯⎯
     D   E

10. Since we are both hungry, shall we go somewhere for lunch?   10. A
    ⎯⎯⎯⎯⎯   ⎯⎯⎯⎯⎯   ⎯⎯⎯⎯⎯⎯⎯⎯⎯   ⎯⎯
      A   B   C   D
    No error
    ⎯⎯⎯⎯⎯⎯⎯⎯
       E

11. Will you please bring this book down to the library and   11. B
    ⎯⎯⎯⎯   ⎯⎯⎯⎯⎯   ⎯⎯⎯⎯⎯⎯⎯
     A   B   C
    give it to my friend, who is waiting for it?   No error
    ⎯⎯⎯⎯⎯⎯⎯⎯⎯⎯⎯⎯⎯⎯⎯   ⎯⎯⎯⎯⎯⎯⎯⎯
            D   E

12. You may have the book; I am finished with it.   No error   12. E
        ⎯⎯⎯ ⎯⎯⎯⎯   ⎯⎯   ⎯⎯⎯⎯   ⎯⎯⎯⎯⎯⎯⎯⎯
         A   B   C   D   E

13. I don't know if I should mention it to her or not.   13. B
      ⎯⎯⎯⎯⎯ ⎯⎯   ⎯⎯⎯⎯⎯⎯   ⎯⎯
        A   B   C   D
    No error
    ⎯⎯⎯⎯⎯⎯⎯⎯
       E

14. Philosophy is not a subject which has to do with philo-   14. D
                   ⎯⎯⎯⎯⎯⎯⎯⎯ ⎯⎯⎯⎯⎯ ⎯⎯⎯⎯⎯⎯⎯
                       A   B   C
    sophers and mathematics only.   No error
                          ⎯⎯⎯⎯   ⎯⎯⎯⎯⎯⎯⎯⎯
                           D   E

15. The thoughts of the scholar in his library are little   15. B
                               ⎯⎯⎯⎯⎯⎯⎯⎯⎯⎯⎯⎯⎯⎯
                                       A
    different than the old woman who first said, "It's no use
              ⎯⎯⎯⎯   ⎯⎯⎯⎯⎯⎯⎯⎯⎯⎯⎯
               B   C
    crying over spilt milk."   No error
                        ⎯⎯⎯⎯   ⎯⎯⎯⎯⎯⎯⎯⎯
                          D   E

16. A complete system of philosophical ideas are implied in   16. C
               ⎯⎯⎯⎯⎯⎯   ⎯⎯⎯ ⎯⎯⎯⎯⎯⎯⎯
                 A   B   C
    many simple utterances.   No error
               ⎯⎯⎯⎯⎯⎯⎯⎯⎯   ⎯⎯⎯⎯⎯⎯⎯⎯
                  D   E

17. Even if one has never put them into words, his ideas   17. B
         ⎯⎯   ⎯⎯⎯⎯   ⎯⎯⎯
          A   B   C
    compose a kind of a philosophy.   No error
    ⎯⎯⎯⎯⎯⎯⎯   ⎯⎯⎯⎯⎯⎯⎯⎯
       D   E

18. Perhaps it is well enough that most people do not attempt   18. D
              ⎯⎯ ⎯⎯⎯⎯⎯⎯⎯⎯⎯   ⎯⎯⎯⎯⎯⎯
               A   B   C
    this formulation.   No error
         ⎯⎯⎯⎯⎯⎯⎯⎯⎯⎯⎯   ⎯⎯⎯⎯⎯⎯⎯⎯
              D   E

19. Leading their ordered lives, this confused body of ideas   19.___
          A   B   C
and feelings is sufficient.   No error
                    D   E

20. Why should we insert upon them formulating it?   No error   20.___
          A   B   C   D   E

21. Since it includes something of the wisdom of the ages, it   21.___
       A   B
is adequate for the purposes of ordinary life.   No error
       C   D   E

22. Therefore, I have sought to make a pattern of mine, and so   22.___
                    A   B   C
there were early moments of my trying to find out what were
                                       D
the elements with which I had to deal.   No error
                                                    E

23. I wanted to get what knowledge I could about the general   23.___
       A   B   C   D
structure of the universe.   No error
                                    E

24. I wanted to know if life per se had any meaning or   24.___
                    A   B   C
whether I must strive to give it one.   No error
       D   E

25. So, in a desultory way, I began to read.   No error   25.___
       A   B   C   D   E

KEY (CORRECT ANSWERS)

1. C			11. B	
2. A			12. C	
3. A			13. B	
4. C			14. D	
5. B			15. B	
6. A			16. B	
7. D			17. A	
8. A			18. C	
9. A			19. A	
10. E			20. C	

21. E
22. C
23. C
24. B
25. E

WORD MEANING
EXAMINATION SECTION
TEST 1

DIRECTIONS: Each question or incomplete statement is followed by several suggested answers or completions. Select the one that BEST answers the question or completes the statement. *PRINT THE LETTER OF THE CORRECT ANSWER IN THE SPACE AT THE RIGHT.*

1. He implied that he would work overtime if necessary.   1. D
   In this sentence, the word *implied* means
     A. denied   B. explained
     C. guaranteed   D. hinted

2. The bag of the vacuum cleaner was inflated.   2. A
   In this sentence, the word *inflated* means
     A. blown up with air   B. filled with dirt
     C. loose   D. torn

3. Burning material during certain hours is prohibited.   3. B
   In this sentence, the word *prohibited* means
     A. allowed   B. forbidden   C. legal   D. required

4. He was rejected when he applied for the job.   4. D
   In this sentence, the word *rejected* means
     A. discouraged   B. put to work
     C. tested   D. turned down

5. The foreman was able to substantiate his need for extra 5. C
   supplies.
   In this sentence, the word *substantiate* means
     A. estimate   B. meet   C. prove   D. reduce

6. The new instructions supersede the old ones.   6. D
   In this sentence, the word *supersede* means
     A. explain   B. improve   C. include   D. replace

7. Shake the broom free of surplus water and hang it up to 7. B
   dry.
   In this sentence, the word *surplus* means
     A. dirty   B. extra   C. rinse   D. soapy

8. When a crack is filled, the asphalt must be tamped.   8. C
   In this sentence, the word *tamped* means
     A. cured   B. heated
     C. packed down   D. wet down

9. The apartment was left vacant.   9. B
   In this sentence, the word *vacant* means
     A. clean   B. empty   C. furnished D. locked

10. The caretaker spent the whole day doing various repairs. 10. A
    In this sentence, the word *various* means
      A. different   B. necessary   C. small   D. special

11. He came back to assist his partner.
    In this sentence, the word *assist* means
       A. call   B. help   C. stop   D. question

11. B

12. A person who is biased cannot be a good foreman.
    In this sentence, the word *biased* means
       A. easy-going   B. prejudiced
       C. strict   D. uneducated

12. B

13. The lecture for the new employees was brief.
    In this sentence, the word *brief* means
       A. educational   B. free
       C. interesting   D. short

13. D

14. He was asked to clarify the order.
    In this sentence, the word *clarify* means
       A. follow out   B. make clear
       C. take back   D. write out

14. B

15. The employee was commended by his foreman.
    In this sentence, the word *commended* means
       A. assigned   B. blamed   C. picked   D. praised

15. D

16. Before the winter, the lawnmower engine was dismantled.
    In this sentence, the word *dismantled* means
       A. oiled   B. repaired
       C. stored away   D. taken apart

16. D

17. They excavated a big hole on the project lawn.
    In this sentence, the word *excavated* means
       A. cleaned out   B. discovered
       C. dug out   D. filled in

17. C

18. The new man was told to sweep the exterior area.
    In this sentence, the word *exterior* means
       A. asphalt   B. nearby   C. outside   D. whole

18. C

19. The officer refuted the statement of the driver.
    As used in this sentence, the word *refuted* means MOST
    NEARLY
       A. disproved   B. elaborated upon
       C. related   D. supported

19. A

20. The mechanism of the parking meter is not intricate.
    As used in this sentence, the word *intricate* means MOST
    NEARLY
       A. cheap   B. complicated
       C. foolproof   D. strong

20. B

21. The weight of each box fluctuates.
    As used in this sentence, the word *fluctuates* means MOST
    NEARLY
       A. always changes   B. decreases
       C. increases gradually   D. is similar

21. A

22. The person chosen to investigate the new procedure should be impartial.
    As used in this sentence, the word *impartial* means MOST NEARLY
        A. experienced   B. fair
        C. forward looking   D. important

22. B

23. Carelessness in the safekeeping of keys will not be tolerated.
    As used in this sentence, the word *tolerated* means MOST NEARLY
        A. forgotten   B. permitted
        C. punished lightly   D. understood

23. B

24. The traffic was easily diverted.
    As used in this sentence, the word *diverted* means MOST NEARLY
        A. controlled   B. speeded up
        B. stopped   D. turned aside

24. D

25. A transcript of the report was prepared in the office.
    As used in this sentence, the word *transcript* means MOST NEARLY
        A. brief   B. copy
        C. record   D. translation

25. B

26. The change was authorized by the supervisor.
    As used in this sentence, the word *authorized* means MOST NEARLY
        A. completed B. corrected C. ordered   D. permitted

26. D

27. The supervisor read the excerpt of the collector's report.
    According to this sentence, the supervisor read _____ the report.
        A. a passage from   B. a summary of
        C. the original of   D. the whole of

27. A

28. During the probation period, the worker proved to be inept.
    The word *inept* means MOST NEARLY
        A. incompetent   B. insubordinate
        C. satisfactory   D. uncooperative

28. A

29. The putative father was not living with the family.
    The word *putative* means MOST NEARLY
        A. reputed   B. unemployed
        C. concerned   D. indifferent

29. A

30. The adopted child researched various documents of vital statistics in an effort to discover the names of his natural parents.
    The words *vital statistics* mean MOST NEARLY statistics relating to
        A. human life   B. hospitals
        C. important facts   D. health and welfare

30. C

31. Despite many requests for them, there was a scant supply   31. C
    of new blotters.
    The word *scant* means MOST NEARLY
       A. adequate   B. abundant
       C. insufficient   D. expensive

32. Did they replenish the supply of forms in the cabinet?   32. B
    The word *replenish* means MOST NEARLY
       A. straighten up   B. refill
       C. sort out   D. use

33. Employees may become bored if they are assigned diverse   33. B
    duties.
    The word *diverse* means MOST NEARLY
       A. interesting   B. different
       C. challenging   D. enjoyable

Questions 34-37.

DIRECTIONS: Each of Questions 34 through 37 consists of a
            capitalized word followed by four suggested meanings
            of the word. Select the word or phrase which means
            MOST NEARLY the same as the capitalized word.

34. PROFICIENCY   34. B
       A. vocation   B. competency
       C. repugnancy   D. prominence

35. BIBLIOGRAPHY   35. D
       A. description   B. stenography
       C. photograph   D. compilation of books

36. FIDELITY   36. D
       A. belief   B. treachery
       C. strength   D. loyalty

37. ACCELERATE   37. C
       A. adjust   B. press   C. quicken   D. strip

38. One of the machinists in your shop enjoys the reputation   38. C
    of being a great equivocator.
    This means MOST NEARLY that he
       A. takes pride and is happy in his work
       B. generally hedges and often gives misleading answers
       C. is a strong union man with great interest in his
          fellow workers' welfare
       D. is good at resolving disputes

39. When a person has the reputation of persistently making   39. B
    foolish or silly remarks, it may be said that he is
       A. inane   B. meticulous
       C. a procrastinator   D. a prevaricator

40. When two mechanics, called A and B, make measurements of   40. _D_
    the same workpiece and find significant discrepancies in
    their measurements, it is MOST NEARLY correct to state
    that
    A. mechanic B made an erroneous reading
    B. mechanic A was careless in making his measurements
    C. both mechanics made their measurements correctly
    D. there was considerable difference in the two sets
       of measurements

41. A foreman who *expedites* a job,   41. ___
    A. abolishes it   B. makes it bigger
    C. slows it down   D. speeds it up

42. If a man is working at a *uniform* speed, it means he is   42. _D_
    working at a speed which is
    A. changing   B. fast   C. slow   D. steady

43. To say that a caretaker is *obstinate* means that he is   43. _C_
    A. cooperative   B. patient
    C. stubborn   D. willing

44. To say that a caretaker is *negligent* means that he is   44. _A_
    A. careless   B. neat   C. nervous   D. late

45. To say that something is *absurd* means that it is   45. _C_
    A. definite   B. not clear
    C. ridiculous   D. unfair

46. To say that a foreman is *impartial* means that he is   46. _A_
    A. fair   B. improving C. in a hurry D. watchful

47. A man who is *lenient* is one who is   47. _D_
    A. careless   B. harsh
    C. inexperienced   D. mild

48. A man who is *punctual* is one who is   48. _C_
    A. able   B. polite   C. prompt   D. sincere

49. If you think one of your men is too *awkward* to do a job,   49. _A_
    it means you think he is too
    A. clumsy   B. lazy   C. old   D. weak

50. A person who is *seldom* late, is late   50. _D_
    A. always   B. never   C. often   D. rarely

KEY (CORRECT ANSWERS)

1. D	11. B	21. A	31. C	41. D
2. A	12. B	22. B	32. B	42. D
3. B	13. D	23. B	33. B	43. C
4. D	14. B	24. D	34. B	44. A
5. C	15. D	25. B	35. D	45. C
6. D	16. D	26. D	36. D	46. A
7. B	17. C	27. A	37. C	47. D
8. C	18. C	28. A	38. B	48. C
9. B	19. A	29. A	39. B	49. A
10. A	20. B	30. A	40. D	50. D

TEST 2

1. The Department of Health can certify that conditions in a housing accommodation are detrimental to life or health.
   As used in the above sentence, the word *detrimental* means MOST NEARLY

   A. injurious   B. serious
   C. satisfactory   D. necessary

   1. A

2. The Administrator shall have the power to revoke any adjustment in rents granted either the landlord or the tenant.
   As used in the above sentence, the word *revoke* means MOST NEARLY

   A. increase   B. decrease   C. rescind   D. restore

   2. C

Questions 3-5.

DIRECTIONS: Each of Questions 3 through 5 consists of a capitalized word followed by four suggested meanings of the word. Select the word which means MOST NEARLY the same as the capitalized word.

3. DOGMATISM
   A. dramatism   B. positiveness
   C. doubtful   D. tentativeness

   3. B

4. ELECTRODE
   A. officer   B. electrolyte
   C. terminal   D. positive

   4. C

5. EMIT
   A. return   B. enter   C. omit   D. discharge

   5. D

6. The word *inflammable* means MOST NEARLY
   A. burnable   B. acid   C. poisonous   D. explosive

   6. A

7. The word *disinfect* means MOST NEARLY
   A. deodorize   B. sterilize   C. bleach   D. dissolve

   7. B

8. He wanted to ascertain the facts before arriving at a conclusion.
   The word *ascertain* means MOST NEARLY
   A. disprove   B. determine   C. convert   D. provide

   8. B

9. Did the supervisor assent to her request for annual leave?   9. C
   The word *assent* means MOST NEARLY
       A. allude   B. protest   C. agree   D. refer

10. The new worker was fearful that the others would rebuff   10. D
    her.
    The word *rebuff* means MOST NEARLY
        A. ignore   B. forget   C. copy   D. snub

11. The supervisor of that office does not condone lateness.   11. B
    The word *condone* means MOST NEARLY
        A. mind   B. excuse   C. punish   D. remember

12. Each employee was instructed to be as concise as possible   12. D
    when preparing a report.
    The word *concise* means MOST NEARLY
        A. exact   B. sincere   C. flexible   D. brief

13. The shovelers should not distribute the asphalt faster   13. C
    than it can be properly handled by the rakers.
    As used above, *distribute* means MOST NEARLY
        A. dump   B. pick-up   C. spread   D. heat

14. Any defective places should be cut out.   14. D
    As used above, *defective* means MOST NEARLY
        A. low   B. hard   C. soft   D. faulty

15. *Sphere of authority* is called   15. C
        A. constituency   B. dictatorial
        C. jurisdiction   D. vassal

16. Rollers are made in several sizes.   16. D
    As used above, *several* means MOST NEARLY
        A. large   B. heavy   C. standard   D. different

17. Sometimes a roller is run over an old surface to detect   17. C
    weak spots.
    As used above, *detect* means MOST NEARLY
        A. compact   B. remove   C. find   D. strengthen

18. Reconstruction of the old base is sometimes required as   18. A
    a preliminary operation.
    As used above, *preliminary* means MOST NEARLY
        A. first   B. necessary   C. important   D. local

19. If a man makes an *absurd* remark, he makes one which is   19. B
    MOST NEARLY
        A. misleading   B. ridiculous
        C. unfair   D. wicked

20. A worker who is *adept* at his job is one who is MOST   20. D
    NEARLY
        A. cooperative   B. developed
        C. diligent   D. skilled

21. If a man states a condition is *general*, he means it is   21. B
    MOST NEARLY
       A. artificial   B. prevalent
       C. timely   D. transient

Questions 22-50.

DIRECTIONS: Each of Questions 22 through 50 consists of a sentence
              in which a word is italicized. Of the four words
              following each sentence, select the word whose meaning
              is MOST NEARLY the same as the meaning of the italicized
              word.

22. The agent's first *assignment* was to patrol on Hicks   22. C
    Avenue.
       A. test   B. sign   C. job   D. deadline

23. Agents get many *inquiries* from the public.   23. D
       A. complaints   B. suggestions
       C. compliments   D. questions

24. The names of all fifty states were written in *abbreviated*   24. A
    form.
       A. shortened   B. corrected
       C. eliminated   D. illegible

25. The meter was examined and found to be *defective*.   25. D
       A. small   B. operating   C. destroyed   D. faulty

26. Agent Roger's reports are *legible*, but Agent Baldwin's   26. B
    are not.
       A. similar   B. readable   C. incorrect   D. late

27. The time allowed, as shown by the meter, had *expired*.   27. C
       A. started   B. broken   C. ended   D. violated

28. The busy *commercial* area is quiet in the evenings.   28. C
       A. deserted   B. growing   C. business   D. local

29. The district office *authorized* the giving of summonses   29. B
    to illegally parked trucks.
       A. suggested   B. approved
       C. prohibited   D. recorded

30. Department property must be used *exclusively* for official   30. C
    business.
       A. occasionally   B. frequently
       C. only   D. properly

31. The District Commander *banned* driving in the area.   31. D
       A. detoured   B. permitted
       C. encouraged   D. prohibited

32. Two copies of the summons are *retained* by the Enforcement Agent.   32. A
    A. kept   B. distributed
    C. submitted   D. signed

33. The Agent *detected* a parking violation.   33. B
    A. cancelled   B. discovered
    C. investigated   D. reported

34. *Pedestrians* may be given summonses for violating traffic   34. D
    regulations.
    A. Bicycle riders   B. Horsemen
    C. Motorcyclists   D. Walkers

35. Parked cars are not allowed to *obstruct* traffic.   35. C
    A. direct   B. lead   C. block   D. speed

36. It was *obvious* to the Agent that the traffic light was   36. D
    broken.
    A. uncertain   B. surprising
    C. possible   D. clear

37. The signs stated that parking in the area was *restricted*   37. D
    to vehicles of foreign diplomats.
    A. allowed   B. increased   C. desired   D. limited

38. Each violation carries an *appropriate* fine.   38. A
    A. suitable   B. extra   C. light   D. heavy

39. Strict enforcement of parking regulations helps to   39. C
    alleviate traffic congestion.
    A. extend   B. build   C. relieve   D. increase

40. The Bureau has a rule which states that an Agent shall   40. A
    speak and act *courteously* in any relationship with the
    public.
    A. respectfully   B. timidly
    C. strangely   D. intelligently

41. City traffic regulations prohibit parking at *jammed*   41. A
    meters.
    A. stuck   B. timed   C. open   D. installed

42. A *significant* error was made by the collector.   42. C
    A. doubtful   B. foolish   C. important   D. strange

43. It is better to *disperse* a crowd.   43. C
    A. hold back   B. quiet   C. scatter   D. talk to

44. Business groups wish to *expand* the program.   44. C
    A. advertise   B. defeat   C. enlarge   D. expose

45. The procedure was *altered* to assist the storekeepers.   45. B
    A. abolished   B. changed
    C. improved   D. made simpler

46. The collector was instructed to *survey* the damage to the parking meter.   46.__
    A. examine   B. give the reason for
    C. repair   D. report

47. It is *imperative* that a collector's report be turned in after each collection.   47.__
    A. desired   B. recommended
    C. requested   D. urgent

48. The collector was not able to *extricate* the key.   48.__
    A. find   B. free
    C. have a copy made of   D. turn

49. Parking meters have *alleviated* one of our major traffic problems.   49.__
    A. created   B. lightened
    C. removed   D. solved

50. Formerly drivers with learners' permits could drive only on *designated* streets.   50.__
    A. dead-end   B. not busy   C. one way   D. specified

KEY (CORRECT ANSWERS)

1. A	11. B	21. B	31. D	41. A
2. C	12. D	22. C	32. A	42. C
3. B	13. C	23. D	33. B	43. C
4. C	14. D	24. A	34. D	44. C
5. D	15. C	25. D	35. C	45. B
6. A	16. D	26. B	36. D	46. A
7. B	17. C	27. C	37. D	47. D
8. B	18. A	28. C	38. A	48. B
9. C	19. B	29. B	39. C	49. B
10. D	20. D	30. C	40. A	50. D

TEST 3

DIRECTIONS: Each question or incomplete statement is followed by several suggested answers or completions. Select the one that BEST answers the question or completes the statement. *PRINT THE LETTER OF THE CORRECT ANSWER IN THE SPACE AT THE RIGHT.*

1. Sprinkler systems in buildings can retard the spread of fires.
   As used in this sentence, the word *retard* means MOST NEARLY
       A. quench   B. slow   C. reveal   D. aggravate

   1. B

2. Although there was widespread criticism, the director refused to curtail the program.
   As used in this sentence, the word *curtail* means MOST NEARLY
       A. change   B. discuss   C. shorten   D. expand

   2. C

3. Argon is an inert gas.
   As used in this sentence, the word *inert* means MOST NEARLY
       A. unstable   B. uncommon   C. volatile   D. inactive

   3. D

4. The firemen turned their hoses on the shed and the main building simultaneously.
   As used in this sentence, the word *simultaneously* means MOST NEARLY
       A. in turn   B. without hesitation
       C. with great haste   D. at the same time

   4. D

5. The officer was rebuked for his failure to act promptly.
   As used in this sentence, the word *rebuked* means MOST NEARLY
       A. demoted   B. reprimanded
       C. discharged   D. reassigned

   5. B

6. Parkways in the city may be used to facilitate responses to fire alarms.
   As used in this sentence, the word *facilitate* means MOST NEARLY
       A. reduce   B. alter   C. complete   D. ease

   6. D

7. Fire extinguishers are most effective when the fire is incipient.
   As used in this sentence, the word *incipient* means MOST NEARLY
       A. accessible   B. beginning
       C. red hot   D. confined

   7. B

8. It is important to convey to new members the fundamentals   8. D
    of the procedure.
    As used in this sentence, the words *convey to* means MOST
    NEARLY
       A. prove for   B. confirm for
       C. suggest to   D. impart to

9. The explosion was a graphic illustration of the effects   9. D
    of neglect and carelessness.
    As used in this sentence, the word *graphic* means MOST
    NEARLY
       A. terrible   B. typical   C. unique   D. vivid

10. The worker was assiduous in all things relating to his   10. ___
    duties.
    As used in this sentence, the word *assiduous* means MOST
    NEARLY
       A. aggressive   B. careless
       C. persistent   D. cautious

11. A worker must be adept to be successful at his work.   11. D
    As used in this sentence, the word *adept* means MOST NEARLY
       A. ambitious   B. strong   C. agile   D. skillful

12. The extinguisher must be inverted before it will operate.   12. A
    As used in this sentence, the word *inverted* means MOST
    NEARLY
       A. turned over   B. completely filled
       C. lightly shaken   D. unhooked

13. Assume that the bridge operator may at times be assigned   13. C
    to the task of coordinating the bridge crew for the
    various routine jobs.
    As used in this sentence, the word *coordinating* means
    MOST NEARLY
       A. ordering   B. testing
       C. scheduling   D. instructing

14. The worker made an insignificant error.   14. D
    As used in this sentence, the word *insignificant* means
    MOST NEARLY
       A. latent   B. serious
       C. accidental   D. minor

15. An Assistant Supervisor should be attentive.   15. A
    As used in this sentence, the word *attentive* means MOST
    NEARLY
       A. watchful   B. prompt   C. negligent   D. willing

16. The Assistant Supervisor reported a cavity in the roadway.   16. C
    As used in this sentence, the word *cavity* means MOST
    NEARLY
       A. lump   B. wreck   C. hollow   D. oil-slick

17. Anyone working in traffic must be cautious.
As used in this sentence, the word *cautious* means MOST NEARLY
    A. brave   B. careful   C. expert   D. fast
17._B_

Questions 18-20.

DIRECTIONS: Each of Questions 18 through 20 consists of a capitalized word followed by four suggested meanings of the word. Select the word or phrase which means MOST NEARLY the same as the capitalized word.

18. OSMOSIS
    A. combining   B. diffusion
    C. ossification   D. incantation
18._____

19. COLLOIDAL
    A. mucinous   B. powdered   C. hairy   D. beautiful
19._____

20. PRETEXT
    A. ritual   B. fictitious reason
    C. sermon   D. truthful motive
20._B_

21. *Easily broken or snapped* defines the word
    A. brittle   B. pliable   C. cohesive   D. volatile
21._A_

22. *At right angles to a given line or surface* defines the word
    A. horizontal   B. oblique
    C. perpendicular   D. adjacent
22._C_

23. *Tools with cutting edges for enlarging or shaping holes* are
    A. screwdrivers   B. pliers
    C. reamers   D. nippers
23._____

24. *An instrument used for measuring very small distances* is called a
    A. gage   B. compass
    C. slide ruler   D. micrometer
24._____

25. When the phrase *acrid smoke* is used, it refers to smoke that is
    A. irritating   B. dense
    C. black   D. very hot
25._A_

26. The officer gave explicit directions on how the work was to be done.
As used in this sentence, the word *explicit* means MOST NEARLY
    A. implied   B. clear   C. vague   D. brief
26._B_

27. After the fire had been extinguished, the debris was taken outside and soaked.
As used in this sentence, the word *debris* means MOST NEARLY
    A. wood   B. rubbish   C. couch   D. paper

27. B

28. The trapped man blanched when he saw the life net below him.
As used in this sentence, the word *blanched* means MOST NEARLY
    A. turned pale   B. sprang forward
    C. flushed   D. fainted

28. A

29. The worker and his supervisor discussed the problem candidly.
As used in this sentence, the word *candidly* means MOST NEARLY
    A. angrily   B. frankly
    C. tolerantly   D. understandingly

29. B

30. The truck came careening down the street.
As used in this sentence, the word *careening* means MOST NEARLY
    A. with sirens screaming
    B. at a slow speed
    C. swaying from side to side
    D. out of control

30. C

31. The population of the province is fairly homogeneous.
As used in this sentence, the word *homogeneous* means MOST NEARLY
    A. devoted to agricultural pursuits
    B. conservative in outlook
    C. essentially alike
    D. sophisticated

31. C

32. The reports of injuries during the past month are being tabulated.
As used in this sentence, the word *tabulated* means MOST NEARLY
    A. analyzed
    B. placed in a file
    C. put in the form of a table
    D. verified

32. C

33. The terms offered were tantamount to surrender.
As used in this sentence, the word *tantamount* means MOST NEARLY
    A. equivalent   B. opposite
    C. preferable   D. preliminary

33. A

34. The man's injuries were superficial.
As used in this sentence, the word *superficial* means MOST NEARLY
    A. on the surface   B. not fatal
    C. free from infection   D. not painful

34. A

35. This experience warped his outlook on life.
    As used in this sentence, the word *warped* means MOST
    NEARLY
    A. changed   B. improved
    C. strengthened   D. twisted

    35. D

36. Hotel guests usually are transients.
    As used in this sentence, the word *transients* means MOST
    NEARLY
    A. persons of considerable wealth
    B. staying for a short time
    C. visitors from other areas
    D. untrustworthy persons

    36. B

37. The pupil's work specimen was considered unsatisfactory
    because of his failure to observe established tolerances.
    As used in this sentence, the word *tolerances* means MOST
    NEARLY
    A. safety precautions
    B. regard for the rights of others
    C. allowable variations in dimensions
    D. amount of waste produced in an operation

    37. C

38. Punishment was severe because the act was considered
    willful.
    As used in this sentence, the word *willful* means MOST
    NEARLY
    A. brutal   B. criminal
    C. harmful   D. intentional

    38. D

39. The malfunctioning of the system was traced to a defective
    thermostat.
    As used in this sentence, the word *thermostat* means MOST
    NEARLY a device that reacts to changes in
    A. amperage   B. water pressure
    C. temperature   D. atmospheric pressure

    39. C

40. His garden contained a profusion of flowers, shrubs, and
    bushes.
    As used in this sentence, the word *profusion* means MOST
    NEARLY
    A. abundance   B. display
    C. representation   D. scarcity

    40. A

41. The inspector would not approve the work because it was
    out of plumb.
    As used in this sentence, the words *out of plumb* means
    MOST NEARLY not
    A. properly seasoned   B. of the required strength
    C. vertical   D. fireproof

    41. C

42. The judge admonished the witness for his answer.
    As used in this sentence, the word *admonished* means MOST
    NEARLY
    A. complimented   B. punished
    C. questioned   D. warned

    42. D

43. A millimeter is a measure of length.
    The length represented by *one millimeter* is
    A. one-thousandth of a meter
    B. one thousand meters
    C. one-millionth of a meter
    D. one million meters

    43. A

44. It is not possible to misconstrue his letter.
    As used in this sentence, the word *misconstrue* means
    MOST NEARLY
    A. decipher   B. forget
    C. ignore   D. misinterpret

    44. D

45. The wire connecting the two terminals must be kept taut.
    As used in this sentence, the word *taut* means MOST NEARLY
    without
    A. defects   B. slack
    C. electrical charge   D. pressure

    45. B

46. Reaching the summit appeared beyond the capacity of the
    hikers.
    As used in this sentence, the word *summit* means MOST NEARLY
    A. canyon   B. peak   C. plateau   D. ravine

    46. B

47. The plot was thwarted by the quick action of the police.
    As used in this sentence, the word *thwarted* means MOST
    NEARLY
    A. blocked   B. discovered
    C. punished   D. solved

    47. A

48. An abrasive was required by the machinist to complete his
    task.
    As used in this sentence, the word *abrasive* means a
    substance used for
    A. coating   B. lubricating
    C. measuring   D. polishing

    48. D

49. The facades of the building were dirty and grimy.
    As used in this sentence, the word *facades* means MOST
    NEARLY
    A. cellars   B. fronts
    C. residents   D. surroundings

    49. B

50. Several firemen were injured by the detonation.
    As used in this sentence, the word *detonation* means MOST
    NEARLY
    A. accident   B. collapse   C. collision   D. explosion

    50. D

KEY (CORRECT ANSWERS)

1. B	11. D	21. A	31. C	41. C
2. C	12. A	22. C	32. C	42. D
3. D	13. C	23. C	33. A	43. A
4. D	14. D	24. D	34. A	44. D
5. B	15. A	25. A	35. D	45. B
6. D	16. C	26. B	36. B	46. B
7. B	17. B	27. B	37. C	47. A
8. D	18. B	28. A	38. D	48. D
9. D	19. A	29. B	39. C	49. B
10. C	20. B	30. C	40. A	50. D

WORD MEANING
EXAMINATION SECTION
TEST 1

Questions 1-20.

DIRECTIONS: Each question consists of a statement. You are to indicate whether the statement is TRUE (T) or FALSE (F). *PRINT THE LETTER OF THE CORRECT ANSWER IN THE SPACE AT THE RIGHT.*

1. *To eliminate hand pumping* means NEARLY the same as *to do away with hand pumping.* 1. T

2. *Discarding a ladder with a cracked rung* means NEARLY the same as *repairing a ladder with a cracked rung.* 2. F

3. A *projecting* stub is USUALLY a stub which sticks out. 3. T

4. A *nitrogen deficiency* in the soil is an oversupply of nitrogen in the soil. 4. F

5. Saying that a soil has a heavy *texture* is NEARLY the same as saying that the soil has a deep color. 5. F

6. A *neutral* soil is one in which no useful plants will grow. 6. F

7. A plant which is *dormant* is USUALLY in an inactive period of growth. 7. T

8. Saying that sun is *detrimental* to ferns is NEARLY the same as saying that sun is harmful to ferns. 8. T

9. *Vendors are permitted only in certain park areas.* In this sentence, the word *vendors* means NEARLY the same as *sellers.* 9. T

10. *The Assistant Gardener was confident that he would be able to learn the new work quickly.* In this sentence, the word *confident* means NEARLY the same as *sure.* 10. T

11. *The employee's behavior on the job was improper.* In this sentence, the word *improper* means NEARLY the same as *good.* 11. F

12. *The foreman's oral instructions were always clear and to the point.* In this sentence, the word *oral* means NEARLY the same as *spoken.* 12. T

13. *A covering with paper will prevent excessive loss of moisture from the surface soil.* In this sentence, the word *excessive* means NEARLY the same as *unnecessary.* 13. F

14. *In making a permanent hotbed, the ground should be excavated to a depth of fifteen inches.* In this sentence, the word *excavated* means NEARLY the same as *dug out.* 14. T

15. *After the seed has been sown, an application of water will help it to germinate. In this sentence, the word germinate means NEARLY the same as start growing.*   15. _T_

16. *A sandy soil may be greatly improved through the incorporation of organic materials. In this sentence, the word incorporation means NEARLY the same as removal.*   16. _F_

17. *Manures are considered a concentrated form of fertilizer. In this sentence, the word concentrated means NEARLY the same as natural.*   17. _F_

18. *Ventilation of some kind must be given the plants. In this sentence, the word ventilation means NEARLY the same as heat.*   18. _F_

19. *When rain water enters soil, it penetrates air spaces. In this sentence, the word penetrates means NEARLY the same as fills.*   X19. _T_

20. *The metal was corroded. In this sentence, the word corroded means NEARLY the same as polished.*   20. _F_

Questions 21-40.

DIRECTIONS: In answering Questions 21 through 40, select the lettered word which means MOST NEARLY the same as the capitalized word. *PRINT THE LETTER OF THE CORRECT ANSWER IN THE SPACE AT THE RIGHT.*

21. ACCURATE   21. _A_
    A. correct   B. useful   C. afraid   D. careless

22. ALTER   22. _B_
    A. copy   B. change   C. repeat   D. agree

23. DOCUMENT   23. _D_
    A. outline   B. agreement   C. blueprint   D. record

24. INDICATE   24. _B_
    A. listen   B. show   C. guess   D. try

25. INVENTORY   25. _D_
    A. custom   B. discovery   C. warning   D. list

26. ISSUE   26. _C_
    A. annoy   B. use up   C. give out   D. gain

27. NOTIFY   27. _A_
    A. inform   B. promise   C. approve   D. strengthen

28. ROUTINE   28. _C_
    A. path   B. mistake   C. habit   D. journey

2

29. TERMINATE
    A. rest   B. start   C. deny   D. end

29. D

30. TRANSMIT
    A. put in   B. send   C. stop   D. go across

30. B

31. QUARANTINE
    A. feed   B. keep separate
    C. clean   D. give an injection to

31. B

32. HERD
    A. group   B. pair   C. person   D. ear

32. A

33. SPECIES
    A. few   B. favorite   C. kind   D. small

33. C

34. INJURE
    A. hurt   B. need   C. protect   D. help

34. A

35. ANNOY
    A. like   B. answer   C. rest   D. bother

35. D

36. EXTINCT
    A. likely   B. no longer exists
    C. tired   D. gradually dying out

36. D

37. CONFINE
    A. fly about freely   B. free
    C. keep within limits   D. care

37. C

38. ENVIRONMENT
    A. distant   B. surroundings
    C. disease   D. lake

38. B

39. AVIARY
    A. pig pen   B. large bird cage
    C. elephant cage   D. snake pit

39. B

40. CRATE
    A. make   B. report   C. box   D. truck

40. C

TEST 2

Questions 1-6.

DIRECTIONS: Questions 1 through 6 are to be answered on the basis
              of the following paragraph.

It is important that traffic signals be regularly and <u>effective-ly</u> maintained. Signals with <u>impaired</u> efficiency cannot be expected to command <u>desired</u> respect. Poorly maintained traffic signs create disrespect in the minds of those who are to obey them and thereby reduce the effectiveness and authority of the signs. Maintenance should receive <u>paramount</u> consideration in the design and purchase of traffic signal equipment. The <u>initial</u> step in a good maintenance program for traffic signals is the establishment of a maintenance record. This record should show the cost of operation and mainte-nance of different types of equipment. It should give complete information regarding signal operations and indicate where <u>defective</u> planning exists in maintenance programs.

1. The word *effectively*, as used in the above paragraph,   1. B
   means MOST NEARLY
      A. occasionally   B. properly
      C. expensively   D. cheaply

2. The word *impaired*, as used in the above paragraph, means   2. A
   MOST NEARLY
      A. reduced   B. increased   C. constant   D. high

3. The word *desired*, as used in the above paragraph, means   3. C
   MOST NEARLY
      A. public   B. complete   C. wanted   D. enough

4. The word *paramount*, as used in the above paragraph, means   4. B
   MOST NEARLY
      A. little   B. chief   C. excessive   D. some

5. The word *initial*, as used in the above paragraph, means   5. A
   MOST NEARLY
      A. first   B. final
      C. determining   D. most important

6. The word *defective*, as used in the above paragraph, means   6. D
   MOST NEARLY
      A. suitable   B. real   C. good   D. faulty

Questions 7-31.

DIRECTIONS: Each of Questions 7 through 31 consists of a capitalized word followed by four suggested meanings of the word. For each question, choose the word or phrase which means MOST NEARLY the same as the capitalized word.

7. ABOLISH   7. _B_
    A. count up   B. do away with
    C. give more   D. pay double for

8. ABUSE   8. _B_
    A. accept   B. mistreat   C. respect   D. touch

9. ACCURATE   9. _A_
    A. correct   B. lost   C. neat   D. secret

10. ASSISTANCE   10. _C_
    A. attendance   B. belief
    C. help   D. reward

11. CAUTIOUS   11. _B_
    A. brave   B. careful   C. greedy   D. hopeful

12. COURTEOUS   12. _C_
    A. better   B. easy   C. polite   D. religious

13. CRITICIZE   13. _B_
    A. admit   B. blame   C. check on   D. make dirty

14. DIFFICULT   14. _D_
    A. capable   B. dangerous   C. dull   D. hard

15. ENCOURAGE   15. _C_
    A. aim at   B. beg for   C. cheer on   D. free from

16. EXTENT   16. _B_
    A. age   B. size   C. truth   D. wildness

17. EXTRAVAGANT   17. _C_
    A. empty   B. helpful   C. over   D. wasteful

18. FALSE   18. _D_
    A. absent   B. colored
    C. not enough   D. wrong

19. INDICATE   19. _A_
    A. point out   B. show up
    C. shrink from   D. take to

20. NEGLECT   20. _A_
    A. disregard   B. flatten
    C. likeness   D. thoughtfulness

5

21. PENALIZE   21. D
    A. make   B. notice   C. pay   D. punish

22. POSTPONED   22. A
    A. put off   B. repeated   C. taught   D. went to

23. PUNCTUAL   23. D
    A. bursting   B. catching
    C. make a hole in   D. on time

24. RARE   24. C
    A. large   B. ride up   C. unusual   D. young

25. REVEAL   25. D
    A. leave   B. renew   C. soften   D. tell

26. EXCESSIVE   26. B
    A. excusable   B. immoderate
    C. ethereal   D. intentional

27. VOLUNTARY   27. D
    A. common   B. paid   C. sharing   D. willing

28. WHOLESOME   28. B
    A. cheap   B. healthful   C. hot   D. together

29. SERIOUS   29. A
    A. important   B. order   C. sharp   D. tight

30. TRIVIAL   30. C
    A. alive   B. empty   C. petty   D. troublesome

31. VENTILATE   31. A
    A. air out   B. darken
    C. last   D. take a chance

Questions 32-40.

DIRECTIONS: Each question consists of a statement. You are to
             indicate whether the statement is TRUE (T) or FALSE (F).

32. *The price of this merchandise fluctuates from day to day.*   32. T
    In this sentence, the word *fluctuates* means the OPPOSITE
    of *remains steady.*

33. *The patient was in acute pain.* In this sentence, the   33. T
    word *acute* means the OPPOSITE of *slight.*

34. *The essential data appear in the report.* In this   34. F
    sentence, the word *data* means the OPPOSITE of *facts.*

35. *The open lounge is spacious.* In this sentence, the word   35. F
    spacious means the OPPOSITE of *well-lighted.*

6

36. *The landscaping work was a prolonged task.* In this   36. F
    sentence, the word *prolonged* means NEARLY the same as
    difficult.

37. *A transparent removable cover was placed over the flower*   37. F
    bed. In this sentence, the word *transparent* means NEARLY
    the same as *wooden.*

38. *The prompt action of the employee saved many lives.* In   38. T
    this sentence, the word *prompt* means NEARLY the same as
    quick.

39. *The attendant's request for a vacation was approved.* In   39. F
    this sentence, the word *approved* means NEARLY the same
    as *refused.*

40. *The paycheck was received in the mail.* In this sentence,   40. F
    the word *received* means NEARLY the same as *lost.*

———

TEST 3

Questions 1-50.

DIRECTIONS: Each question consists of a statement. You are to
indicate whether the statement is TRUE (T) or FALSE (F).
PRINT THE LETTER OF THE CORRECT ANSWER IN THE SPACE AT
THE RIGHT.

1. *A few men were assisting the attendant.* In this sentence,   1. T
   the word *assisting* means NEARLY the same as *helping.*

2. *He opposed the idea of using a vacuum cleaner for this job.*   2. F
   In this sentence, the word *opposed* means NEARLY the same
   as *suggested.*

3. *Four employees were selected.* In this sentence, the word   3. T
   selected means NEARLY the same as *chosen.*

4. *This man is constantly supervised.* In this sentence, the   4. F
   word *constantly* means NEARLY the same as *rarely.*

5. *One part of soap to two parts of water is sufficient.* In   5. T
   this sentence, the word *sufficient* means NEARLY the same
   as *enough.*

6. *The fire protection system was inadequate.* In this   6. F
   sentence, the word *inadequate* means NEARLY the same as
   very good.

7. *The nozzle of the hose was clogged.* In this sentence, the word *clogged* means NEARLY the same as *brass*.

    7. F

8. *He resembles the man who worked here before.* In this sentence, the word *resembles* means NEARLY the same as *replaces*.

    8. F

9. *They eliminated a number of items.* In this sentence, the word *eliminated* means NEARLY the same as *bought*.

    9. F

10. *He is a dependable worker.* In this sentence, the word *dependable* means NEARLY the same as *poor*.

    10. F

11. *Some wood finishes color the wood and conceal the natural grain.* In this sentence, the word *conceal* means NEARLY the same as *hide*.

    11. T

12. *Paint that is chalking sometimes retains its protective value.* In this sentence, the word *retains* means NEARLY the same as *keeps*.

    12. T

13. *Wood and trash had accumulated.* In this sentence, the word *accumulated* means NEARLY the same as *piled up*.

    13. T

14. An *inflammable* liquid is one that is easily set on fire.

    14. T

15. *The amounts were then compared.* In this sentence, the word *compared* means NEARLY the same as *added*.

    15. F

16. *The boy had fallen into a shallow pool.* In this sentence, the word *shallow* means NEARLY the same as *deep*.

    16. F

17. *He acquired a new instrument.* In this sentence, the word *acquired* means NEARLY the same as *got*.

    17. T

18. *Several men were designated for this activity.* In this sentence, the word *designated* means NEARLY the same as *laid off*.

    18. F

19. *The drawer had been converted into a file.* In this sentence, the word *converted* means NEARLY the same as *changed*.

    19. T

20. *The patient has recuperated.* In this sentence, the word *recuperated* means NEARLY the same as *died*.

    20. F

21. *A rigid material should be used.* In this sentence, the word *rigid* means NEARLY the same as *stiff*.

    21. T

22. *Only half the supplies were utilized.* In this sentence, the word *utilized* means NEARLY the same as *used*.

    22. T

23. *In all these years, he had never obstructed any change.* In this sentence, the word *obstructed* means NEARLY the same as *suggested*.

    23. F

8

24. *Conditions were aggravated when he left.* In this sentence, the word *aggravated* means NEARLY the same as *improved.*   24. F

25. *The autopsy room is now available.* In this sentence, the word *available* means NEARLY the same as *clean.*   25. F

26. An investigation which *precedes* a report is one which comes before the report.   26. T

27. *Another word was inserted.* In this sentence, the word *inserted* means NEARLY the same as *put in.*   27. T

28. *He reversed the recommended steps in the procedure.* In this sentence, the word *reversed* means NEARLY the same as *explained.*   28. F

29. *His complaint was about a trivial matter.* In this sentence, the word *trivial* means NEARLY the same as *petty.*   29. T

30. *Using the proper tool will aid a worker in doing a better job.* In this sentence, the word *aid* means NEARLY the same as *help.*   30. T

31. *The application form has a space for the name of the former employer.* In this sentence, the word *former* means NEARLY the same as *new.*   31. F

32. *The exterior of the building needed to be painted.* In this sentence, the word *exterior* means NEARLY the same as *inside.*   32. F

33. *The smoke from the fire was dense.* In this sentence, the word *dense* means NEARLY the same as *thick.*   33. T

34. *Vacations should be planned in advance.* In this sentence, vacations should be planned ahead of time.   34. T

35. *The employee denied that he would accept another job.* In this sentence, the word *denied* means NEARLY the same as *admitted.*   35. F

36. *An annual report is made by the central stockroom.* In this sentence, the word *annual* means NEARLY the same as *monthly.*   36. F

37. *Salaries were increased in the new budget.* In this sentence, the word *increased* means NEARLY the same as *cut.*   37. F

38. *All excess oil is to be removed from tools.* In this sentence, the word *excess* means NEARLY the same as *extra.*   38. T

39. *The new employee did similar work on his last job.* In this sentence, the word *similar* means NEARLY the same as *interesting.*   39. F

40. *Helpful employees make favorable impressions on the public.* In this sentence, the word *favorable* means NEARLY the same as *poor*.   40. F

41. *Some plants are grown for the decorative value of their leaves.* In this sentence, the word *decorative* means NEARLY the same as *ornamental*.   41. T

42. *They made a circular flower garden.* In this sentence, the word *circular* means NEARLY the same as *square*.   42. F

43. *The gardener was a conscientious worker.* In this sentence, the word *conscientious* means NEARLY the same as *lazy*.   43. F

44. *The instructions received were contradictory.* In this sentence, the word *contradictory* means NEARLY the same as *alike*.   44. F

45. *His application for the job was rejected.* In this sentence, the word *rejected* means NEARLY the same as *accepted*.   45. F

46. *This plant reaches maturity quickly.* In this sentence, the word *maturity* means NEARLY the same as *full development*.   46. T

47. *The garden was provided with a system of underground irrigation.* In this sentence, the word *irrigation* means NEARLY the same as *watering*.   47. T

48. *In some plants, the flowers often appear before the foliage.* In this sentence, the word *foliage* refers to the leaves of the plant.   48. T

49. *The new horticultural society was organized through the merger of two previous groups.* In this sentence, the word *merger* means NEARLY the same as *breakup*.   49. F

50. *The stem of the plant measured three inches in diameter.* In this sentence, the word *diameter* means NEARLY the same as *height*.   50. F

———

KEY (CORRECT ANSWERS)

TEST 1

1. T	11. F	21. A	31. B
2. F	12. T	22. B	32. A
3. T	13. F	23. D	33. C
4. F	14. T	24. B	34. A
5. F	15. T	25. D	35. D
6. F	16. F	26. C	36. B
7. T	17. F	27. A	37. C
8. T	18. F	28. C	38. B
9. T	19. F	29. D	39. B
10. T	20. F	30. B	40. C

TEST 2

1. B	11. B	21. D	31. A
2. A	12. C	22. A	32. T
3. C	13. B	23. D	33. T
4. B	14. D	24. C	34. F
5. A	15. C	25. D	35. F
6. D	16. B	26. B	36. F
7. B	17. D	27. D	37. F
8. B	18. D	28. B	38. T
9. A	19. A	29. A	39. F
10. C	20. A	30. C	40. F

TEST 3

1. T	11. T	21. T	31. F	41. T
2. F	12. T	22. T	32. F	42. F
3. T	13. T	23. F	33. T	43. F
4. F	14. T	24. F	34. T	44. F
5. T	15. F	25. F	35. F	45. F
6. F	16. F	26. T	36. F	46. T
7. F	17. T	27. T	37. F	47. T
8. F	18. F	28. F	38. T	48. T
9. F	19. T	29. T	39. F	49. F
10. F	20. F	30. T	40. F	50. F

WORD MEANING
EXAMINATION SECTION
TEST 1

DIRECTIONS: Each question consists of a statement. You are to
indicate whether the statement is TRUE (T) or FALSE (F).
*PRINT THE LETTER OF THE CORRECT ANSWER IN THE SPACE AT
THE RIGHT.*

1. *The foreman had received a few requests.* In this
sentence, the word *requests* means NEARLY the same as
complaints.   1._F_

2. *The procedure for doing the work was modified.* In this
sentence, the word *modified* means NEARLY the same as
discovered.   2._F_

3. *He stressed the importance of doing the job right.* In
this sentence, the word *stressed* means NEARLY the same
as *discovered.*   3._F_

4. *He worked with rapid movements.* In this sentence, the
word *rapid* means NEARLY the same as *slow.*   4._F_

5. *The man resumed his work when the foreman came in.* In
this sentence, the word *resumed* means NEARLY the same as
stopped.   5._F_

6. *The interior door would not open.* In this sentence, the
word *interior* means NEARLY the same as *inside.*   6._T_

7. *He extended his arm.* In this sentence, the word *extended*
means NEARLY the same as *stretched out.*   7._T_

8. *He answered promptly.* In this sentence, the word *promptly*
means NEARLY the same as *quickly.*   8._T_

9. *He punctured a piece of rubber.* In this sentence, the
word *punctured* means NEARLY the same as *bought.*   9._F_

10. *Education curbs crime.* In this sentence, the word *curb*
means NEARLY the same as *checks.*   10.____

11. *Badges were distributed to the attendants.* In this
sentence, the word *distributed* means NEARLY the same as
given out.   11._T_

12. *The attendant lifted the pail without assistance.* In
this sentence, the word *assistance* means NEARLY the same
as *delay.*   12._F_

13. *The alert attendant notices unusual happenings.* In this
sentence, the word *alert* means NEARLY the same as *busy.*   13._F_

14. *Several bottles of ammonia were required for cleaning windows.* In this sentence, the word *required* means NEARLY the same as *needed.* 14. T

15. *The building had an efficient heating system.* In this sentence, the word *efficient* means NEARLY the same as *faulty.* 15. F

16. *An attendant never operates a motor vehicle.* In this sentence, the word *operates* means NEARLY the same as *fixes.* 16. F

17. *The new employee was praised for his work.* In this sentence, the word *praised* means NEARLY the same as *blamed.* 17. F

18. *Cooperation makes the work of all the employees easier.* In this sentence, the word *cooperation* means NEARLY the same as *working together.* 18. T

18. *All the people in the building had the same problems.* In this sentence, the word *problems* means NEARLY the same as *wages.* 18. F

20. *The employee was transferred to special work for the day.* In this sentence, the word *transferred* means NEARLY the same as *shifted.* 20. T

21. *Your supervisor will tell you of the different responsibilities of your job.* In this sentence, the word *responsibilities* means NEARLY the same as *tools.* 21. F

22. *A damper regulates the air flowing through a furnace.* In this sentence, the word *regulates* means NEARLY the same as *controls.* 22. T

23. *The wounded man was perspiring.* In this sentence, the word *perspiring* means NEARLY the same as *sweating.* 23. T

24. *This mop absorbs water better than a sponge.* In this sentence, the word *absorbs* means NEARLY the same as *spreads.* 24. F

25. *A metal box contained all the cleaning material.* In this sentence, the word *contained* means NEARLY the same as *held.* 25. T

26. *The stock of paper towels had gone down.* In this sentence, the word *stock* means NEARLY the same as *bond.* 26. F

27. *The Governor today urged all citizens to prevent fires.* In this sentence, the word *urged* means NEARLY the same as *ordered.* 27. F

28. *The news did not disturb the foreman.* In this sentence, the word *disturb* means NEARLY the same as *upset.* 28. T

2

29. *The Commissioner said that sixty men registered for the training course.* In this sentence, the word *registered* means NEARLY the same as *were eligible.*   29. F

30. *New York City attracts many people because of its opportunities.* In this sentence, the word *attracts* means NEARLY the same as *employs.*   30. F

31. *Five systems were suggested for helping the work of attendants.* In this sentence, the word *systems* means NEARLY the same as *methods.*   31. T

32. *It is not easy to select a foreman from such a fine group.* In this sentence, the word *select* means NEARLY the same as *pick.*   32. T

33. *The power of the public is in its freedom.* In this sentence, the word *power* means NEARLY the same as *strength.*   33. T

34. *The rescue was made quickly by the attendant.* In this sentence, the word *rescue* means NEARLY the same as *report.*   34. F

35. *The attendant avoided a quarrel.* In this sentence, the word *avoided* means NEARLY the same as *started.*   35. F

36. *A decaying branch is dangerous to the life of a tree.* In this sentence, the word *decaying* means NEARLY the same as *rotting.*   36. T

37. *Shearing helps keep the plants in the shape required.* In this sentence, the word *shearing* means NEARLY the same as *watering.*   37. F

38. *Some shrubs have vigorous growth and early flowering.* In this sentence, the word *vigorous* means NEARLY the same as *weak.*   38. F

39. *The lawn retained its healthy green color.* In this sentence, the word *retained* means NEARLY the same as *kept.*   39. T

40. *The soil is combined with an acid plant food.* In this sentence, the word *combined* means NEARLY the same as *mixed.*   40. T

41. *Gardening can be tiring without the right tools.* In this sentence, the word *tiring* means NEARLY the same as *amusing.*   41. F

42. *With the ground saturated, the roots may die.* In this sentence, the word *saturated* means NEARLY the same as *soaked.*   42. T

43. *Air can penetrate freely if holes are made in the soil.* In this sentence, the word *penetrate* means NEARLY the same as *follows.*   43. F

44. *With some plants, flowers precede the growth of leaves.* In this sentence, the word *precede* means NEARLY the same as *follow*.

44. F

45. *The gardener anticipated frost.* In this sentence, the word *anticipated* means NEARLY the same as *expected*.

45. T

46. *Tools are assembled when the job is finished.* In this sentence, the word *assembled* means NEARLY the same as *cleaned*.

46. F

47. *Part of the area was set aside for a miniature rock garden.* In this sentence, the word *miniature* means NEARLY the same as *beautiful*.

47. F

48. *Cheap tools are seldom durable.* In this sentence, the word *durable* means NEARLY the same as *long lasting*.

48. T

49. *Concrete walks are maintained clean easily.* In this sentence, the word *maintained* means NEARLY the same as *kept*.

49. T

50. *Each morning the assistant gardener was punctual in reporting to work.* In this sentence, the word *punctual* means NEARLY the same as *prompt*.

50. T

TEST 2

1. *Formal shearing destroys the plant's individuality.* In this sentence, the word *formal* means NEARLY the same as *irregular*.

1. F

2. *The entire tree is covered with a film which is flexible, colorless, and lasting.* In this sentence, the word *flexible* means NEARLY the same as *tough*.

2. F

3. *All of the equipment is mobile.* In this sentence, the word *mobile* means NEARLY the same as *movable*.

3. T

4. *Just enough asphalt adheres to make a mat.* In this sentence, the word *adheres* means NEARLY the same as *sticks*.

4. T

5. *Efforts at proper maintenance were nullified by this act.* In this sentence, the word *nullified* means NEARLY the same as *brought to nothing*.

5. T

6. Saying that a hose is *perforated* is another way of saying that a hose is *bent*.

6. F

7. *Do not injure the foliage of a plant* means NEARLY the same as *do not injure the plant's roots*.

7. F

4

8. *Pulverizing* soil is breaking it down into very small bits. 8. T

9. Humus is the part of the soil which is very often called 9. F
    clay in gardening practice.

10. *Aerating* a turf area is NEARLY the same as *sodding* the 10. F
    area.

11. *To mechanically agitate* means NEARLY the same as *to seed* 11. F
    by mechanical power.

12. *Ashes are transported from Department of Sanitation* 12. T
    incinerators to points of ultimate disposal. In this
    sentence, the word *ultimate* means NEARLY the same as
    final.

13. *In some areas where mechanical sweepers are used,* 13. T
    supplementary manual cleaning is required. In this
    sentence, the word *supplementary* means NEARLY the same
    as *additional*.

14. *It was stipulated that ferrous metals should be used.* ? 14. F
    In this sentence, the word *stipulated* means NEARLY the
    same as *agreed*.

15. *We find a different type of residue here.* In this 15. F
    sentence, the word *residue* means NEARLY the same as
    inhabitant.

16. *Several giant segments lay there.* In this sentence, the 16. T
    word *segments* means NEARLY the same as *parts*.

17. *The number of usable fill properties continues to dwindle.* 17. F
    In this sentence, the word *dwindle* means NEARLY the same
    as *multiply*.

18. *The salient provisions were given.* In this sentence, ? 18. F
    the word *salient* means NEARLY the same as *prominent*.

19. *Rate of putrefaction must be considered.* In this sentence, 19. T
    the word *putrefaction* means NEARLY the same as *rotting*.

20. *The supervisor gave a brief talk on the importance on* 20. F
    safety. In this sentence, the word *brief* means NEARLY
    the same as *interesting*.

21. *The supervisor made a thorough study of the problem.* 21. T
    In this sentence, the word *thorough* means NEARLY the
    same as *complete*.

22. *It is essential that all employees work together as a* 22. T
    team. In this sentence, the word *essential* means NEARLY
    the same as *absolutely necessary*.

5

23. *Employees are occasionally required to work overtime.* In this sentence, the word *occasionally* means NEARLY the same as *often.*

23. F

24. *The form is to be submitted in duplicate.* According to this sentence, three copies of the form are to be submitted.

24. F

25. *The benches should be wiped free of dirt and moisture each day.* In this sentence, the word *moisture* means NEARLY the same as *oil.*

25. F

26. *She omitted her name at the bottom of the application.* In this sentence, the word *omitted* means NEARLY the same as *left out.*

26. T

27. *The employee's excuse for being absent was absurd.* In this sentence, the word *absurd* means NEARLY the same as *sensible.*

27. F

28. *The attendant was instructed to reverse the mop head at the end of each stroke.* In this sentence, the word *reverse* means NEARLY the same as *clean.*

28. F

29. *The supervisor was in accord with the employee's suggestion.* In this sentence, the word *accord* means NEARLY the same as *agreement.*

29. T

30. *The mail clerk inserted the letter in the envelope.* In this sentence, the word *inserted* means NEARLY the same as *found.*

30. F

31. *If a tenant does not comply with the rules of the Housing Project, report this to your supervisor.* In this sentence, the words *comply with* mean NEARLY the same as *obey.*

31. T

32. *Surplus water on a floor should be wiped up with a mop.* In this sentence, the word *surplus* means NEARLY the same as *dirty.*

32. F

33. *An employee who is hurt should turn in an accident report immediately.* In this sentence, the word *immediately* means NEARLY the same as *right away.*

33. T

34. *A new employee is expected to learn his job gradually.* In this sentence, the word *gradually* means NEARLY the same as *correctly.*

34. F

35. *The Commissioner said it was an immense job to keep New York City clean.* In this sentence, the word *immense* means NEARLY the same as *very big.*

35. T

36. *The foreman could tell right away that the caretaker had swept the hall thoroughly.* In this sentence, the word *thoroughly* means NEARLY the same as *poorly*.   36. F

37. *The caretaker could not make permanent repairs.* In this sentence, the word *permanent* means NEARLY the same as *plumbing*.   37. F

38. *The employee requested a summer vacation.* In this sentence, the word *requested* means NEARLY the same as *asked for*.   38. I

39. *The caretaker could not open the door because the lock was jammed.* In this sentence, the word *jammed* means NEARLY the same as *loose*.   39. F

40. *Jones and Smith were rivals in the section's clean-up campaign.* In this sentence, the word *rivals* means NEARLY the same as *partners*.   40. F

41. *The caretaker persuaded the children to keep the playground clean.* In this sentence, the word *persuaded* means NEARLY the same as *warned*.   41. F

42. *All elevators should be operating during the morning rush hour to avoid crowding in the lobby.* In this sentence, the word *lobby* means NEARLY the same as *entrance hall*.   42. I

43. *The caretaker used a liquid polish on the brass trim.* In this sentence, the word *liquid* means NEARLY the same as *paste*.   43. F

44. *Report all minor accidents to your supervisor.* In this sentence, the word *minor* means NEARLY the same as *serious*.   44. F

45. *The attendant obtained the towels from the supply room.* In this sentence, the word *obtained* means NEARLY the same as *inspected*.   45. F

46. *Ten men were needed for the normal work of the section.* In this sentence, the word *normal* means NEARLY the same as *regular*.   46. I

47. *The swimming pool can accommodate 100 people.* In this sentence, the word *accommodate* means NEARLY the same as *hold without crowding*.   47. I

48. *The elevator operator did not recognize the new tenant.* In this sentence, the word *recognize* means NEARLY the same as *like*.   48. F

49. *The new playground swings were installed carefully.* In this sentence, the word *installed* means NEARLY the same as *put in*.   49. I

50. *Kerosene or benzine will ruin asphalt tile.* In this sentence, the word *ruin* means NEARLY the same as *spoil*.

50. T

TEST 3

1. *His ideas about the best method of doing the work were flexible.* In this sentence, the word *flexible* means NEARLY the same as *unchangeable*.

1. F

2. *Many difficulties were encountered.* In this sentence, the word *encountered* means NEARLY the same as *met*.

2. T

3. *The different parts of the refuse must be segregated.* In this sentence, the word *segregated* means NEARLY the same as *combined*.

3. F

4. *The child was obviously hurt.* In this sentence, the word *obviously* means NEARLY the same as *accidentally*.

4. F

5. *Some kind of criteria for judging service necessity must be established.* In this sentence, the word *criteria* means NEARLY the same as *standards*.

5. T

6. *A small segment of the membership favored the amendment.* In this sentence, the word *segment* means NEARLY the same as *part*.

6. T

7. *The effectiveness of any organization depends upon the quality and integrity of its rank and file.* In this sentence, the word *integrity* means NEARLY the same as *quantity*.

7. F

8. *He adhered to his opinion.* In this sentence, the word *adhered* means NEARLY the same as *stuck to*.

8. T

9. *The suspects were interrogated at the police station.* In this sentence, *interrogated* means NEARLY the same as *identified*.

9. F

10. *Flanking the fireplace are shelves holding books.* In this sentence, the word *flanking* means NEARLY the same as *above*.

10. F

11. *He refused to comment on the current Berlin crisis.* In this sentence, the word *current* means NEARLY the same as *shocking*.

11. F

12. *Nothing has been done to remedy the situation.* In this sentence, the word *remedy* means NEARLY the same as *correct*.

12. T

13. *The reports had been ignored.* In this sentence, the word *ignored* means NEARLY the same as *prepared.* 13. F

14. *A firm was hired to construct the building.* In this sentence, the word *construct* means NEARLY the same as *build.* 14. T

15. *The Commissioner spoke about the operations of his department.* In this sentence, the word *operations* means NEARLY the same as *problems.* 15. F

16. *The increase in the number of accidents is negligible.* In this sentence, the word *negligible* means NEARLY the same as *serious.* 16. F

17. *He received monetary assistance.* In this sentence, the word *monetary* means NEARLY the same as *temporary.* 17. F

18. *Litigation delayed construction of the new incinerator.* In this sentence, the word *litigation* means NEARLY the same as *rising costs.* 18. F

19. *Proximity of the site is important.* In this sentence, the word *proximity* means NEARLY the same as *closeness.* 19. T

20. *At sanitary landfills, refuse is not dumped indiscriminately.* In this sentence, the word *indiscriminately* means NEARLY the same as *before burning.* 20. F

21. *Improvised equipment is seldom used.* In this sentence, the word *improvised* means NEARLY the same as *worn out.* 21. F

22. *At marine loading stations, refuse barges are loaded by gravity.* In this sentence, the word *gravity* means NEARLY the same as *shovel.* 22. F

23. *Many difficulties were encountered in the operation.* In this sentence, the word *encountered* means NEARLY the same as *met.* 23. T

24. *Traffic control facilitates the collection of waste in a large city.* In this sentence, the word *facilitates* means NEARLY the same as *eases.* 24. T

25. *Four persons were extricated immediately.* In this sentence, the word *extricated* means NEARLY the same as *treated.* 25. F

26. *Large objects produce extensive damage to mechanical equipment of furnaces.* In this sentence, the word *extensive* means NEARLY the same as *slight.* 26. F

27. *The car's headlights flickered on the dark street.* In this sentence, the word *flickered* means NEARLY the same as *shone brightly.* 27. F

9

28. *The sweeper was retained when the vacuum cleaners were installed.* In this sentence, the word *retained* means NEARLY the same as *kept*.

28. T

29. *Several men had dismantled the engine.* In this sentence, the word *dismantled* means NEARLY the same as *inspected*.

29. F

30. *The switch should be pushed down when the car approaches.* In this sentence, the word *approaches* means NEARLY the same as *comes near*.

30. T

31. *There is a possibility of ground water contamination.* In this sentence, the word *contamination* means NEARLY the same as *radioactivity*.

31. F

32. *The components of refuse must be segregated.* In this sentence, the word *components* means NEARLY the same as *containers*.

? 32. F

33. *The arrival of the tractor coincided with that of the dump truck.* In this sentence, the word *coincided* means NEARLY the same as *interfered*.

33. F

34. *Every idea sent to the Employee Suggestion Program is appraised.* In this sentence, the word *appraised* means NEARLY the same as *judged*.

34. T

35. *An adjacent garage maintained snow equipment.* In this sentence, the word *adjacent* means NEARLY the same as *neighboring*.

35. T

36. *Check all facts before analyzing a report.* In this sentence, the word *analyzing* means NEARLY the same as *submitting*.

36. F

37. *The abatement of odors affects living conditions.* In this sentence, the word *abatement* means NEARLY the same as *reduction*.

T
37. T

38. *For proper growth, the plant needs plenty of water, supplemented with liquid manure.* In this sentence, the word *supplemented* means NEARLY the same as *replaced*.

38. F

39. *One reason why aphids are undesirable is that they transmit plant diseases.* In this sentence, the word *transmit* means NEARLY the same as *pass on*.

39. T

40. *When the trees are young, the spaces between them may be utilized for other plantings.* In this sentence, the word *utilized* means NEARLY the same as *used*.

40. T

41. *The cuttings will take root readily.* In this sentence, the word *readily* means NEARLY the same as *quickly*.

41. T

10

42. *The seedlings should be transplanted at least once to stimulate growth.* In this sentence, the word *stimulate* means NEARLY the same as *encouraged.*

42. T

43. *The water evaporates through cracks in the soil.* In this sentence, the word *evaporates* means NEARLY the same as *flows in.*

43. F

44. *Hardy, native vines were planted.* In this sentence, the word *hardy* means NEARLY the same as *few.*

44. F

45. *The insects were present in moderate numbers.* In this sentence, the word *moderate* means NEARLY the same as *large.*

45. F

46. *The beetle is injurious to garden crops.* In this sentence, the word *injurious* means NEARLY the same as *harmful.*

46. T

47. *With proper care, the plants will survive the winter.* In this sentence, the word *survive* means NEARLY the same as *live through.*

47. T

48. *An arbor should be inconspicuous.* In this sentence, the word *inconspicuous* means NEARLY the same as *made of wood.*

48. F

49. *The plants are indifferent as to soil.* In this sentence, the word *indifferent* means NEARLY the same as *not particular.*

49. T

50. *The plant produces fragrant flowers.* In this sentence, the word *fragrant* means NEARLY the same as *sweet smelling.*

50. T

KEY (CORRECT ANSWERS)

TEST 1

1. F	11. T	21. F	31. T	41. F
2. T	12. F	22. T	32. T	42. T
3. F	13. F	23. T	33. T	43. F
4. F	14. T	24. F	34. F	44. F
5. F	15. F	25. T	35. F	45. T
6. T	16. F	26. F	36. T	46. F
7. T	17. F	27. F	37. F	47. F
8. T	18. T	28. T	38. F	48. T
9. F	19. F	29. F	39. T	49. T
10. T	20. T	30. F	40. T	50. T

TEST 2

1. F	11. F	21. T	31. T	41. F
2. F	12. T	22. T	32. F	42. T
3. T	13. T	23. F	33. T	43. F
4. T	14. T	24. F	34. F	44. F
5. T	15. F	25. F	35. T	45. F
6. F	16. T	26. T	36. F	46. T
7. F	17. F	27. F	37. F	47. T
8. T	18. T	28. F	38. T	48. F
9. F	19. T	29. T	39. F	49. T
10. F	20. F	30. F	40. F	50. T

TEST 3

1. F	11. F	21. F	31. F	41. T
2. T	12. T	22. F	32. F	42. T
3. F	13. F	23. T	33. F	43. F
4. F	14. T	24. T	34. T	44. F
5. T	15. F	25. F	35. T	45. F
6. T	16. F	26. F	36. F	46. T
7. F	17. F	27. F	37. T	47. T
8. T	18. F	28. T	38. F	48. F
9. F	19. T	29. F	39. T	49. T
10. F	20. F	30. T	40. T	50. T

READING
EXAMINATION SECTION

Questions 1-40.
DIRECTIONS: Read the following passages, and select the most appropriate word from the five alternatives provided for each deleted word. Print the letter of the correct answer in the space at the right.

PASSAGE I

Bridges are built to allow a continuous flow of highway and railway traffic across water lying in their paths. But engineers cannot forget the fact that river traffic, too, is essential to our economy. The role of __1__ is important. To keep these vessels moving freely, bridges are built high enough, when possible, to let them pass underneath. Sometimes, however, channels must accommodate very tall ships. It may be uneconomical to build a tall enough bridge. The __2__ would be too high. To save money, engineers build movable bridges.

1. A. wind   B. boats   C. weight   1. B
    D. wires   E. experience
2. A. levels   B. cost   C. standards   2. B
    D. waves   E. deck

In the swing bridge, the middle part pivots or swings open. When the bridge is closed, this section joins the two ends of the bridge, blocking tall vessels. But this section __3__. When swung open, it is perpendicular to the ends of the bridge, creating two free channels for river traffic. With swing bridges, channel width is limited by the bridge's piers. The largest swing bridge provides only a 75-meter channel. Such channels are sometimes too __4__. In such cases, a bascule bridge may be built.

3. A. stands   B. floods   C. wears   3. A
    D. turns   E. supports
4. A. narrow   B. rough   C. long   4. A
    D. deep   E. straight

Bascule bridges are drawbridges with two arms that swing upward. They provide an opening as wide as the span. They are also versatile. These bridges are not limited to being fully opened or fully closed. They can be __5__ in many ways. They can be fixed at different angles to accommodate different vessels.

5. A. approached   B. crossed   C. lighted   5. E
    D. planned   E. positioned

In vertical lift bridges, the center remains horizontal. Towers at both ends allow the center to be lifted like an elevator. One interesting variation of this kind of bridge was built during World War II. A lift bridge was desired, but there were wartime shortages of the steel and machinery needed for the towers. It was hard to find enough __6__. An ingenious engineer designed the bridge so that it did not have to be raised above traffic. Instead it was __7__. It could be submerged seven meters below the river surface. Ships sailed over it.

6. A. work   B. material   C. time   6. B
    D. power   E. space
7. A. burned   B. emptied   C. secured   7. E
    D. shared   E. lowered

1

PASSAGE II

Before anesthetics were discovered, surgery was carried out under very severe time restrictions. Patients were awake, tossing and screaming in terrible pain. Surgeons were forced to hurry in order to constrain suffering and minimize shock. __8__ was essential. Haste, however, did not make for good outcomes in surgery. No surprise, then, that the __9__ were often poor.

8.   A. Blood   B. Silence   C. Speed   8. C.
      D. Water   E. Money
9.   A. quarters   B. teeth   C. results   9. C.
      D. materials   E. families

The discovery of anesthetics happened, in part, by accident. During the early 1800's, nitrous oxide and ether were used for entertainment. At "ether frolics" in theaters, volunteers would breathe these gases, become lightheaded, and run around the stage laughing and dancing. By chance, a Connecticut dentist saw such a __10__. One volunteer banged his leg against a sharp edge. But he did not __11__. He paid no attention to his wound, as though he felt nothing. This gave the dentist the idea of using gas to kill pain.

10.   A. show   B. machine   C. face   10. A.
       D. source   E. growth
11.   A. dream   B. recover   C. succeed   11. E.
       D. agree   E. notice

At first, using the "open drip method," ether and chloroform were filtered through a cotton pad placed over the mouth and nose. This direct dose was difficult to regulate and irritating to the nose and throat. Patients would hold their breath, cough, or gag. This made it impossible for them to relax, let alone sleep. Consequently, surgery was often __12__. It couldn't begin until the patient had quieted and the anesthesia had taken hold.

12.   A. delayed   B. required   C. blamed   12. A.
       D. observed   E. repeated

Today's procedures are safer and more accurate. In the "closed method," a fixed amount of gas is released from sealed bottles into an inhalator bag when the patient exhales. He inhales this gas through tubes with his next breath. In this way, the gas is __13__. The system carefully regulates how much gas reaches the patient.

13.   A. heated   B. controlled   C. cleaned   13. B.
       D. selected   E. wasted

For dentistry and minor operations, patients need not be asleep. Newer anesthetics can be used which deaden nerves only in the affected part of the body. These __14__ anesthetics offer several advantages. For instance, since the anesthesia is fairly light and patients remain awake, they can cooperate with their doctors.

14.   A. local   B. natural   C. ancient   14. A.
       D. heavy   E. three

PASSAGE III

An indispensable element in the development of telephony was the continual improvement of telephone station instruments, those operating units located at the client's premises. Modern units normally consist of a transmitter, receiver, and transformer. They also contain a bell or equivalent summoning device, a mechanism for controlling the unit's connection to the client's line, and various associated items, like

dials. All of these 15 have changed over the years. The transmitter, especially, has undergone enormous refinement during the last
century.

15.   A. parts   B. costs   C. services   15. ..A
      D. models   E. routes

Bell's original electromagnetic transmitter functioned likewise
as receiver, the same instrument being held alternately to mouth and
ear. But having to 16 the instrument this way was inconvenient.
Suggestions understandably emerged for mounting the transmitter and
receiver onto a common handle, thereby creating what are now known
as handsets. Transmitter and receiver were, in fact, later 17 his
way. Combination handsets were produced for commercial utilization
late in the nineteenth century, but prospects for their acceptance
were uncertain as the initial quality of transmissions with the handsets was disappointing. But 18 transmissions followed. With ade-
quately high transmission standards attained, acceptance of handsets
was virtually assured.

16.   A. store   B. use   C. test   16. B.
      D. strip   E. clean
17.   A. grounded   B. marked   C. covered   17. E..
      D. priced   E. coupled
18.   A. shorter   B. fewer   C. better   18. C.
      D. faster   E. cheaper

Among the most significant improvements in transmitters has been
the enormous amplification (up to a thousandfold) of speech sounds.
This increased 19 has benefited tele-communications enormously.
Nineteenth century telephone conversations frequently were only
marginally audible, whereas nowadays even murmured conversations
can be transmitted successfully, barring unusual atmospheric or
electronic disturbances.

19.   A. distance   B. speed   C. market   19. D..
      D. volume   E. number

Vocal quality over nineteenth century instruments was distorted,
the speaker not readily identifiable. By comparison, current sound
is characterized by considerably greater naturalism. Modern telephony produces speech sounds more nearly resembling an individual's
actual voice. Thus it is easier to 20 the speaker. A considerable
portion of this improvement is attributable to practical applications
of laboratory investigations concerning the mechanisms of human
speech and audition. These 21 have exerted a profound influence.
Their results prompted technical innovations in modern transmitter
design which contributed appreciably to the excellent communication
available nowadays.

20.   A. time   B. help   C. bill   20. E..
      D. stop   E. recognize
21.   A. studies   B. rates   C. materials   21. .A.
      D. machines   E. companies

3

The dramatic events of December 7, 1941, plunged this nation into war. The full 22 of the war we can not even now comprehend, but one of the effects stands out in sharp relief -- the coming of the air age. The airplane, which played a relatively 23 part in World War I, has already soared to heights undreamed of save by the few with mighty vision.

In wartime the airplane is the 24 on wings and the battleship that flies. To man in his need it symbolizes deadly extremes: friend or foe; deliverance or 25 .

It is a powerful instrument of war revolutionizing military strategy, but its peacetime role is just as 26. This new master of time and space, fruit of man's inventive genius, has come to stay, smalling the earth and smoothing its surface.

To all of us, then, to youth, and to 27 alike, comes the winged challenge to get ourselves ready--to 28 ourselves for living in an age which the airplane seems destined to mold.

22. A. destruction B. character   C. history   D. import   22. D.
    E. pictur

23. A. important   B. dull C. vast D. unknown E. minor   23. E.

24. A. giant B. ant   C. monster   D. artillery E. robot   24. D.

25. A. ecstasy B. bombardment C. death D. denial   25. C.
    E. survival

26. A. revolting B. revolutionary C. residual D. reliable 26. B
    E. regressive

27. A. animals B. nations C. women D. men E. adult   27. E.

28. A. distract B. engage C. determine D. deter E. orient 28. E

PASSAGE V

Let us consider how voice training may contribute to 29 development and an improved social 30 .

In the first place, it has been fairly well established that individuals tend to become what they believe 31 people think them to be.

When people react more favorably toward us because our voices 32 the impression that we are friendly, competent, and interesting, there is a strong tendency for us to develop those 33 in our personality.

If we are treated with respect by others, we soon come to have more respect for 34 .

Then, too, one's own consciousness of having a pleasant, effective voice of which he does not need to be ashamed contributes materially to a feeling of poise, self-confidence, and a just pride in himself.

A good voice, like good clothes, can do much for an 35 that otherwise might be inclined to droop.

29. A. facial B. material C. community D. personality   29. D.
    E. physical

30. A. adjustment B. upheaval C. development D. bias   30. A.
    E. theories

31. A. some B. hostile C. jealous D. inferior E. other   31. E
32. A. betray B. imply C. destroy D. transfigure   32. E
    E. convey
33. A. defects B. qualities C. techniques D. idiosyncrasies 33. B
    E. quirks
34. A. others B. their children C. their teachers   34. D
    D. ourselves   E. each other
35. A. mind B. heart C. brain D. feeling E. ego   35. E

——

PASSAGE VI

How are symphony orchestras launched, kept going, and built up in smaller communities? Recent reports from five of them suggest that, though the __36__ changes, certain elements are fairly common. One thing shines out; __37__ is essential.

Also, aside from the indispensable, instrumentalists who play, the following personalities, either singly, or preferably in __38__, seem to be the chief needs: a conductor who wants to conduct so badly he will organize his own orchestra if it is the only way he can get one; a manager with plenty of resourcefulness in rounding up audiences and finding financial support; an energetic community leader, general-ly a woman, who will take up locating the orchestra as a __39__; and generous visiting soloists who will help draw those who are __40__ that anything local can be used.

36. A. world B. pattern C. reason D. scene E. cast   36. B
37. A. hatred B. love C. enthusiasm D. participation   37. C
    E. criticism
38. A. combination B. particular C. isolation D. sympathy   38. A
    E. solitary
39. A. chore B. duty C. hobby D. delight E. career   39. C
40. A. convinced B. skeptical C. happy D. unhappy   40. B
    E. unsure

——

KEY (CORRECT ANSWERS)

1.	B	11.	E	21.	A	31.	E
2.	B	12.	A	22.	D	32.	E
3.	D	13.	B	23.	E	33.	B
4.	A	14.	A	24.	D	34.	D
5.	E	15.	A	25.	C	35.	E
6.	B	16.	B	26.	B	36.	B
7.	E	17.	E	27.	E	37.	C
8.	C	18.	C	28.	E	38.	A
9.	C	19.	D	29.	D	39.	C
10.	A	20.	E	30.	A	40.	B

——

5

READING COMPREHENSION

UNDERSTANDING AND INTERPRETING WRITTEN MATERIAL

EXAMINATION SECTION

DIRECTIONS: Each question or incomplete statement is followed by several suggested answers or completions. Select the one that BEST answers the question or completes the statement. *PRINT THE LETTER OF THE CORRECT ANSWER IN THE SPACE AT THE RIGHT.*

TEST 1

Skiing has recently become one of the more popular sports in the United States. Because of its popularity, thousands of winter vacationers are flying north rather than south. In many areas, reservations are required months ahead of time.

I discovered the accommodation shortage through an unfortunate experience. On a sunny Saturday morning, I set out from Denver for the beckoning slopes of Aspen, Colorado. After passing signs for other ski areas, I finally reached my destination. Naturally, I lost no time in heading for the nearest tow. After a stimulating after-noon of miscalculated stem turns, I was famished. Well, one thing led to another, and it must have been eight o'clock before I concerned myself with a bed for my bruised and aching bones.

It took precisely one phone call to ascertain the lack of lodgings in the Aspen area. I had but one recourse. My auto and I started the treacherous jaunt over the pass and back towards Denver. Along the way, I went begging for a bed. Finally, a jolly tavernkeeper took pity, and for only thirty dollars a night allowed me the privilege of staying in a musty, dirty, bathless room above his tavern.

1. The author's problem would have been avoided if he had   1. D
    A. not tired himself out skiing
    B. taken a bus instead of driving
    C. looked for food as soon as he arrived
    D. arranged for accommodations well ahead of his trip
    E. answer cannot be determined from the information given

TEST 2

Helen Keller was born in 1880 in Tuscumbia, Alabama. When she was two years old, she lost her sight and hearing as the result of an illness. In 1886, she became the pupil of Anne Sullivan, who taught Helen to *see* with her fingertips, to *hear* with her feet and hands, and to communicate with other people. Miss Sullivan succeeded in arousing Helen's curiosity and interest by spelling the names of objects into her hand. At the end of three years, Helen had mastered the manual and the braille alphabet and could read and write.

2. When did Helen Keller lose her sight and hearing?   2. B
    A. 1880   B. 1882   C. 1886   D. 1890   E. 1900

TEST 3

Sammy got to school ten minutes after the school bell had rung. He was breathing hard and had a black eye. His face was dirty and scratched. One leg of his pants was torn.

Tommy was late to school, too; however, he was only five minutes late. Like Sammy, he was breathing hard, but he was happy and smiling.

3. Sammy and Tommy had been fighting.
    Who probably won?
      A. Sammy   B. Tommy
      C. Cannot tell from story   D. The teacher
      E. The school

3. B

TEST 4

This is like a game to see if you can tell what the nonsense word in the paragraph stands for. The nonsense word is just a silly word for something that you know very well. Read the paragraph and see if you can tell what the underlined nonsense word stands for.

You can wash your hands and face in zup. You can even take a bath in it. When people swim, they are in the zup. Everyone drinks zup.

4. Zup is PROBABLY
      A. milk   B. pop   C. soap   D. water   E. soup

4. D

TEST 5

After two weeks of unusually high-speed travel, we reached Xeno, a small planet whose population, though never before visited by Earthmen, was listed as *friendly* in the INTERSTELLAR GAZETTEER.

On stepping lightly (after all, the gravity of Xeno is scarcely more than twice that of our own moon) from our spacecraft, we saw that *friendly* was an understatement. We were immediately surrounded by Frangibles of various colors, mostly pinkish or orange, who held out their *hands* to us. Imagine our surprise when their *hands* actually merged with ours as we tried to shake them!

Then, before we could stop them (how could we have stopped them?), two particularly pink Frangibles simply stepped right into two eminent scientists among our party, who immediately lit up with the same pink glow. While occupied in this way, the scientists reported afterwards they suddenly discovered they *knew* a great deal about Frangibles and life on Xeno.

Apparently, Frangibles could take themselves apart atomically and enter right into any other substance. They communicated by thought waves, occasionally merging *heads* for greater clarity. Two Frangibles who were in love with each other would spend most of their time merged into one; they were a bluish-green color unless they were having a lover's quarrel, when they turned gray.

5. In order to find out about an object which interested   5. B
    him, what would a Frangible MOST likely do?
    A. Take it apart
    B. Enter into it
    C. Study it scientifically
    D. Ask earth scientists about it
    E. Wait to see if it would change color

TEST 6

This is like a game to see if you can tell what the nonsense word in the paragraph stands for. The nonsense word is just a silly word for something that you know very well. Read the paragraph and see if you can tell what the underlined nonsense word stands for.

Have you ever smelled a <u>mart</u>? They smell very good. Bees like <u>marts</u>. They come in many colors. <u>Marts</u> grow in the earth, and they usually bloom in the spring.

6. Marts are PROBABLY   6. B
    A. bugs   B. flowers   C. perfume
    D. pies   E. cherries

TEST 7

Christmas was only a few days away. The wind was strong and cold. The walks were covered with snow. The downtown streets were crowded with people. Their faces were hidden by many packages as they went in one store after another. They all tried to move faster as they looked at the clock.

7. When did the story PROBABLY happen?   7. C
    A. November 28   B. December 1   C. December 21
    D. December 25   E. December 28

TEST 8

THE WAYFARER

The wayfarer,
Perceiving the pathway to truth,
Was struck with astonishment.
It was thickly grown with weeds.
Ha, he said,
I see that no one has passed here
In a long time.
Later he saw that each weed
Was a singular knife,
Well, he mumbled at last,
Doubtless there are other roads.

8. *I see that no one has passed here*
    In a long time.
    What do the above lines from the poem mean?
     A. The way of truth is popular.
     B. People are fascinated by the truth.
     C. Truth comes and goes like the wind.
     D. The truth is difficult to recognize.
     E. Few people are searching for the truth.

8. ___

TEST 9

Any attempt to label an entire generation is unrewarding, and yet the generation which went through the last war, or at least could get a drink easily once it was over, seems to possess a uniform, general quality which demands an adjective. It was John Kerouac, the author of a fine, neglected novel, THE TOWN AND THE CITY, who finally came up with it. It was several years ago, when the face was harder to recognize, but he had a sharp, sympathetic eye, and one day he said, *You know, this is really a* beat *generation*. The origins of the word *beat* are obscure, but the meaning is only too clear to most Americans. More than mere weariness, it implies the feeling of having been used, of being raw. It involves a sort of nakedness of mind, and ultimately, of soul; a feeling of being reduced to the bedrock of consciousness. In short, it means being undramatically pushed up against the wall of oneself. A man is beat whenever he goes for broke and waters the sum of his resources on a single number; and the young generation has done that continually from early youth.

9. What does the writer suggest when he mentions a *fine, neglected novel*?
     A. Kerouac had the right idea about the war
     B. Kerouac had a clear understanding of the new post-war generation
     C. Kerouac had not received the recognition of THE TOWN AND THE CITY that was deserved
     D. Kerouac had the wrong idea about the war.
     E. All of the above

9. ___

TEST 10

One spring, Farmer Brown had an unusually good field of wheat. Whenever he saw any birds in this field, he got his gun and shot as many of them as he could. In the middle of the summer, he found that his wheat was being ruined by insects. With no birds to feed on them, the insects had multiplied very fast. What Farmer Brown did not understand was this: A bird is not simply an animal that eats food the farmer may want for himself. Instead, it is one of many links in the complex surroundings, or environment, in which we live.

How much grain a farmer can raise on an acre of ground depends on many factors. All of these factors can be divided into two big groups. Such things as the richness of the soil, the amount of rainfall, the amount of sunlight, and the temperature belong together in one of these groups. This group may be called <u>nonliving factors</u>. The second group may be called <u>living factors</u>. The living factors in any plant's environment are animals and other plants. Wheat, for example, may be damaged by wheat rust, a tiny plant that feeds on wheat, or it may be eaten by plant-eating animals such as birds or grasshoppers...

It is easy to see that the relations of plants and animals to their environment are very complex, and that any change in the environment is likely to bring about a whole series of changes.

10. What does the passage suggest a good farmer should understand about nature?   10. E
    A. Insects are harmful to plants
    B. Birds are not harmful to plants
    C. Wheat may be damaged by both animals and other plants
    D. The amount of wheat he can raise depends on two factors: birds and insects
    E. A change in one factor of plants' surroundings may cause other factors to change

11. What important idea about nature does the writer want us to understand?   11. E
    A. Farmer Brown was worried about the heavy rainfall
    B. Nobody needs to have such destructive birds around
    C. Farmer Brown did not want the temperature to change
    D. All insects need not only wheat rust but grasshoppers
    E. All living things are dependent on other living things

TEST 11

For a 12-year-old, I've been around a lot because my father's in the Army. I have been to New York and to Paris. When I was nine, my parents took me to Rome. I didn't like Europe very much because the people don't speak the same language I do. When I am older, my mother says I can travel by myself. I think I will like that. Ever since I was 13, I have wanted to go to Canada.

12. Why can't everything this person said be TRUE?   12.___
    A. 12-year-olds can't travel alone
    B. No one can travel that much in 12 years
    C. There is a conflict in the ages used in the passage
    D. 9-year-olds can't travel alone
    E. He is a liar

TEST 12

Between April and October, the Persian Gulf is dotted with the small boats of pearl divers. Some seventy-five thousand of them are busy diving down and bringing up pearl-bearing oysters. These oysters are not the kind we eat. The edible oyster produces pearls of little or no value. You may have heard tales of divers who discovered pearls and sold them for great sums of money. These stories are entertaining but not accurate.

13. The Persian Gulf has many   13.___
    A. large boats of pearl divers
    B. pearl divers who eat oysters
    C. edible oysters that produce pearls
    D. non-edible oysters that produce pearls
    E. edible oysters that do not produce pearls

TEST 13

Art says that the polar ice cap is melting at the rate of 3% per year. Bert says that this isn't true because the polar ice cap is really melting at the rate of 7% per year.

14. We know for certain that   14.___
    A. Art is wrong
    B. Bert is wrong
    C. they are both wrong
    D. they both might be right
    E. they can't both be right

TEST 14

FORTUNE AND MEN'S EYES
Shakespeare

1. When, in disgrace with fortune and men's eyes,
2. I all alone beweep my outcast state,
3. And trouble deaf heaven with my bootless cries,
4. And look upon myself and curse my fate,
5. Wishing me like to one more rich in hope,
6. Featured like him, like him with friends possessed
7. Desiring this man's art, and that man's scope,
8. With what I most enjoy contented least;
9. Yet in these thoughts myself almost despising,
10. Haply I think on thee; and then my state,
11. Like to the lark at break of day arising
12. From sullen earth, sings hymns at heaven's gate;
13. For thy sweet love remembered, such wealth brings
14. That then I scorn to change my state with kings.

15. What saves this man from wishing to be different than he   15. D
    is?
    A. Such wealth brings
    B. Hymns at heaven's gate
    C. The lark at break of day
    D. Thy sweet love remembered
    E. Change my state with kings

TEST 15

My name is Gregory Gotrocks, and I live in Peoria, Illinois. I sell tractors. In June 1952, the Gotrocks Tractor Company (my dad happens to be the president) sent me to Nepal-Tibet to check on our sales office there.

Business was slow, and I had a lot of time to kill. I decided to see Mt. Everest so that I could tell everyone back in Peoria that I had seen it.

It was beautiful; I was spellbound. I simply had to see what the view looked like from the top. So I started up the northwest slope. Everyone know that this is the best route to take. It took me three long hours to reach the top, but the climb was well worth it.

16. Gregory Gotrocks went to see Mt. Everest so that he could   16. E
    A. see some friends
    B. sell some tractors
    C. take a picture of it
    D. plant a flag at its base
    E. entertain his friends back home

TEST 16

Suburbanites are not irresponsible. Indeed, what is striking about the young couples' march along the abyss is the earnestness and precision with which they go about it. They are extremely budget-conscious. They can rattle off most of their monthly payments down to the last penny; one might say that even their impulse buying is deliberately planned. They are conscientious in meeting obligations and rarely do they fall delinquent in their accounts.

They are exponents of what could be called <u>budgetism</u>. This does not mean that they actually keep formal budgets - quite the contrary. The beauty of budgetism is that one doesn't have to keep a budget at all. It's done automatically. In the new middle-class rhythms of life, obligations are homogenized, for the overriding aim is to have oneself precommitted to regular, unvarying monthly payments on all the major items.

Americans used to be divided into three sizable groups: those who thought of money obligations in terms of the week, of the month, and of the year. Many people remain at both ends of the scale; but with the widening of the middle class, the mortgage payments are firmly geared to a thirty-day cycle, and any dissonant peaks and valleys are anathema. Just as young couples are now paying winter fuel bills in equal monthly fractions through the year, so they seek to spread out all the other heavy seasonal obligations they can anticipate. If vendors will not oblige by accepting equal monthly installments, the purchasers will smooth out the load themselves by floating loans.

It is, suburbanites cheerfully explain, a matter of psychology. They don't trust themselves. In self-entrapment is security. They try to budget so tightly that there is no unappropriated funds, for they know these would burn a hole in their pocket. Not merely out of greed for goods, then, do they commit themselves; it is protection they want, too. And though it would be extreme to say that they go into debt to be secure, carefully chartered debt does give them a certain peace of mind - and in suburbia this is more coveted than luxury itself.

17. What is the *abyss* along which the young couples are marching?   17. D
    A. Nuclear war   B. Unemployment
    C. Mental breakdown   D. Financial disaster
    E. Catastrophic illness

18. What conclusion does the author reach concerning carefully   18. C
    chartered debt among young couples in the United States today?
    It
    A. is a symbol of love
    B. brings marital happiness
    C. helps them to feel secure
    D. enables them to acquire wealth
    E. provides them with material goods

___
TEST 16

TEST 17

Read the verse and fill in the space beside the object described in the verse.

You see me when I'm right or wrong;
My face I never hide.
My hands move slowly round and round
And o'er me minutes glide.

19. A. ___ Book   B. ___ Clock   C. ___ Record   19. ___
     D. ___ Table   E. ___ Lock

———

TEST 18

Until about thirty years ago, the village of Nayon seems to have been a self-sufficient agricultural community with a mixture of native and sixteenth century Spanish customs. Lands were abandoned when too badly eroded. The balance between population and resources allowed a minimum subsistence. A few traders exchanged goods between Quito and the villages in the tropical barrancas, all within a radius of ten miles. Houses had dirt floors, thatched roofs, and pole walls that were sometimes plastered with mud. Guinea pigs ran freely about each house and were the main meat source. Most of the population spoke no Spanish. Men wore long hair and concerned themselves chiefly with farming.

The completion of the Guayaquil-Quito railway in 1908 brought the first real contacts with industrial civilization to the high inter-Andean valley. From this event gradually flowed not only technological changes but new ideas and social institutions. Feudal social relationships no longer seemed right and immutable; medicine and public health improved; elementary education became more common; urban Quito began to expand; and finally, and perhaps least important so far, modern industries began to appear, although even now on a most modest scale.

In 1948-49, the date of our visit, only two men wore their hair long; and only two old-style houses remained. If guinea pigs were kept, they were penned; their flesh was now a luxury food, and beef the most common meat. Houses were of adobe or fired brick, usually with tile roofs, and often contained five or six rooms, some of which had plank or brick floors. Most of the population spoke Spanish. There was no resident priest, but an appointed government official and a policeman represented authority. A six-teacher school provided education. Clothing was becoming citified; for men it often included overalls for work and a tailored suit, white shirt, necktie, and felt hat for trips to Quito. Attendance at church was low, and many festivals had been abandoned. Volleyball or soccer was played weekly in the plaza by young men who sometimes wore shorts, blazers, and berets. There were few shops, for most purchases were made in Quito, and from there came most of the food, so that there was a far more varied diet than twenty-five years ago. There were piped water and sporadic health services; in addition, most families patronized Quito doctors' in emergencies.

The crops and their uses had undergone change. Maize, or Indian corn, was still the primary crop, but very little was harvested as grain. Almost all was sold in Quito as green corn to eat boiled on the cob, and a considerable amount of the corn eaten as grain in Nayon was imported. Beans, which do poorly here, were grown on a small scale for household consumption. Though some squash was eaten, most was exported. Sweet potatoes, tomatoes, cabbage, onions, peppers, and, at lower elevations, sweet yucca, and arrowroot were grown extensively for export; indeed, so export-minded was the community that it was almost impossible to buy locally grown produce in the village. People couldn't be bothered with retail scales.

20. Why was there primitiveness and self-containment in Nayon before 1910?   20.___
    A. Social mores   B. Cultural tradition
    C. Biological instincts   D. Geographical factors
    E. Religious regulations

21. By 1948, the village of Nayon was   21.___
    A. a self-sufficient village
    B. out of touch with the outside world
    C. a small dependent portion of a larger economic unit
    D. a rapidly growing and sound social and cultural unit
    E. a metropolis

22. Why was Nayon originally separated from its neighbors?   22.___
    A. Rich arable land
    B. Long meandering streams
    C. Artificial political barriers
    D. Broad stretches of arid desert
    E. Deep rugged gorges traversed by rock trails

————

TEST 19

Read the verse and fill in the space beside the object described in the verse.

    I have two eyes and when I'm worn
    I give the wearer four.
    I'm strong or weak or thick or thin -
    Need I say much more?

23. A.___ Clock   B. ___ Eyeglasses   C.___ Piano   23.___
    D.___ Thermometer   E. ___ I don't know

————

TEST 20

Scarlet fever begins with fever, chills, headache, and sore throat. A doctor diagnoses the illness as scarlet fever when a characteristic rash erupts on the skin. This rash appears on the neck and chest in three to five days after the onset of the illness and spreads rapidly over the body. Sometimes the skin on the palm of the hands and soles of the feet shreds in flakes. Scarlet fever is usually treated with penicillin and, in severe cases, a convalescent serum. The disease may be accompanied by infections of the ear and throat, inflammation of the kidneys, pneumonia, and inflammation of the heart.

24. How does the author tell us that scarlet fever may be a serious disease?   24. D
    A. He tells how many people die of it.
    B. He tells that he once had the disease.
    C. He tells that hands and feet may fall off.
    D. He tells how other infections may come with scarlet fever.
    E. None of the above

TEST 21

Read the verse and fill in the space beside the object described in the verse.

I have no wings but often fly:
I come in colors many.
From varied nationalities
Respect I get a-plenty.

25. A.___ Deck of cards   B. ___ Eyeglasses   C. ___ Flag   25. C
     D.___ Needles   E. ___ None of the above

KEY (CORRECT ANSWERS)

1. D	6. B	11. E	16. E	21. C
2. B	7. C	12. C	17. D	22. E
3. B	8. E	13. D	18. C	23. B
4. D	9. C	14. E	19. B	24. D
5. B	10. E	15. D	20. D	25. C

READING COMPREHENSION
UNDERSTANDING AND INTERPRETING WRITTEN MATERIAL
COMMENTARY

The ability to read and understand written materials -- texts, publications, newspapers, orders, directions, expositions -- is a skill basic to a functioning democracy and to an efficient business or viable government.

That is why almost all examinations -- for beginning, middle, and senior levels -- test reading comprehension, directly or indirectly.

The reading test measures how well you understand what you read. This is how it is done: You read a short paragraph and five statements. From the five statements, you choose the one statement, or answer, that is BEST supported by, or best matches, what is said in the paragraph.

SAMPLE QUESTIONS

DIRECTIONS: Each question has five suggested answers, lettered A,B,C,D, and E. Decide which one is the BEST answer. *PRINT THE LETTER OF THE CORRECT ANSWER IN THE SPACE AT THE RIGHT.*

1. The prevention of accidents makes it necessary not only that safety devices be used to guard exposed machinery but also that mechanics be instructed in safety rules which they must follow for their own protection and that the light in the plant be adequate.
   The paragraph BEST supports the statement that industrial accidents
   A. are always avoidable
   B. may be due to ignorance
   C. usually result from inadequate machinery
   D. cannot be entirely overcome
   E. result in damage to machinery

ANALYSIS
Remember what you have to do --
   First - Read the paragraph.
   Second - Decide what the paragraph means.
   Third - Read the five suggested answers.
   Fourth - Select the one answer which BEST matches what the paragraph says or is BEST supported by something in the paragraph. (Sometimes you may have to read the paragraph again in order to be sure which suggested answer is best.)
This paragraph is talking about three steps that should be taken to prevent industrial accidents --
   1. use safety devices on machines
   2. instruct mechanics in safety rules
   3. provide adequate lighting.

SELECTION
With this in mind let's look at each suggested answer. Each one starts with "Industrial accidents ..."

SUGGESTED ANSWER A.
   Industrial accidents (A) are always avoidable.
   (The paragraph talks about how to avoid accidents, but does not say that accidents are always avoidable.)

1

SUGGESTED ANSWER B.
   Industrial accidents (b) may be due to ignorance.
   (One of the steps given in the paragraph to prevent accidents is to instruct mechanics on safety rules. This suggests that lack of knowledge or ignorance of safety rules causes accidents. This suggested answer sounds like a good possibility for being the right answer.)

SUGGESTED ANSWER C.
   Industrial accidents (C) usually result from inadequate machinery.
   (The paragraph does suggest that exposed machines cause accidents, but it doesn't say that it is the usual cause of accidents. The word *usually* makes this a wrong answer.)

SUGGESTED ANSWER D.
   Industrial accidents (D) cannot be entirely overcome.
   (You may know from your own experience that this is a true statement. But that is not what the paragraph is talking about. Therefore it is NOT the correct answer.)

SUGGESTED ANSWER E.
   Industrial accidents (E) result in damage to machinery.
   (This is a statement that may or may not be true, but in any case it is NOT covered by the paragraph.)

   Looking back, you see that the one suggested answer of the five given that BEST matches what the paragraph says is --
      Industrial accidents (B) may be due to ignorance.
   The CORRECT answer then is B.
   Be sure you read ALL the possible answers before you make your choice. You may think that none of the five answers is really good, but choose the BEST one of the five.

2. Probably few people realize, as they drive on a concrete road, that steel is used to keep the surface flat in spite of the weight of the busses and trucks. Steel bars, deeply embedded in the concrete, provide sinews to take the stresses so that the stresses cannot crack the slab or make it wavy.
   The paragraph BEST supports the statement THAT a concrete road
      A. is expensive to build
      B. usually cracks under heavy weights
      C. looks like any other road
      D. is used only for heavy traffic
      E. is reinforced with other material

ANALYSIS
This paragraph is commenting on the fact that --
   1. few people realize, as they drive on a concrete road, that steel is deeply embedded
   2. steel keeps the surface flat
   3. steel bars enable the road to take the stresses without cracking or becoming wavy.

SELECTION
Now read and think about the possible answers:
   A. A concrete road is expensive to build.
      (Maybe so but that is not what the paragraph is about.)
   B. A concrete road usually cracks under heavy weights.
      (The paragraph talks about using steel bars to prevent heavy weights from cracking concrete roads. It says nothing about how usual it is for the roads to crack. The word *usually* makes this suggested answer wrong.)

2

C. A concrete road looks like any other road.
(This may or may not be true. The important thing to note is that it has nothing to do with what the paragraph is about.)
D. A concrete road is used only for heavy traffic.
(This answer at least has something to do with the paragraph -- concrete roads are used with heavy traffic but it does not say "used only.")
E. A concrete road is reinforced with other material.
(This choice seems to be the correct one on two counts: *First*, the paragraph does suggest that concrete roads are made stronger by embedding steel bars in them. This is another way of saying "concrete roads are reinforced with steel bars." *Second*, by the process of elimination, the other four choices are ruled out as correct answers simply because they do not apply.)

You can be sure that not all the reading questions will be so easy as these.

_____

HINTS FOR ANSWERING READING QUESTIONS

1. Read the paragraph carefully. Then read each suggested answer carefully. Read every word, because often one word can make the difference between a right and a wrong answer.
2. Choose that answer which is supported in the paragraph itself. Do not choose an answer which is a correct statement unless it is based on information in the paragraph.
3. Even though a suggested answer has many of the words used in the paragraph, it may still be wrong.
4. Look out for words -- such as *always, never, entirely, or only* -- which tend to make a suggested answer wrong.
5. Answer first those questions which you can answer most easily. Then work on the other questions.
6. If you can't figure out the answer to the question, guess.

EXAMINATION SECTION

DIRECTIONS FOR THIS SECTION:
   Each question has five suggested answers, lettered A to E. Decide which one is the BEST answer. *PRINT THE LETTER OF THE CORRECT ANSWER IN THE SPACE AT THE RIGHT.*

TEST 1

1. Some specialists are willing to give their services to the Government entirely free of charge; some feel that a nominal salary, such as will cover traveling expenses, is sufficient for a position that is recognized as being somewhat honorary in nature; many other specialists value their time so highly that they will not devote any of it to public service that does not repay them at a rate commensurate with the fees that they can obtain from a good private clientele.
The paragraph BEST supports the statement that the use of specialists by the Government
   A. is rare because of the high cost of securing such persons
   B. may be influenced by the willingness of specialists to serve
   C. enables them to secure higher salaries in private fields
   D. has become increasingly common during the past few years
   E. always conflicts with private demands for their services

1. .B.

3

2. The fact must not be overlooked that only about one-half of   2. D.
   the international trade of the world crosses the oceans. The
   other half is merely exchanges of merchandise between coun-
   tries lying alongside each other or at least within the same
   continent.
   The paragraph BEST supports the statement that
   A. the most important part of any country's trade is trans-
      oceanic
   B. domestic trade is insignificant when compared with for-
      eign trade
   C. the exchange of goods between neighborhing countries is
      not considered international trade
   D. foreign commerce is not necessarily carried on by water
   E. about one-half of the trade of the world is international   A

3. Individual differences in mental traits assume importance in   3. ...
   fitting workers to jobs because such personal characteristics
   are persistent and are relatively little influenced by train-
   ing and experience.
   *The paragraph BEST supports the statement that training and
   experience*
   A. are limited in their effectiveness in fitting workers
      to jobs
   B. do not increase a worker's fitness for a job
   C. have no effect upon a person's mental traits
   D. have relatively little effect upon the individual's
      chances for success
   E. should be based on the mental traits of an individual

4. The competition of buyers tends to keep prices up, the com-   4. D ...
   petition of sellers to send them down. Normally the pressure
   of competition among sellers is stronger than that among buy-
   ers since the seller has his article to sell and must get rid
   of it, whereas the buyer is not committed to anything.
   *The paragraph BEST supports the statement that low prices
   are caused by*
   A. buyer competition
   B. competition of buyers with sellers
   C. fluctuations in demand
   D. greater competition among sellers than among buyers
   E. more sellers than buyers

5. In seventeen states, every lawyer is automatically a member   5. A ...
   of the American Bar Association. In some other states and lo-
   calities, truly representative organizations of the Bar have
   not yet come into being, but are greatly needed.
   The paragraph IMPLIES that
   A. representative Bar Associations are necessary in states
      where they do not now exist
   B. every lawyer is required by law to become a member of
      the Bar
   C. the Bar Association is a democratic organization
   D. some states have more lawyers than others
   E. every member of the American Bar Association is automa-
      tically a lawyer in seventeen states.

4

TEST 2

1. We hear a great deal about the new education, and see a great 1. *B.*
deal of it in action. But the school house, though prodigious-
ly magnified in scale, is still very much the same old school
house.
   The paragraph IMPLIES that
   A. the old education was, after all, better than the new
   B. although the modern school buildings are larger than
   the old ones, they have not changed very much in other
   respects
   C. the old school houses do not fit in with modern educational theories
   D. a fine school building does not make up for poor teachers
   E. schools will be schools

2. No two human beings are of the same pattern --not even twins-- 2. *A.*
and the method of bringing out the best in each one necessar-
ily varies according to the nature of the child.
   The paragraph IMPLIES that
   A. individual differences should be considered in dealing
   with children
   B. twins should be treated impartially
   C. it is an easy matter to determine the special abilities
   of children
   D. a child's nature varies from year to year
   E. we must discover the general technique of dealing with
   children

3. Man inhabits today a world very different from that which en- 3. *B.*
compassed even his parents and grandparents. It is a world
geared to modern machinery - automobiles, airplanes, power
plants; it is linked together and served by electricity.
   The paragraph IMPLIES that
   A. the world has not changed much during the last few
   generations
   B. modern inventions and discoveries have brought about
   many changes in man's way of living
   C. the world is run more efficiently today than it was in
   our grandparents' time
   D. man is much happier today than he was a hundred years ago
   E. we must learn to see man as he truly is, underneath the
   veneers of man's contrivances

4. Success in any study depends largely upon the interest taken 4. *C.*
in that particular subject by the student. This being the case,
each teacher earnestly hopes that her students will realize at
the very outset that shorthand can be made an intensely fascina-
ting study.
   The paragraph IMPLIES that
   A. everyone is interested in shorthand
   B. success in a study is entirely impossible unless the
   student finds the study very interesting
   C. if a student is eager to study shorthand, he is likely
   to succeed in it
   D. shorthand is necessary for success
   E. anyone who is not interested in shorthand will not suc-
   ceed in business

5. The primary purpose of all business English is to move the   5. .D.
   reader to agreeable and mutually profitable action. This action may be indirect or direct, but in either case a highly
   competitive appeal for business should be clothed with inci-
   sive diction tending to replace vagueness and doubt with clarity, confidence, and appropriate action.
   The paragraph IMPLIES that the
     A. ideal business letter uses words to conform to the read-
        er's language level
     B. business correspondent should strive for conciseness in
        letter writing
     C. keen competition of today has lessened the value of the
        letter as an appeal for business
     D. writer of a business letter should employ incisive dic-
        tion to move the reader to compliant and gainful action
     E. the writer of a business letter should be himself clear,
        confident, and forceful

TEST 3

1. To serve the community best, a comprehensive city plan must 1. .B.
   coordinate all physical improvements, even at the possible
   expense of subordinating individual desires, to the end that
   a city may grow in a more orderly way and provide adequate
   facilities for its people.
   The paragraph IMPLIES that
     A. city planning provides adequate facilities for recreation
     B. a comprehensive city plan provides the means for a city
        to grow in a more orderly fashion
     C. individual desires must always be subordinated to civic
        changes
     D. the only way to serve a community is to adopt a compre-
        hensive city plan
     E. city planning is the most important function of city
        government
2. Facility in writing letters, the knack of putting into these 2. ...
   quickly written letters the same personal impression that
   would mark an interview, and the ability to boil down to a
   one-page letter the gist of what might be called a five or
   ten minute conversation – all these are essential to effective
   work under conditions of modern business organization.
   The paragraph IMPLIES that
     A. letters are of more importance in modern business activi-
        ties than ever before
     B. letters should be used in place of interviews
     C. the ability to write good letters is essential to effec-
        tive work in modern business organization
     D. business letters should never be more than one page in
        length
     E. the person who can write a letter with great skill will
        get ahead more readily than others

3. The general rule is that it is the city council which deter-   3. .B
mines the amount to be raised by taxation and which therefore
determines, within the law, the tax rates. As has been pointed
out, however, no city council or city authority has the power
to determine what kinds of taxes should be levied.
The paragraph IMPLIES that
   A. the city council has more authority than any other munici-
      pal body
   B. while the city council has a great deal of authority in
      the levying of taxes, its power is not absolute
   C. the kinds of taxes levied in different cities vary great-
      ly
   D. the city council appoints the tax collectors
   E. the mayor determines the kinds of taxes to be levied

4. The growth of modern business has made necessary mass produc-   4. ...C
tion, mass distribution, and mass selling. As a result, the
problems of personnel and industrial relations have increased
so rapidly that grave injustices in the handling of personal
relationships have frequently occurred. Personnel administration is complex because, as in all human problems, many intangible elements are involved. Therefore a thorough, systema-
tic, and continuous study of the psychology of human behavior
is essential to the intelligent handling of personnel.
The paragraph IMPLIES that
   A. complex modern industry makes impossible the personal re-
      lationships which formerly existed between employer and
      employee
   B. mass decisions are successfully applied to personnel
      problems
   C. the human element in personnel administration makes con-
      tinuous study necessary to its intelligent application
   D. personnel problems are less important than the problems
      of mass production and mass distribution
   E. since personnel administration is so complex and costly,
      it should be subordinated to the needs of good industrial
      relations

5. The Social Security Act is striving toward the attainment of   5. ...E
economic security for the individual and for his family. It was
stated, in outlining this program, that security for the individual and for the family concerns itself with three factors:
(1) decent homes to live in; (2) development of the natural resources of the country so as to afford the fullest opportunity
to engage in productive work; and (3) safeguards against the major misfortunes of life. The Social Security Act is concerned
with the third of these factors —"safeguards against misfortunes
which cannot be wholly eliminated in this man-made world of ours."
The paragraph IMPLIES that
   A. the Social Security Act is concerned primarily with supply-
      ing to families decent homes in which to live
   B. the development of natural resources is the only means of
      offering employment to the masses of the unemployed
   C. the Social Security Act has attained absolute economic
      security for the individual and for his family
   D. the Social Security Act deals with the first (1) factor
      as stated in the paragraph above
   E. the Social Security Act deals with the third (3) factor
      as stated in the paragraph above

TEST 4

Free unrhymed verse has been practiced for some thousands of years and reaches back to the incantation which linked verse with the ritual dance. It provided a communal emotion; the aim of the cadenced phrases was to create a state of mind. The general coloring of free rhythms in the poetry of today is that of speech rhythm, composed in the sequence of the musical phrase, not in the sequence of the metronome, the regular beat. In the twenties, conventional rhyme fell into almost complete disuse. This liberation from rhyme became as well a liberation of rhyme. Freed of its exacting task of supporting lame verse, it would be applied with greater effect where wanted for some special effect. Such break in the tradition of rhymed verse had the healthy effect of giving it a fresh start, released from the hampering convention of too familiar cadences. This refreshing and subtilizing of the use of rhyme can be seen everywhere in the poetry today.

1. The title below that BEST expresses the ideas of this paragraph is:
    A. Primitive poetry
    B. The origin of poetry
    C. Rhyme and rhythm in modern verse
    D. Classification of poetry
    E. Purposes in all poetry

    1. C

2. Free verse had its origin in primitive
    A. fairy tales   B. literature C. warfare D. chants
    E. courtship

    2. D

3. The object of early free verse was to
    A. influence the mood of the people B. convey ideas
    C. produce mental pictures   D. create pleasing sounds
    E. provide enjoyment

    3. A

Control of the Mississippi had always been goals of nations having ambitions in the New World. La Salle claimed it for France in 1682. Iberville appropriated it to France when he colonized Louisiana in 1700. Bienville founded New Orleans, its principal port, as a French city in 1718. The fleur-de-lis were the blazon of the delta country until 1762. Then Spain claimed all of Louisiana. The Spanish were easy neighbors. American products from western Pennsylvania and the Northwest Territory were barged down the Ohio and Mississippi to New Orleans, here they were reloaded on ocean-going vessels that cleared for the great seaports of the world.

1. The title below that BEST expresses the ideas of this paragraph is:
    A. Importance of seaports
    B. France and Spain in the New World
    C. Early control of the Mississippi
    D. Claims of European nations
    E. American trade on the Mississippi

    1. C

2. Until 1762 the lower Mississippi area was held by
    A. England   B. Spain   C. the United States
    D. France   E. Indians

    2. D

3. In doing business with Americans the Spaniards were   3. B.
   A. easy to outsmart   B. friendly to trade
   C. inclined to charge high prices for use of their ports
   D. shrewd   E. suspicious

PASSAGE 3

Our humanity is by no means so materialistic as foolish talk is continually asserting it to be. Judging by what I have learned about men
and women, I am convinced that there is far more in them of idealistic
willpower than ever comes to the surface of the world. Just as the water of streams is small in amount compared to that which flows underground, so the idealism which becomes visible is small in amount compared with that which men and women bear locked in their hearts, un-
released or scarcely released. To unbind what is bound, to bring the
underground waters to the surface -- mankind is waiting and longing
for men who can do that.

1. The title below that BEST expresses the ideas of this para-   1. ....
   graph is: D
      A. Releasing underground riches
      B. The good and bad in man
      C. Materialism in humanity
      D. The surface and the depths of idealism
      E. Unreleased energy
2. Human beings are more idealistic than   2. C.
      A. the water in underground streams
      B. their waiting and longing proves
      C. outward evidence shows
      D. the world
      E. other living creatures

PASSAGE 4

The total impression made by any work of fiction cannot be rightly
understood without a sympathetic perception of the artistic aims of the
writer. Consciously or unconsciouly, he has accepted certain facts, and
rejected or suppressed other facts, in order to give unity to the particular aspect of human life which he is depicting. No novelist possesses
the impartiality, the indifference, the infinite tolerance of nature.
Nature displays to use, with complete unconcern, the beautiful and the
ugly, the precious and the trivial, the pure and the impure. But a writer must select the aspects of nature and human nature which are demanded
by the work in hand. He is forced to select, to combine, to create.

1. The title below that BEST expresses the ideas of this para-   1. D.
   graph is:
      A. Impressionists in literature
      B. Nature as an artist
      C. The novelist as an imitator
      D. Creative technic of the novelist
      E. Aspects of nature
2. A novelist rejects some facts because they   2. E.
      A. are impure and ugly
      B. would show he is not impartial
      C. are unrelated to human nature
      D. would make a bad impression
      E. mar the unity of his story

3. It is important for a reader to know 3. A...
    A. the purpose of the author
    B. what facts the author omits
    C. both the ugly and the beautiful
    D. something about nature
    E. what the author thinks of human nature

PASSAGE 5

If you watch a lamp which is turned very rapidly on and off, and you keep your eyes open, "persistence of vision" will bridge the gaps of darkness between the flashes of light, and the lamp will seem to be continuously lit. This "topical afterglow" explains the magic produced by the stroboscope, a new instrument which seems to freeze the swiftest motions while they are still going on, and to stop time itself dead in its tracks. The "magic" is all in the eye of the beholder.

1. The "magic" of the stroboscope is due to 1. D..
    A. continuous lighting   B. intense cold
    C. slow motion   D. behavior of the human eye
    E. a lapse of time
2. "Persistence of vision" is explained by 2. E..
    A. darkness   B. winking   C. rapid flashes
    D. gaps   E. after impression

TEST 5

PASSAGE 1

During the past fourteen years, thousands of top-lofty United States elms have been marked for death by the activities of the tiny European elm bark beetle. The beetles, however, do not do fatal damage. Death is caused by another importation, Dutch elm disease, a fungus infection which the beetles carry from tree to tree. Up to 1941, quarantine and tree-sanitation measures kept the beetles and the disease pretty well confined within 510 miles around metropolitan New York. War curtailed these measures and made Dutch elm disease a wider menace. Every household and village that prizes an elm-shaded lawn or commons must now watch for it. Since there is as yet no cure for it, the infected trees must be pruned or felled, and the wood must be burned in order to protect other healthy trees.

1. The title below that BEST expresses the ideas of this para- 1. A...
   graph is:
    A. A menace to our elms   B. Pests and diseases of the elm
    C. Our vanishing elms   D. The need to protect Dutch elms
    E. How elms are protected
2. The danger of spreading the Dutch elm disease was increased 2. B...
   by
    A. destroying infected trees B. the war
    C. the lack of a cure   D. a fungus infection
    E. quarantine measures
3. The European elm bark beetle is a serious threat to our elms 3. D...
   because it
    A. chews the bark   B. kills the trees
    C. is particularly active on the eastern seaboard
    D. carries infection   E. cannot be controlled

PASSAGE 2

It is elemental that the greater the development of man, the greater the problems he has to concern him. When he lived in a cave with stone implements, his mind no less than his actions was grooved into simple channels. Every new invention, every new way of doing things posed fresh problems for him. And, as he moved along the road, he questioned each step, as indeed he should, for he trod upon the beliefs of his ancestors. It is equally clemental to say that each step upon this later road posed more questions than the earlier ones. It is only the edcated man who realizes the results of his actions; it is only the thoughtful one who questions his own decisions.

1. The title below that BEST expresses the ideas of this para- 1. ....
   graph is:
   - A. Channels of civilization
   - B. The mark of a thoughtful man
   - C. The cave man in contrast with man today
   - D. The price of early progress
   - E. Man's never-ending challenge

PASSAGE 3

Spring is one of those things that man has no hand in, any more than he has a part in sunrise or the phases of the moon. Spring came before man was here to enjoy it, and it will go right on coming even if man isn't here some time in the future. It is a matter of solar mechanics and celestial order. And for all our knowledge of astronomy and terrestrial mechanics, we haven't yet been able to do more than bounce a radar beam off the moon. We couldn't alter the arrival of the spring equinox by as much as one second, if we tried.

Spring is a matter of growth, of chlorophyll, of bud and blossom. We can alter growth and change the time of blossoming in individual plants; but the forests still grow in nature's way, and the grass of the plains hasn't altered its nature in a thousand years. Spring is a magnificent phase of the cycle of nature; but man really hasn't any guiding or controlling hand in it. He is here to enjoy it and benefit by it. And April is a good time to realize it; by May perhaps we will want to take full credit.

1. The title below that BEST expresses the ideas of this passage 1. ....
   is:
   - A. The marvels of the Spring equinox
   - B. Nature's dependence on mankind
   - C. The weakness of man opposed to nature
   - D. The glories of the world
   - E. Eternal growth
2. The author of the passage states that 2. ....
   - A. man has a part in the phases of the moon
   - B. April is a time for taking full-credit
   - C. April is a good time to enjoy nature
   - D. man has a guiding hand in spring
   - E. spring will cease to be if civilization ends

PASSAGE 4

The walled medieval town was as characteristic of its period as the cut of a robber baron's beard. It sprang out of the exigencies of war, and it was not without its architectural charm, whatever its hygienic deficiencies may have been. Behind its high, thick walls not only the normal inhabitants but the whole countryside fought and cowered in an hour of need. The capitals of Europe now forsake the city when the sirens scream and death from the sky seems imminent. Will the fear of bombs accelerate the slow decentralization which began with the automobile and the wide distribution of electrical energy and thus reverse the medieval flow to the city?

1. The title below that BEST expresses the ideas in this paragraph is.   1. A.
    A. A changing function of the town B. The walled medieval town
    C. The automobile's influence on city life D. Forsaking the city
    E. Bombs today and yesterday
2. Conditions in the Middle Ages made the walled town   2. A.
    A. a natural development B. the most dangerous of all places
    C. a victim of fires   D. lacking in architectural charm
    E. healthful
3. Modern conditions may   3. D.
    A. make cities larger   B. make cities more hygienic
    C. protect against floods
    D. cause people to move from population centers
    E. encourage good architecture

___

PASSAGE 5

The literary history of this nation began when the first settler from abroad of sensitive mind paused in his adventure long enough to feel that he was under a different sky, breathing new air, and that a New World was all before him with only his strength and Providence for guides. With him began a new emphasis upon an old theme in literature, the theme of cutting loose and faring forth, renewed, under the powerful influence of a fresh continent for civilized man. It has provided, ever since those first days, a strong current in our native literature, whose other flow has come from a nostalgia for the rich culture of Europe, so much of which was perforce left behind.

1. The title below that BEST expresses the ideas of this paragraph is: 1. A.
    A. America's distinctive literature B. Pioneer authors
    C. The dead hand of the past D. Europe's literary grandchild
    E. America comes of age
2. American writers, according to the author, because of their colonial experiences   2. E.
    A. were antagonistic to European writers
    B. cut loose from Old World influences
    C. wrote only on New World events and characters
    D. created new literary themes
    E. gave fresh interpretation to an old literary idea

___

TEST 6

1. Any business not provided with capable substitutes to fill 1. ..E..
all important positions is a weak business. Therefore a fore-
man should train each man not only to perform his own particular duties but also to do those of two or three positions.
The paragraph BEST supports the statement that
   A. dependence on substitutes is a sign of weak organization
   B. training will improve the strongest organization
   C. the foreman should be the most expert at any particular
   job under him
   D. every employee can be trained to perform efficiently
   work other than his own
   E. vacancies in vital positions should be provided for in
   advance

2. The coloration of textile fabrics composed of cotton and   2. .E..
wool generally requires two processes, as the process used
in dyeing wool is seldom capable of fixing the color upon
cotton. The usual method is to immerse the fabric in the re-
quisite baths to dye the wool and then to treat the partial-
ly dyed material in the manner found suitable for cotton.
The paragraph BEST supports the statement that the dyeing
of textile fabrics composed of cotton and wool
   A. is less complicated than the dyeing of wool alone
   B. is more successful when the material contains more
   cotton than wool
   C. is not satisfactory when solid colors are desired
   D. is restricted to two colors for any one fabric
   E. is usually based upon the methods required for dyeing
   the different materials

3. The serious investigator must direct his whole effort toward3. .B.
success in his work. If he wishes to succeed in each inves-
tigation, his work will be by no means easy, smooth, or peace-
ful; on the contrary, he will have to devote himself complete-
ly and continuously to a task that requires all his ability.
The paragraph BEST supports the statement that an investiga-
tor's success depends most upon
   A. ambition to advance rapidly in the service
   B. persistence in the face of difficulty
   C. training and experience
   D. willingness to obey orders without delay
   E. the number of investigations which he conducts

4. Honest people in one nation find it difficult to understand 4. .A.
the viewpoint of honest people in another. State departments
and their ministers exist for the purpose of explaining the
viewpoints of one nation in terms understood by another. Some
of their most important work lies in this direction.
The paragraph BEST supports the statement that
   A. people of different nations may not consider matters
   in the same light
   B. it is unusual for many people to share similar ideas
   C. suspicion prevents understanding between nations
   D. the chief work of state departments is to guide relations between nations united by a common cause
   E. the people of one nation must sympathize with the view-
   points of others

5. Economy once in a while is just not enough. I expect to find   5. E...
it at every level of responsibility, from cabinet member to
the newest and youngest recruit. Controlling waste is some-
thing like bailing a boat; you have to keep at it. I have no
intention of easing up on my insistence on getting a dollar
of value for each dollar we spend.
The paragraph BEST supports the statement that
   A. we need not be concerned about items which cost less
      than a dollar
   B. it is advisable to buy the cheaper of two items
   C. the responsibility of economy is greater at high levels
      than at low levels
   D. economy becomes easy with practice
   E. economy is a continuing responsibility

TEST 7

1. On all permit imprint mail the charge for postage has been   1. B...
printed by the mailer before he presents it for mailing and
pays the postage. Such mail of any class is mailable only at
the post office that issued a permit covering it. Since the
postage receipts for such mail represent only the amount of
permit imprint mail detected and verified, employees in re-
ceiving, handling, and outgoing sections must be alert constantly to route such mail to the weighing section before it
is handled or dispatched.
The paragraph BEST supports the statement that, at post offices where permit mail is received for dispatch,
   A. dispatching units make a final check on the amount of
      postage payable on permit imprint mail
   B. employees are to check the postage chargeable on mail
      received under permit
   C. neither more nor less postage is to be collected than
      the amount printed on permit imprint mail
   D. the weighing section is primarily responsible for fail-
      ure to collect postage on such mail
   E. unusual measures are taken to prevent unstamped mail
      from being accepted
2. Education should not stop when the individual has been pre-   2. B...
pared to make a livelihood and to live in modern society.
Living would be mere existence were there no appreciation
and enjoyment of the riches of art, literature, and science.
The paragraph BEST supports the statement that true education
   A. is focused on the routine problems of life
   B. prepares one for full enjoyment of life
   C. deals chiefly with art, literature and science
   D. is not possible for one who does not enjoy scientific
      literature
   E. disregards practical ends
3. Insured and c.o.d. air and surface mail is accepted with   3. B...
the understanding that the sender guarantees any necessary
forwarding or return postage. When such mail is forwarded or
returned, it shall be rated up for collection of postage; except that insured or c.o.d. air mail weighing 8 ounces or less

14

and subject to the 10 cents an ounce rate shall be forwarded by air if delivery will be advanced, and returned by surface means, without additional postage.

The paragraph BEST supports the statement that the return postage for undeliverable insured mail is

    A. included in the original prepayment on air mail parcels

    B. computed but not collected before dispatching surface patrol post mail to sender

    C. not computed or charged for any air mail that is returned by surface transportation

    D. included in the amount collected when the sender mails parcel post

    E. collected before dispatching for return if any amount due has been guaranteed

4. All undeliverable first-class mail, except first-class parcels and parcel post paid with first-class postage, which cannot be returned to the sender, is sent to a dead-letter branch. Undeliverable matter of the third-and fourth-classes of obvious value for which the sender does not furnish return postage and undeliverable first-class parcels and parcel-post matter bearing postage of the first-class, which cannot be returned, is sent to a dead parcel-post branch.

The paragraph BEST supports the statement that matter that is sent to a dead parcel-post branch includes all undeliverable

    A. mail, except first-class letter mail, that appears to be valuable

    B. mail, except that of the first-class, on which the sender failed to prepay the original mailing costs

    C. parcels on which the mailer prepaid the first-class rate of postage

    D. third- and fourth-class matter on which the required return postage has not been paid

    E. parcels on which first-class postage has been prepaid, when the sender's address is not known

5. Civilization started to move rapidly when man freed himself of the shackles that restricted his search for truth.

The paragraph BEST supports the statement that the progress of civilization

    A. came as a result of man's dislike for obstacles

    B. did not begin until restrictions on learning were removed

    C. has been aided by man's efforts to find the truth

    D. is based on continually increasing efforts

    E. continues at a constantly increasing rate

TEST 8

1. Telegrams should be clear, concise, and brief. Omit all unnecessary words. The parts of speech most often used in telegrams are nouns,verbs,adjectives,and adverbs. If possible,do without pronouns,prepositions,articles,and copulative verbs. Use simple sentences, rather than complex and compound.

The paragraph BEST supports the statement that in writing telegrams one should always use

    A. common and simple words

    B. only nouns, verbs, adjectives, and adverbs
    C. incomplete sentences
    D. only words essential to the meaning
    E. the present tense of verbs

2. The function of business is to increase the wealth of the country and the value and happiness of life. It does this by supplying the material needs of men and women. When the nation's business is successfully carried on, it renders public service of the highest value.   2. D

The paragraph BEST supports the statement that
    A. all businesses which render public service are successful
    B. human happiness is enhanced only by the increase of material wants
    C. the value of life is increased only by the increase of wealth
    D. the material needs of men and women are supplied by well-conducted business
    E. business is the only field of activity which increases happiness

3. In almost every community, fortunately, there are certain men and women known to be public-spirited. Others, however, may be selfish and act only as their private interests seem to require.   3. E

The paragraph BEST supports the statement that those citizens who disregard others are
    A. fortunate   B. needed
    C. found only in small communities   D. not known
    E. not public-spirited

KEY (CORRECT ANSWERS)

TEST 1		TEST 4		TEST 5		TEST 6	
1. B		PASSAGE 1		PASSAGE 1		1. E	
2. D		1. C		1. A		2. E	
3. A		2. D		2. B		3. B	
4. D		3. A		3. D		4. A	
5. A		PASSAGE 2		PASSAGE 2		5. E	
		1. C		1. E			
TEST 2		2. D		PASSAGE 3		TEST 7	
1. B		3. B		1. C		1. B	
2. A		PASSAGE 3		2. C		2. B	
3. B		1. D		PASSAGE 4		3. B	
4. C		2. C		1. A		4. E	
5. D		PASSAGE 4		2. A		5. C	
		1. D		3. D			
TEST 3		2. E		PASSAGE 5		TEST 8	
1. B		2. A		1. A		1. D	
2. C		PASSAGE 5		2. E		2. D	
3. B		1. D				3. E	
4. C		2. E					
5. E							

MATHEMATICS
EXAMINATION SECTION

Questions 1-60.
DIRECTIONS: For problems No. 1 through 22, compute an answer for each. For problems No. 23 through 60, select an answer from among the four choices given. Print the letter of the correct answer in the space at the right.

1. Add: 215
          86
         193

2. From 761 subtract 257.

3. Multiply: 206
            x 57

4. Divide: 25) 4175

5. Divide: 408 ÷ 4

6. Multiply: 1/2 X 3/4

7. Add: 3.4 and 1.16

8. Find the product of 3.4 and 7.8.

9. If 12.36 is divided by 6, what is the quotient?

10. What is 2/3 of 30?

11. Subtract: 9.67
              4.85

12. Divide: 8 ÷ 1/3

13. If John spends $6.45, how much change should he receive from a $10 bill?

14. What is the average (mean) of 81, 72, and 78?

15. How many cubic centimeters are in the volume of a rectangular box 6 cm long, 4 cm wide, and 4 cm high?

16. What is the perimeter of a rectangle with length 6 and width 2?

17. A number of test scores are arranged as follows: 58, 65, 65, 75, 85, 85, 99. What is the median score?

18. Solve for x: $4x + 1 = 17$

19. Solve for x: $\frac{6}{10} = \frac{x}{30}$

20. A team lost 40% of its games. If the team played 30 games, how many games were lost?

21. On a map, 1 centimeter represents 12 kilometers. How many kilometers does 2½ centimeters on the map represent?

22. What is the area of a square with each side of length 5?

In the following group of questions, students are to select the correct answer from among the four choices given. Print the letter of the correct answer in the space at the right.

23. Which number makes this open sentence true?
    ☐ - 186 = 54
    A. 132   B. 238   C. 240   D. 250

24. The sum of 3/5 and 2/3 is
    A. 5/8   B. 5/15   C. 19/15   D. 6/8

25. What is the least common denominator of the fractions 1/2, 2/3, and 5/6?
    A. 36   B. 18   C. 12   D. 6

26. Which has the same value as $\frac{17}{5}$?
    A. 12   B. 2 2/5   C. 3 2/5   D. 5 2/3

1. ...
2. ...
3. ...
4. ...
5. ...
6. ...
7. ...
8. ...
9. ...
10. ...
11. ...
12. ...
13. ...
14. ...
15. ...
16. ...
17. ...
18. ...
19. ...
20. ...
21. ...
22. ...
23. ...
24. ...
25. ...
26. ...

1

27. When written as a percent, the fraction 3/4 is   27. ...
   A. 25%   B. 66 2/3%   C. 75%   D. 87 1/2%
28. If 46,534 people were at a football game, what would be   28. ...
    the total attendance, reported to the nearest thousand?
    A. 40,000   B. 46,000   C. 47,000   D. 50,000
29. Which number represents seventy thousand eight hundred?   29. ...
    A. 7,080   B. 70,080   C. 70,800   D. 78,000
30. When listed in order from smallest to largest, which   30. ...
    fraction would be the first?
    A. 1/5   B. 1/2   C. 1/3   D. 1/4
31. The cost of a telephone call was listed as: 31. ...
    $1.00 for the first 3 minutes
    $0.30 for each additional minute
    What would be the total cost of a telephone call that
    was 6 minutes long?
    A $1.80   B. $1.90   C. $2.00   D. $2.80

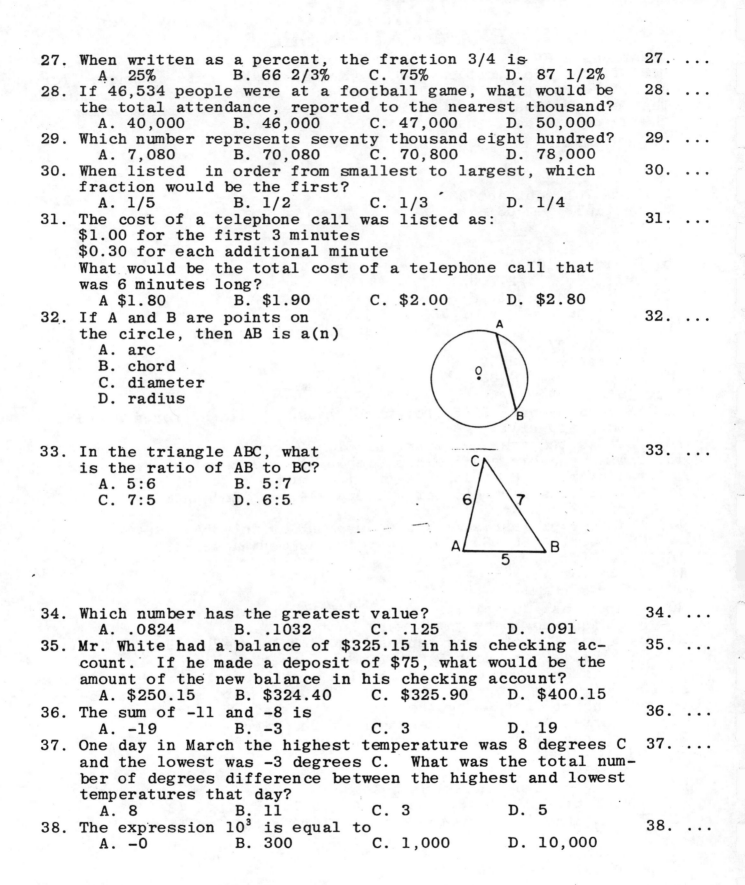

32. If A and B are points on   32. ...
    the circle, then AB is a(n)
       A. arc
       B. chord
       C. diameter
       D. radius

33. In the triangle ABC, what   33. ...
    is the ratio of AB to BC?
       A. 5:6   B. 5:7
       C. 7:5   D. 6:5

34. Which number has the greatest value?   34. ...
    A. .0824   B. .1032   C. .125   D. .091
35. Mr. White had a balance of $325.15 in his checking ac-   35. ...
    count. If he made a deposit of $75, what would be the
    amount of the new balance in his checking account?
    A. $250.15   B. $324.40   C. $325.90   D. $400.15
36. The sum of -11 and -8 is   36. ...
    A. -19   B. -3   C. 3   D. 19
37. One day in March the highest temperature was 8 degrees C   37. ...
    and the lowest was -3 degrees C. What was the total num-
    ber of degrees difference between the highest and lowest
    temperatures that day?
    A. 8   B. 11   C. 3   D. 5
38. The expression 10^3 is equal to   38. ...
    A. -0   B. 300   C. 1,000   D. 10,000

2

39. On the accompanying graph,
    point A has coordinates
    A. (0,3)
    B. (1,3)
    C. (3,0)
    D. (3,1)

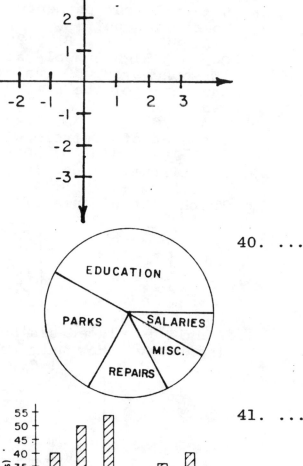

39. ...

40. The circle graph to the right
    shows how each tax dollar is
    spent in Salt City. What is
    the largest part of the tax
    dollar spent for?
    A. Repairs
    B. Salaries
    C. Education
    D. Parks

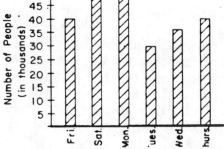

40. ...

41. The graph to the right shows
    the number of people attend-
    ing each game of the World
    Series one year. On which
    day did the fewest number of
    people attend a World Series
    game?
    A. Friday   B. Monday
    C. Tuesday   D. Thursday

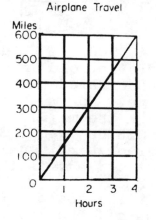

41. ...

42. The graph to the right repre-
    sents the relationship between
    distance traveled and flying
    time for a certain airplane.
    How many hours of flying time
    did the airplane require to
    travel 450 miles?
    A. $2\frac{1}{2}$ B. 2
    C. 3   D. $3\frac{1}{2}$

Airplane Travel

42. ...

43. Which is the prime number?
    A. 21   B. 99   C. 101   D. 126

43. ...

44. Mr. Ford bought a jacket for $15.00 and had to pay a
    7% sales tax. If he gave the clerk $20, what should
    his change be?
    A. $1.05   B. $3.95   C. $4.95   D. $16.05

44. ...

45. If carpeting costs $9.50 a square meter, what is the
    total cost of carpeting an entire room floor which is
    3 meters by 4 meters?
    A. $133   B. $114   C. $85.50 $66.50

45. ...

46. Ruby buys a television set with a $25 downpayment and 6 installment payments of $20. The total cost of the television set is

    A. $95   B. $120   C. $145   D. $150

47. Carver High School has an enrollment of 50 freshmen, 40 sophomores, 60 juniors, and 30 seniors. What is the ratio of the number of juniors to the total enrollment?

    A. 1/6   B. 1/4   C. 2/3   D. 1/3

48. The area of a circle with a radius of 5 centimeters is

    A. 10π cm^2 B. 20π cm^2 C. 25π cm^2 D. 100π cm^2

49. The circumference of a circle with a radius of 4 is

    A. 2π B. 4π C. 8π D. 16π

50. Which is a picture of a cylinder?

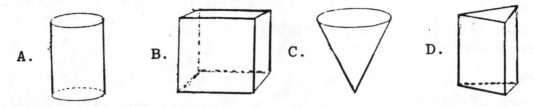

    A.   B.   C.   D.

51. A nail is placed against a ruler as shown in the drawing below. How many centimers long is the nail?

    A. 7.0   B. 6.5   C. 6.0   D. 5.5

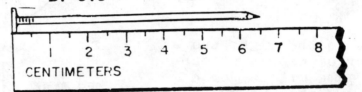

52. A race began at 11:00 a.m. The winner ran the course in 2 hours and 19 minutes. At what time did the winner cross the finish line?

    A. 8:41 a.m.   B. 12:19 p.m.   C. 1:19 p.m.   D. 2:19 p.m.

53. Each house below represents 10,000 homes. What is the total number of homes represented by the figures?

    A. 40,500   B. 45,000   C. 405,000   D. 450,000

54. A radio is sold in a store for $54.50. The same radio can be ordered through the mail for $24.50 plus $1.50 for postage. How much would be saved by buying the radio through the mail?

    A. $28.50   B. $30.00   C. $30.50   D. $53.00

55. A stereo which usually sells for $450 is on sale for 1/3 off. What is the sale price?

    A. $33   B. $150   C. $300   D. $417

56. Mary has a board $12\frac{1}{2}$ inches long. If she cuts $1\frac{1}{4}$ inches off the board, how long will the board be?

    A. $10\frac{1}{4}$ inches   B. 11 inches
    C. $11\frac{1}{4}$ inches   D. $11\frac{1}{2}$ inches

57. If 3 cases of canned fruit cost $27, then 1 of these cases would cost

    A. $81   B. $18   C. $3   D. $9

58. Carlo earns $2 per hour at a part-time job. How much does he earn in a day when he works $5\frac{1}{2}$ hours?

    A. $10   B. $11   C. $12   D. $12.50

46. ...
47. ...
48. ...
49. ...
50. ...
51. ...
52. ...
53. ...
54. ...
55. ...
56. ...
57. ...
58. ...

59. How many kilometers are there in the 10,000 meter run?   59. ...
    A. 1   B. 2   C. 10   D. 100
60. What is the probability of obtaining a head when a coin   60. ...
    is tossed?
    A. 1   B. 1/2   C. 1/3   D. 1/4

KEY (CORRECT ANSWERS)

1. 494	13. $3.55	25. D	37. B	49. C
2. 504	14. 77	26. C	38. C	50. A
3. 11,742	15. 96	27. C	39. B	51. B
4. 167	16. 16	28. C	40. C	52. C
5. 102	17. 75	29. C	41. C	53. B
6. 3/8	18. 4	30. A	42. C	54. A
7. 4.56	19. 18	31. B	43. C	55. C
8. 26.52	20. 12	32. B	44. B	56. C
9. 2.06	21. 30	33. B	45. B	57. D
10. 20	22. 25	34. C	46. C	58. B
11. 4.82	23. C	35. D	47. D	59. C
12. 24	24. C	36. A	48. C	60. B

5

SOLUTIONS TO PROBLEMS

1. $215 + 86 + 193 = 494$

2. $761 - 257 = 504$

3. $(206)(57) = 11,742$

4. $4175 \div 25 = 167$

5. $408 \div 4 = 102$

6. $(\frac{1}{2})(\frac{3}{4}) = \frac{3}{8}$

7. $3.40 + 1.16 = 4.56$

8. $(3.4)(7.8) = 26.52$

9. $12.36 \div 6 = 2.06$

10. $(\frac{2}{3})(30) = 20$

11. $9.67 - 4.85 = 4.82$

12. $8 \div \frac{1}{3} = (8)(\frac{3}{1}) = 24$

13. $\$10 - \$6.45 = \$3.55$

14. $(81 + 72 + 78) \div 3 = 77$

15. Volume $= (6)(4)(4) = 96$ cubic cm.

16. Perimeter $= (2)(6 + 2) = 16$

17. Median $= (7 + 1)/2 = $ 4th score $= 75$

18. If $4x + 1 = 17$, then $4x = 16$. Solving, $x = 4$

19. If $\frac{6}{10} = \frac{x}{30}$, then $10x = 180$. Solving, $x = 18$.

20. $(.40)(30) = 12$ games lost

21. $(2\frac{1}{2})(12) = 30$ kilometers

22. Area $= 5^2 = 25$

23. Missing number $= 54 + 186 = 240$

24. $\frac{3}{5} + \frac{2}{3} = \frac{9}{15} + \frac{10}{15} = \frac{19}{15}$

25. Least common denominator of $\frac{1}{2}$, $\frac{2}{3}$, and $\frac{5}{6}$ is 6.

26. $\frac{17}{5} = 3\frac{2}{5}$

27. $\frac{3}{4} = (\frac{3}{4})(100)\% = 75\%$

28. 46,534 is 47,000 to the nearest thousand.

29. Seventy thousand eight hundred = 70,800

30. $\frac{1}{5}$ is smaller than $\frac{1}{2}$, $\frac{1}{3}$, and $\frac{1}{4}$

31. Total cost = \$1.00 + (3)(.30) = \$1.90

32. AB is a chord since it joins 2 points on the circle but does not pass through the center.

33. AB:BC = 5:7

34. .125 is larger than .0824, .1032, and .091.

35. New balance = \$325.15 + \$75 = \$400.15

36. (-11) + (-8) = -19

37. 8 - (-3) = 11 degrees difference

38. $10^3 = (10)(10)(10) = 1000$

39. Point A has coordinates (1,3)

40. Education represents the largest section.

41. On Tuesday, about 30,000 people attended the World Series. This was the lowest attendance figure in the chart.

42. On the graph, 450 miles corresponds to 3 hours.

43. 101 is prime since it can only be divided evenly by itself and 1.

44. \$15 + (.07)(\$15) = \$16.05. Then, \$20 - \$16.05 = \$3.95

45. Total cost = (\$9.50)(3)(4) = \$114.00

46. Total cost = \$25 + (6)(\$20) = \$145

47. Juniors: total enrollment = $60:180 = \frac{1}{3}$

48. Area = $(\pi)(5\ cm)^2 = 25\pi\ cm^2$

49. Circumference = $(2\pi)(4) = 8\Pi$

50. Selection A represents a cylinder. (The other 3 selections are cube, cone, triangular prism.)

51. Length of nail = 6.5 cm

52. 11:00 A.M. + 2 hrs. 19 min. = 1:19 P.M.

53. (10,000)(4.5) = 45,000

54. Amount saved = \$54.50 – \$24.50 – \$1.50 = \$28.50

55. Sale price = $\$450 - (\frac{1}{3})(\$450) = \$300$

56. $12\frac{1}{2}" - 1\frac{1}{4}" = 11\frac{1}{4}$ inches

57. 1 case costs $\$27 \div 3 = \$9$

58. $(\$2)(5\frac{1}{2}) = \$11$

59. Since 1 km = 1000 m, 10 kilometers = 10,000 meters

60. In tossing a coin, the probability of getting a head = $\frac{1}{2}$

———

Basic Mathematics

EXAMINATION SECTION

DIRECTIONS: Each question or incomplete statement is followed by several suggested answers or completions. Select the one that BEST answers the question or completes the statement. *PRINT THE LETTER OF THE CORRECT ANSWER IN THE SPACE AT THE RIGHT.*

1. Add: 5,796 + 6 + 243 + 24   1.___
    A. 6,069   B. 6,079   C. 6,169   D. 6,179

2. Subtract: 8,007 - 6,898   2.___
    A. 1,109   B. 1,119   C. 1,209   D. 2,109

3. Multiply: 3,876 × 904   3.___
    A. 364,344   B. 3,493,904
    C. 3,494,904   D. 3,503,904

4. Divide: 76$\overline{)58,976}$ 4.___
    A. 775   B. 776   C. 786   D. 876

5. Combine: (+4) + (−3) − (−7)   5.___
    A. −6   B. +6   C. +8   D. +14

6. Simplify: [(−8)×(−6)] ÷ (−3)   6.___
    A. −16   B. −14   C. +14   D. +16

7. Add: 1 3/5 + 3 7/8   7.___
    A. 4 10/40   B. 4 10/13   C. 4 19/40   D. 5 19/40

8. Subtract: 4 3/8 − 2 2/3   8.___
    A. 1 17/24   B. 2 1/24   C. 2 1/5   D. 2 17/24

9. Multiply: 3 2/3 × 5$\frac{1}{2}$ 9.___
    A. 15 1/3   B. 16 1/3   C. 20 1/6   D. 21 1/6

10. Divide: 7$\frac{1}{2}$ ÷ 2$\frac{1}{4}$ 10.___
    A. 3/10   B. 3 1/3   C. 3$\frac{1}{2}$ D. 16 7/8

11. Add: 434.7 + .04 + 7.107   11.___
    A. .441847   B. .442207   C. 441.847   D. 442.207

12. Subtract: 986.4 − 34.87   12.___
    A. 6.377   B. 63.77   C. 951.53   D. 9,515.3

13. Multiply: 5.96   13.___
                ×87.4
    A. 51.0904   B. 52.0904   C. 510.904   D. 520.904

14. Divide: .034$\overline{)6.698}$ 14.___
    A. 19.2   B. 19.7   C. 192   D. 197

15. Add: .7 + ½   15.___
    A. .12   B. 1.2   C. 7/2   D. 15/2

16. What is 5.5% of 75?   16.___
    A. 4.125   B. 13.65   C. 41.25   D. 412.5

17. 12 is what percent of 6?   17.___
    A. ½%   B. 5%   C. 50%   D. 200%

18. 14 is 28% of ____.   18.___
    A. 2   B. 5   C. 50   D. 500

19. A record player sells for $92.00. It is discounted 15%   19.___
    for a special sale.
    What is the sale price?
    A. $13.80   B. $68.20   C. $77.00   D. $78.20

20.   Table A - Acme Mortgage Company   20.___
                       $320 Loan - 3/4 of 1% Interest

Month	Payment	Principal Paid/Month	Interest Paid/Month
1	$ 27.98	$ 25.58	$ 2.40
2	27.98	25.77	2.21
3	27.98	25.96	2.02
4	27.98	26.15	1.83
5	27.98	26.35	1.63
6	27.98	26.55	1.43
7	27.98	26.75	1.23
8	27.98	26.95	1.03
9	27.98	27.15	.83
10	27.98	27.35	.63
11	27.98	27.56	.42
12	27.93	27.77	.16
Total	$335.82	$320.00	$15.82

Acme Mortgage Company charges 3/4 of 1% (.0075) on the
unpaid balance per month. Bowman Mortgage Company charges
9% per year on the total loan.
Which company charges the LEAST amount of interest on a
$320 loan held for one year?
    A. Acme charges the least amount.
    B. Bowman charges the least amount.
    C. Acme and Bowman charge the same.
    D. Insufficient information to determine.

21.   Percent of Auto Insurance Discounts for   21.___
                 High School Students with Certain
                         Grade Point Averages

Policy Coverage	Grade Point Average Percent of Discount		
	A	B	C
Liability	33 1/3%	33 1/3%	10%
Comprehensive	20%	10%	-
Collision	25%	20%	-

Frank Verna has a B average. The regular 6-month amounts to be paid for insurance before discount follow:

Liability	$18.00
Comprehensive	$20.00
Collision	$60.00
Total	$98.00

How much does Frank pay for insurance for 6 months?

   A. $20.00   B. $58.00   C. $78.00   D. $156.00

22. Mr. Martinez had a fire in his home. Repairing the damage will cost about $900. His home is valued at $14,000 and is insured for $12,000. Mr. Martinez had paid $32.00 a year for ten years for his insurance. The insurance company has agreed to pay the full amount of the claim ($900).
Which of the following statements are TRUE?
   I. The amount of the claim is more than what has been paid to the company.
  II. The insurance company should pay $14,000 for this claim.
  III. If the house had been completely burned, the insurance company would pay $14,000.
  IV. The maximum claim Mr. Martinez could collect is $12,000.

The CORRECT answer is:
   A. I, II   B. I, III   C. II, III   D. I, IV

22.___

23. When two coins are tossed, what is the chance that both will be heads?
1 in
   A. 1   B. 2   C. 3   D. 4

23.___

24. If 4 teams are in a football league, how many games are necessary to allow each team to play every team one time?
_____ games.
   A. 6   B. 9   C. 12   D. 16

24.___

25. Five people donated money to the Red Cross. The donations were: $52.00, $76.00, $18.00, $94.00, and $120.00.
What was the AVERAGE donation?
   A. $70   B. $72   C. $76   D. $360

25.___

26. From the following statements, determine the CORRECT conclusion.
   I. If Lauraine is a red-head, then Lauraine is hot-tempered.
  II. Lauraine is not hot-tempered.

The CORRECT answer is:
   A. Lauraine is a red-head.
   B. Lauraine is not a red-head.
   C. Lauraine could be a red-head.
   D. All red-heads are hot-tempered.

26.___

27. The graph represents the way the Jones family spends its money (budget).
What is the monthly income if they are spending $4080 per year for food?
    A. $1,020
    B. $1,360
    C. $4,080
    D. $16,320

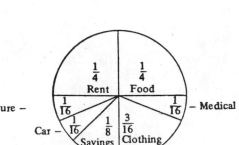

27._____

28.

	S	M	T	W	T	F	S
Charlie Simms	?	8	8	8	8	8	3
Jim Chow	2	9	8	8	9	9	4

Time and one-half is paid on Saturdays and for hours worked beyond 8 hours each day. Double-time is paid for Sunday work.
Mr. Simms would have to work how many hours on Sunday to earn as much as Mr. Chow?
        Regular time - $2.00/hour
        Time and one-half - $3.00/hour
        Double time - $4.00/hour

_____ hours.
    A. 2   B. 5   C. 6   D. 20

28._____

29. Jane Gunther wrote checks for these items:
        $16.95 for a hair dryer
        $125.50 for a car payment
        $33.68 for television repair
        $21.59 for a dress
Jane had a beginning check balance (before she wrote the checks) of $351.76. She also deposited $41.50 into her account.
After the checks were written and the deposit made, what was her new balance?
    A. $154.04   B. $195.54   C. $196.54   D. $239.22

29._____

30. Given the formula I = PRT:
If I = 24, R = .05, T = 3, find P.
    A. .00625   B. 1.6   C. 3.6   D. 160.0

30._____

31. Fencing is needed to enclose a piece of land 26 meters on a side.
How much fencing is needed?
    _____ meters.
    A. 52
    B. 98
    C. 104
    D. 676

31._____

32. The area of figure A is 12 square units, and the area of B is 18 square units.
What is the area of figure C?
_____ square units.
  A. 16
  B. 16½
  C. 17
  D. 17½

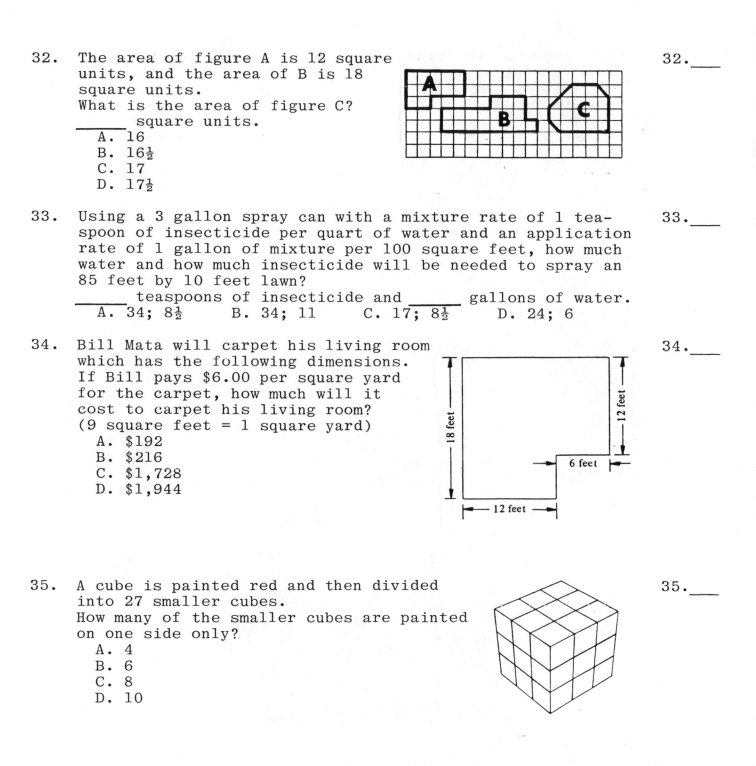

32.____

33. Using a 3 gallon spray can with a mixture rate of 1 teaspoon of insecticide per quart of water and an application rate of 1 gallon of mixture per 100 square feet, how much water and how much insecticide will be needed to spray an 85 feet by 10 feet lawn?
_____ teaspoons of insecticide and _____ gallons of water.
    A. 34; 8½   B. 34; 11   C. 17; 8½   D. 24; 6

33.____

34. Bill Mata will carpet his living room which has the following dimensions.
If Bill pays $6.00 per square yard for the carpet, how much will it cost to carpet his living room?
(9 square feet = 1 square yard)
  A. $192
  B. $216
  C. $1,728
  D. $1,944

34.____

35. A cube is painted red and then divided into 27 smaller cubes.
How many of the smaller cubes are painted on one side only?
  A. 4
  B. 6
  C. 8
  D. 10

35.____

36. John and Frank wish to pour a cement walk 108 feet long, 4 feet wide, and 3 inches deep.
If ready-mix concrete can be delivered on weekdays for $19.50 a cubic yard and on weekends for $22.50 a cubic yard, how much would they save on the complete job if they decide on Thursday rather than on the weekend? (1 cubic yard = 27 cubic feet)
    A. $3.00   B. $12.00   C. $36.00   D. $78.00

36.____

37. Antifreeze may be purchased in different size containers   37.___
     for different prices:
              8 oz. can - 43¢
             10 oz. can - 51¢
             12 oz. can - 62¢
     If exactly 15 pints of antifreeze are needed, how many cans
     of each size are needed for the cost to be minimum? (16 oz.
     = 1 pint)
        A. 12 - 10 oz. cans and 10 - 12 oz. cans
        B. 24 - 10 oz. cans
        C. 18 - 12 oz. cans and 3 - 8 oz. cans
        D. 20 - 12 oz. cans

38. From the graph, assuming   38.___
     the growth rate in the
     senior class is constant,
     how many students will
     be seniors in 1976?
        A. 225
        B. 250
        C. 300
        D. 375

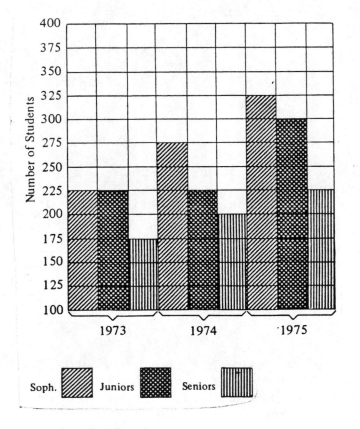

39.

Population in U.S.
1880–1980

Percentage of the U.S.
Population Over 65

Key: Each ■ represents 1% of the population.

In looking at the two graphs, which of the following
conclusions are TRUE?
   I. Both graphs show population growth.
  II. Both graphs cover exactly the same time period.
 III. The percentage of *over 65* population remains the same
      over the 1940 to 1970 period.
  IV. If you were in the retail business, you might expect
      greater sales to the *over 65* population in 1970 than
      in 1940.
   V. In the general population of about 200 million people
      in 1970, 24 million were over 65.
  VI. In 1920, there were only about 7 million people *over 65*
      out of about 100 million people.

The CORRECT answer is:
   A. I, III, IV   B. II, IV, V
   C. II, III, VI   D. I, IV, V

40. Jerry Martin owns a home with a market value of $18,000.   40.___
    Its assessed value is 25% of the market value. The tax
    rate is $5.00 per $100 of assessed value.
    What is the amount of his tax?
       A. $22.50   B. $225.00   C. $450.00   D. $675.00

41. You are governor of the state and you need an additional   41.___
    500 million dollars in tax money. To raise the money,
    an increase in sales tax is required.
    What information would be MOST helpful in determining the
    new tax rate?
      I. Average income per person in the state
     II. Number of people out of work
    III. Population of the state over 18 years of age
     IV. Birth rate in the state
      V. Percent of income spent on taxable goods
     VI. Percent of income spent on non-taxable goods
    VII. Number of people filing income tax returns

    The CORRECT answer is:
       A. I, IV, VI   B. II, III, VII
       C. V, VI   D. I, V

42. <u>Income Tax Table</u> 42.___

If adjusted gross income is –		And the number of exemptions is –					
		1	2	3	4	5	6
At least	But less than	Your tax is –					
$2,450	$2,475	$236	$124	$23	$0	$0	$0
2,475	2,500	240	128	26	0	0	0
2,500	2,525	244	132	30	0	0	0
2,525	2,550	248	136	33	0	0	0
2,550	2,575	253	139	37	0	0	0
2,575	2,600	257	143	40	0	0	0
2,600	2,625	261	147	44	0	0	0
2,625	2,650	265	151	47	0	0	0
2,650	2,675	270	155	51	0	0	0
2,675	2,700	274	159	54	0	0	0
2,700	2,725	278	163	58	0	0	0
2,725	2,750	282	167	61	0	0	0
2,750	2,775	287	171	65	0	0	0
2,775	2,800	291	175	68	0	0	0
2,800	2,825	295	179	72	0	0	0
2,825	2,850	299	183	76	0	0	0
2,850	2,875	304	187	79	0	0	0

Jerry Ladd earned $2,839.00 during the year. To find his adjusted gross income, he must reduce the amount earned by the standard 10% deduction. He had only one exemption, himself.
How much tax did Jerry pay?
   A. $139   B. $183   C. $253   D. $299

43.

Weight in Ounces	2 oz.	4 oz.	12 oz.	21 oz.
Price	5¢	7¢	15¢	24¢

43.___

Using the above table, predict the price if the weight is 32 ounces.
   A. 27¢   B. 28¢   C. 29¢   D. 35¢

44. Given [(0,2),(1,4),(2,6),...(5,y)].
What is the value of y?
   A. 8   B. 10   C. 12   D. 14

44.___

45. If the larger of two numbers is two and one-half times the smaller number, what fraction is the smaller of the larger?
   A. 3/4   B. 4/5   C. 5/8   D. 2/5

45.___

46. John can save 75¢ a week. He has $3.75 in the bank now. How many weeks will it take him to have a total deposit of $12?
   A. 16   B. 9   C. 11   D. 17

46.___

47. Using the approximation of 3.14 for pi, find the area of a circle whose diameter is 20 inches.
_____ square inches.
   A. 31.4   B. 314   C. 628   D. 1256

47.___

48. Express .045 as a percent. 48.___
    A. 45%   B. 4.5%   C. .45%   D. .045%

49. Twenty is what percent of 50? 49.___
    A. 40   B. 60   C. 25   D. 16 2/3

50. Two hundred twenty-five percent of 160 is 50.___
    A. 80   B. 350   C. 360   D. 440

KEY (CORRECT ANSWERS)

1. A	11. C	21. C	31. C	41. C
2. A	12. C	22. D	32. C	42. C
3. D	13. D	23. D	33. A	43. D
4. B	14. D	24. A	34. A	44. C
5. C	15. B	25. B	35. B	45. D
6. A	16. A	26. B	36. B	46. C
7. D	17. D	27. D	37. B	47. B
8. A	18. C	28. B	38. B	48. B
9. C	19. D	29. B	39. D	49. A
10. B	20. A	30. D	40. B	50. C

SOLUTIONS TO PROBLEMS

1. $5796 + 6 + 243 + 24 = 6069$

2. $8007 - 6898 = 1109$

3. $(3876)(904) = 3,503,904$

4. $58,976 \div 76 = 776$

5. $(+4) + (-3) - (-7) = 4 - 3 + 7 = +8$

6. $[(-8)(-6)] \div -3 = 48 \div -3 = -16$

7. $1\frac{3}{5} + 3\frac{7}{8} = 1\frac{24}{40} + 3\frac{35}{40} = 4\frac{59}{40} = 5\frac{19}{40}$

8. $4\frac{3}{8} - 2\frac{2}{3} = 4\frac{9}{24} - 2\frac{16}{24} = 3\frac{33}{24} - 2\frac{16}{24} = 1\frac{17}{24}$

9. $(3\frac{2}{3})(5\frac{1}{2}) = (\frac{11}{3})(\frac{11}{2}) = \frac{121}{6} = 20\frac{1}{6}$

10. $7\frac{1}{2} \div 2\frac{1}{4} = \frac{15}{2} \div \frac{9}{4} = (\frac{15}{2})(\frac{4}{9}) = \frac{60}{18} = 3\frac{1}{3}$

11. $434.7 + .04 + 7.107 = 441.847$

12. $986.4 - 34.87 = 951.53$

13. $(5.96)(87.4) = 520.904$

14. $6.698 \div .034 = 197$

15. $.7 + \frac{1}{2} = .7 + .5 = 1.2$

16. $(.055)(75) = 4.125$

17. $\frac{12}{6} = 2 = 200\%$

18. $14 \div .28 = 50$

19. $\$92 - (.15)(\$92) = \$78.20$

20. Acme's interest charge = $15.82, whereas Bowman's interest charge = $(.09)(\$320) = \$28.80$. Thus, Acme charges less.

21. $(\$18.00)(66\frac{2}{3}\%) + (\$20.00)(90\%) + (\$60.00)(80\%) = \$78.00$

22. Statements I and IV are correct. For 10 years, he has paid $320, but collected $900 on his claim. Also, since the insured value of the home is $12,000, he could not collect more than that amount on any claim.

23. Probability of 2 heads = $(\frac{1}{2})(\frac{1}{2}) = \frac{1}{4}$, which means 1 in 4.

24. The number of required games = $(4)(3) \div 2 = 6$

25. Average donation = ($52.00 + $76.00 + $18.00 + $94.00 + $120.00) $\div$ 5 = $72

26. The correct conclusion is B: Lauraine is not a redhead. Let p = Lauraine is a redhead, q = Lauraine is hot-tempered. The given statement says: *If p, then q.* The contrapositive, which is also true, says, *If not q, then not p.* This corresponds to statement B.

27. Let x = monthly income. Then, $4080 = $\frac{1}{4}$x. Solving, x = $16,320.

28. Mr. Chow's earnings = $(2)($4) + (40)($2) + (7)($3) = 109. For Monday through Saturday, Mr. Simms' earnings = $(40)($2) + (3)($3) = 89. Thus, Mr. Simms would need to earn $109 - 89 = 20 on Sunday. This means Sunday's time = $20 \div $4 = 5$ hours.

29. New balance = $351.76 + $41.50 - $16.95 - $125.50 - $33.68 - $21.59 = $195.54.

30. $24 = (P)(.05)(3)$, $24 = .15P$, so $P = 160$

31. Fencing: $(26)(4) = 104$ meters.

32. Area of C = $(4)(5) - (\frac{1}{2})(1)(1) - (\frac{1}{2})(2)(2) - (\frac{1}{2})(1)(1) = 17$

33. $(85)(10) = 850$ sq.ft. = 8.5 gallons of water. Now, 8.5 gallons = 34 quarts, so 34 teaspoons of insecticide are needed.

34. Area = $(12)(6) + (12)(18) = 288$ sq.ft. = 32 sq.yds. Total cost = $(32)($6) = 192

35. There are 6 cubes painted red on only one side. They are found in the center of each face of the original cube.

36. $(108)(4)(\frac{1}{4}) = 108$ cu.ft. = 4 cu.yds. Savings would be $($22.50)(4) - ($19.50)(4) = 12.00

37. 15 pints = 240 oz. The costs for each selection are: For A: $(12)(.51) + (10)(.62) = 12.32; for B: $(24)(.51) = 12.24; for C: $(18)(.62) + (3)(.43) = 12.45; for D: $(20)(.62) = 12.40. So, selection B is the minimum cost.

38. The number of seniors in 1973, 1974, 1975 are 175, 200, and 225, respectively. If growth is constant, the number of seniors in 1976 is 250.

39. Statements I, IV, V are correct. Statement II is wrong because the 1st graph covers 1800-1970, whereas the 2nd graph covers 1940-1970. Statement III is wrong because the *over 65* population increases in percent from 7% in 1940 to 12% in 1970.

40. (25%)($18,000) = $4500 assessed value. Amount of tax = ($5.00)($4500 ÷ $100) = $225.

41. For increasing sales tax, it would be helpful in knowing the respective percent of income spent on taxable vs. non-taxable goods.

42. Adjusted gross income = ($2839)(.90) = $2555.10. On the tax chart, this figure lies between $2550 and $2575. Using the column for 1 exemption, the tax is $253.

43. Using 2 oz. = .05, note that each additional oz. = 1 cent more. So, 32 oz. = .05 + .30 = .35.

44. (5,y) represents the sixth point in this sequence. Thus, the corresponding y value = (2)(6) = 12

45. Let x = smaller number, 2.5x = larger number.
Then, $\frac{x}{2.5x} = \frac{1}{2.5} = \frac{10}{25} = \frac{2}{5}$

46. $12 - $3.75 = $8.25. Then, $8.25 ÷ .75 = 11 weeks

47. Radius = 10 in. Area ≈ (3.14)(10^2) = 314 sq.in.

48. .045 = 4.5%

49. $\frac{20}{50}$ = 40%

50. (225%)(160) = (2.25)(160) = 360

Basic Mathematics
EXAMINATION SECTION

DIRECTIONS: Each question or incomplete statement is followed by several suggested answers or completions. Select the one that BEST answers the question or completes the statement. *PRINT THE LETTER OF THE CORRECT ANSWER IN THE SPACE AT THE RIGHT.*

1.   534
     18
    +1291
      A. 1733   B. 1743   C. 1833   D. 1843   E. 1853   1.___

2. (17×23) - 16 + 20 =   2.___
      A. 459   B. 427   C. 411   D. 395   E. 355

3. 3/7 + 5/11 =   3.___
      A. 33/35   B. 4/9   C. 8/18   D. 68/77   E. 15/77

4. 4832 ÷ 6 =   4.___
      A. 905 1/3   B. 805 1/3   C. 95 1/3   D. 95   E. 85 1/3

5. 62.3 - 4.9 =   5.___
      A. 5.74   B. 7.4   C. 57.4   D. 58.4   E. 67.4

6. 3/5 × 4/9 =   6.___
      A. 4/15   B. 7/45   C. 27/20   D. 12/14   E. 15/4

7. 14/16 - 5/16 =   7.___
      A. 8/16   B. 9/16   C. 11/16   D. 8   E. 9

8. 5.03 + 2.7 + 40 =   8.___
      A. .570   B. 4.773   C. 5.70   D. 11.73   E. 47.73

9. 5.37 × 21.4 =   9.___
      A. 11491.8   B. 1149.18   C. 114.918   D. 11.4918   E. 1.14918

10. 5 1/4 + 2 7/8 =   10.___
      A. 8¼   B. 8 1/8   C. 7 2/3   D. 7¼   E. 7 1/8

11. -14 + 5 =   11.___
      A. -19   B. -9   C. 9   D. 19   E. 70

12. 2/7 of 28 =   12.___
      A. 98   B. 16   C. 14   D. 8   E. 4

13. 2/5 =   13.___
      A. .10   B. .20   C. .25   D. .40   E. .52

14. 20% of _____ is 38.   14.___
      A. 7.6   B. 19   C. 76   D. 190   E. 760

15. $\frac{8.4}{400}$ =   15.___

    A. .0021   B. .021   C. .21   D. 2.1   E. 21

16. $\frac{4}{5} = \frac{?}{60}$ 16.___

    A. 240   B. 48   C. 20   D. 15   E. 12

17. What is the area of the rectangle shown at the right?   17.___
    A. 47 mm^2
    B. 94 mm^2
    C. 240 mm^2
    D. 480 mm^2
    E. 960 mm^2

18. What number does ☐ represent in this equation?   18.___

$$25 - \square - \square - \square - \square = 13$$

    A. 13   B. 12   C. 7   D. 4   E. 3

19. Approximate lengths are given in the right triangles shown at the right.   19.___
What does length x equal?
    A. 48
    B. 39
    C. 37
    D. 35
    E. 32

20. What is the perimeter of the triangle shown at the right?   20.___
    A. 10 × 15 × 17
    B. 10 + 15 + 17
    C. $\frac{1}{2}$ × 10 × 15
    D. $\frac{1}{2}$ × 10 × 17
    E. $\frac{1}{2}$(10 + 15 + 17)

21. Which of the following expressions will give the same answer as 45 × 9?   21.___
    A. 5 × 3^3 B. (4×9) + (5×9)
    C. (40+9) × 5   D. (45×3) + (45×3)
    E. (45×10) − (45×1)

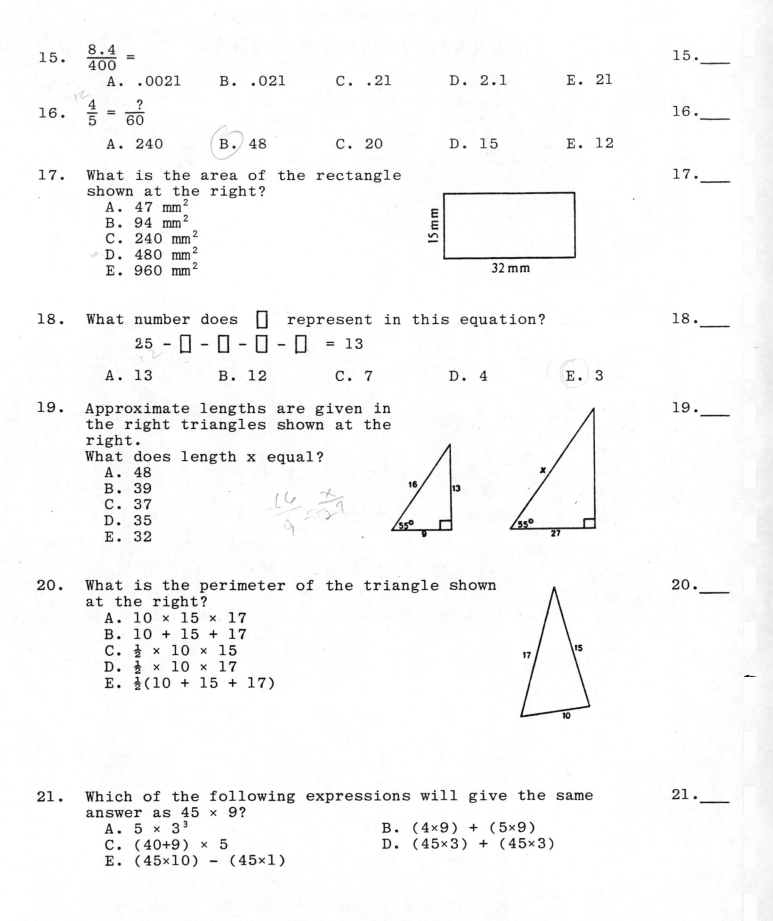

22. Find the average of 19, 21, 21, 22, and 27.   22.___
    A. 23   B. 22   C. 21   D. 20   E. 19

23. In the triangle at the right, how many   23.___
degrees is ∠T?
    A. 75°
    B. 85°
    C. 95°
    D. 115°
    E. 180°

24.   24.___

About how long is the paper clip?
    A. 5 cm   B. 4 cm   C. 3 cm   D. 2 cm   E. 1 cm

25. Five stores sell the same size cans of tomato soup. Their   25.___
prices are listed below.
Which sells the soup for the LOWEST price per can?
_____ cans for _____.
    A. 6; 99¢   B. 6; 90¢   C. 5; 93¢   D. 3; 56¢   E. 3; 50¢

26. Rock star Peter Giles receives $1.97 royalty on each of his   26.___
albums that is sold. 14,127 albums are sold.
Estimate how much Peter Giles will receive.
    A. $7,000   B. $14,000   C. $20,000   D. $26,000   E. $28,000

27. An amplifier is advertised for 20% off the list price of   27.___
$430.
What is the sale price?
    A. $516   B. $454   C. $354   D. $344   E. $215

28. If 9 dozen eggs cost $3.60, what do 25 dozen eggs cost?   28.___
    A. $90.00   B. $10.00   C. $9.00   D. $2.54   E. $.40

29. The distance between New York and San Antonio is 1860 miles.   29.___
If a jet averages 465 miles per hour, how many hours will
it take to travel the distance?
    A. 9   B. 5   C. 4   D. 3   E. 2

30. In a high school homeroom of 32 students, 24 are girls.   30.___
What percent are girls?
    A. 3/4%   B. 24%   C. 25%   D. 75%   E. 80%

31. Which problem could give the answer shown
on the calculator?
    A. 2 + .3
    B. 2 × 3/10
    C. 2 × 1/3
    D. 33333 + .2
    E. 7 ÷ 3

31.___

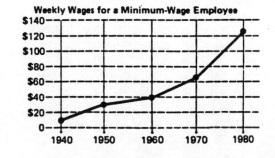

    2.33333

32. According to the table at the
right, how much will it cost in
a typical week for the 3 members
of the Wright family to eat at
home? Mr. Wright is 56 years old;
Mrs. Wright, 52; and their son
Harry, 17.
    A. $125
    B. $52
    C. $49
    D. $42
    E. $40

32.___

Cost of Eating at Home
(one week)

Age	Male	Female
6-11 yrs.	$14	$14
12-19 yrs.	$19	$16
20-54 yrs.	$20	$16
55 and up	$14	$14

33. According to the table shown in the previous question, how
much does it cost in a typical four-week month to feed a
12-year-old girl?
    A. $4   B. $16   C. $48   D. $64   E. $78

33.___

34. Reverend Wilhite jogs for 1½ hours each day, 6 days a week.
If he burns 800 calories per hour of jogging, how many
calories does he burn in a week?
    A. 4800   B. 5600   C. 7200   D. 8400   E. 9000

34.___

35. Ground meat costs 90¢ per pound.
How much does the meat on the scale
cost?
    A. $1.80
    B. $1.60
    C. $1.54
    D. $1.44
    E. $.90

35.___

36. According to the graph at the
right, about when did the
weekly wages for a minimum
wage worker go over $100?
    A. 1965
    B. 1970
    C. 1975
    D. 1979
    E. 1980

36.___

Weekly Wages for a Minimum-Wage Employee

37. According to the bar graph at the right, what is the approximate height of the Crystal Beach Comet?
    A. 40 ft.
    B. 90 ft.
    C. 92 ft.
    D. 94 ft.
    E. 98 ft.

37.____

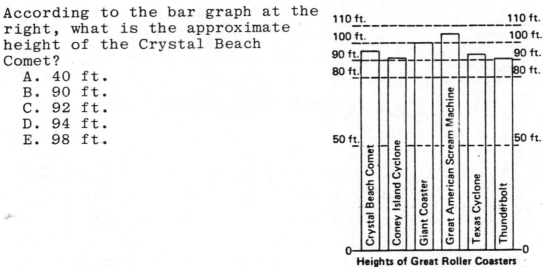

Heights of Great Roller Coasters

38. According to the bar graph shown in the previous question, what is the difference in height between the tallest and shortest roller coasters? ____ feet.

38.____

    A. 5   B. 10   C. 15   D. 20   E. 50

39. How much change will you receive from a $10 bill when you buy 4 grapefruits at 90¢ each and 3 apples at 40¢ each?

39.____

    A. $6.20   B. $5.20   C. $4.80   D. $4.20   E. $4.00

40. A medical supplier packages medicine in boxes. The cost of packaging is computed with the flow chart at the right.
    What is the cost of packaging medicine in a box that is 30 cm long, 20 cm wide, and 20 cm high?
    A. $.20
    B. $.24
    C. $2.00
    D. $2.40
    E. $3.00

40.____

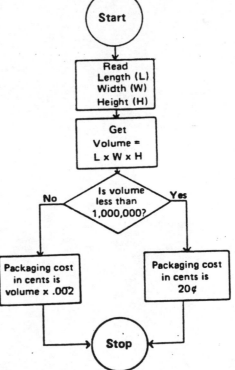

KEY (CORRECT ANSWERS)

1. D	11. B	21. E	31. E
2. D	12. D	22. B	32. C
3. D	13. D	23. B	33. D
4. B	14. D	24. C	34. C
5. C	15. B	25. B	35. D
6. A	16. B	26. E	36. C
7. B	17. D	27. D	37. D
8. E	18. E	28. B	38. C
9. C	19. A	29. C	39. B
10. B	20. B	30. D	40. A

SOLUTIONS TO PROBLEMS

1. $534 + 18 + 1291 = 1843$

2. $(17 \times 23) - 16 + 20 = 391 - 16 + 20 = 395$

3. $\frac{3}{7} + \frac{5}{11} = \frac{33}{77} + \frac{35}{77} = \frac{68}{77}$

4. $4832 \div 6 = 805\frac{1}{3}$

5. $62.3 - 4.9 = 57.4$

6. $\frac{3}{5} \times \frac{4}{9} = \frac{12}{45} = \frac{4}{15}$

7. $\frac{14}{16} - \frac{5}{16} = \frac{9}{16}$

8. $5.03 + 2.7 + 40 = 47.73$

9. $5.37 \times 21.4 = 114.918$

10. $5\frac{1}{4} + 2\frac{7}{8} = 7\frac{9}{8} = 8\frac{1}{8}$

11. $-14 + 5 = -9$

12. $\frac{2}{7}$ of $28 = (\frac{2}{7})(\frac{28}{1}) = 8$

13. $\frac{2}{5} = .40$ as a decimal

14. Let x = missing number. Then, $.20x = 38$. Solving, x = 190

15. $\frac{8.4}{400} = .021$

16. Let x = missing number. Then, $\frac{4}{5} = \frac{x}{60}$. $5x = 240$, so x = 48

17. Area = $(15)(32) = 480mm^2$

18. Let x = □. Then, $25 - 4x = 13$. So, $-4x = -12$. Solving, x = 3

19. $\frac{9}{27} = \frac{16}{x}$. Then, 9x = 432. Solving, x = 48.

20. Perimeter = 17 + 10 + 15 = 42

21. 45 × 9 = 405 = (45×10) – (45×1)

22. 19 + 21 + 21 + 22 + 27 = 110. Then, 110 ÷ 5 = 22

23. ∠T = 180° – 50° – 45° = 85°

24. The paper clip's length is about 5 – 2 = 3 cm.

25. For A: price per can = $\frac{.99}{6}$ = .165;

    For B: price per can = $\frac{.90}{6}$ = .15

    For C: price per can = $\frac{.93}{5}$ = .186

    For D: price per can = $\frac{.56}{3}$ = .18$\overline{6}$

    For E: price per can = $\frac{.50}{3}$ = .1$\overline{6}$

    Lowest price is for B.

26. $1.97 ≈ $2.00. Then, ($2.00)(14,127) = $28,254 ≈ $28,000.

27. Sale price = ($430)(.80) = $344

28. Let x = cost. Then, $\frac{9}{360} = \frac{25}{x}$. 9x = $90, so x = $10.00

29. $\frac{1860}{465}$ = 4 hours

30. $\frac{24}{32}$ = 75%

31. $\frac{7}{3}$ = 2.$\overline{3}$ = 2.33333 on this calculator shown.

32. Total cost = $14 + $16 + $19 = $49

33. Cost = ($16)(4) = $64

34. (800)(1½)(6) = 7200 calories

35. (.90)(1.6) = $1.44

36. Around 1975, the minimum weekly wages exceeded $100.

37. The Crystal Beach Comet's height is about 94 ft.

38. Tallest ≈ 105 ft. and the shortest ≈ 90 ft.
    Difference = 15 ft.

39. $10 − (4)(.90) − (3)(.40) = $5.20 change

40. $(30)(20)(20) = 12,000 \text{ cm}^3$. Since 12,000 < 1,000,000, the price is 20 cents.

INTERPRETING STATISTICAL DATA
GRAPHS, CHARTS AND TABLES

DIRECTIONS: Each question or incomplete statement is followed by
several suggested answers or completions. Select the
one that BEST answers the question or completes the
statement. *PRINT THE LETTER OF THE CORRECT ANSWER IN
THE SPACE AT THE RIGHT.*

Questions 1-12.   **TEST 1**

DIRECTIONS: Questions 1 through 12 are to be answered SOLELY on the
basis of the information given in the graph and chart
below.

ENROLLMENT IN POSTGRADUATE STUDIES

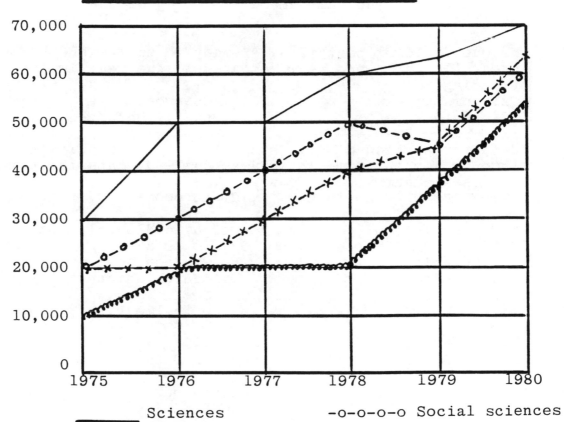

————— Sciences   -o-o-o-o Social sciences

-x-x-x Humanities   ⵡⵡⵡⵡ Professions

Fields	Subdivisions	1979	1980
Sciences	Math	10,000	12,000
	Physical science	22,000	24,000
	Behavioral science	32,000	35,000
Humanities	Literature	26,000	34,000
	Philosophy	6,000	8,000
	Religion	4,000	6,000
	Arts	10,000	16,000
Social sciences	History	36,000	46,000
	Sociology	8,000	14,000
Professions	Law	2,000	2,000
	Medicine	6,000	8,000
	Business	30,000	44,000

1. The number of students enrolled in the social sciences
   and in the humanities was the same in
   A. 1977 and 1979   B. 1975 and 1979
   C. 1979 and 1980   D. 1976 and 1979

2. A comparison of the enrollment of students in the various
   postgraduate studies shows that in every year from 1975
   through 1980, there were MORE students enrolled in the
   _____ than in the _____.
   A. professions; sciences
   B. humanities; professions
   C. social sciencies; professions
   D. humanities; sciences

3. The number of students enrolled in the humanities was
   GREATER than the number of students enrolled in the
   professions by the same amount in _____ of the years.
   A. two   B. three   C. four   D. five

4. The one field of postgraduate study to show a DECREASE
   in enrollment in one year compared to the year immediately
   preceding is
   A. humanities   B. sciences
   C. professions   D. social sciences

5. If the proportion of arts students to all humanities
   students was the same in 1977 as in 1980, then the number
   of arts students in 1977 was
   A. 7,500   B. 13,000   C. 15,000   D. 5,000

6. In which field of postgraduate study did enrollment
   INCREASE by 20 percent from 1977 to 1978?
   A. Humanities   B. Professions
   C. Sciences   D. Social sciences

7. The GREATEST increase in overall enrollment took place
   between
   A. 1975 and 1976   B. 1977 and 1978
   C. 1978 and 1979   D. 1979 and 1980

8. Between 1977 and 1980, the combined enrollment of the
   sciences and social sciences INCREASED by
   A. 40,000   B. 48,000   C. 50,000   D. 54,000

9. If the enrollment in the social sciences had decreased
   from 1979 to 1980 at the same rate as from 1978 to 1979,
   then the social science enrollment in 1980 would have
   differed from the humanities enrollment in 1980 MOST
   NEARLY by
   A. 6,000   B. 8,000   C. 12,000   D. 22,000

10. In the humanities, the GREATEST percentage increase in enrollment from 1979 to 1980 was in
    A. literature   B. philosophy
    C. religion   D. arts

    10.___

11. If the proportion of behavioral science students to the total number of students in the sciences was the same in 1976 as in 1979, then the increase in behavioral science enrollment from 1976 to 1980 was
    A. 5,000   B. 7,000   C. 10,000   D. 14,000

    11.___

12. If enrollment in the professions increased at the same rate from 1980 to 1981 as from 1979 to 1980, the enrollment in the professions in 1981 would be MOST NEARLY
    A. 85,000   B. 75,000   C. 60,000   D. 55,000

    12.___

TEST 2

Questions 1-5.

DIRECTIONS: Questions 1 through 5 involve calculations of annual grade averages for college students who have just completed their junior year. These averages are to be based on the following table showing the number of credit hours for each student during the year at each of the grade levels: A, B, C, D, and F. How these letter grades may be translated into numerical grades is indicated in the first column of the table.

Grade Value	Credit Hours – Junior Year					
	King	Lewis	Martin	Nonkin	Ottly	Perry
A = 95	12	12	9	15	6	3
B = 85	9	12	9	12	18	6
C = 75	6	6	9	3	3	21
D = 65	3	3	3	3	-	-
F = 0	-	-	3	-	-	-

Calculating a grade average for an individual student is a four-step process:

    I. Multiply each grade value by the number of credit hours for which the student received that grade.
   II. Add these multiplication products for each student.
 III. Add the student's total credit hours.
  IV. Divide the multiplication product total by the total number of credit hours.
   V. Round the result, if there is a decimal place, to the nearest whole number. A number ending in .5 would be rounded to the next higher number.

EXAMPLE:

Using student King's grades as an example, his grade average can be calculated by going through the following four steps:

  I.   95 x 12 = 1140   III. 12
       85 x 9 = 765   9
       75 x 6 = 450   6
       65 x 3 = 195   3
        0 x 0 =   0   0
                          30 TOTAL credit hours

  II. TOTAL = 2550

                       IV. Divide 2550 by 30: $\frac{2550}{30} = 85.$

King's grade average is 85.

1. The grade average of Lewis is
   A. 83   B. 84   C. 85   D. 86

2. The grade average of Martin is
   A. 72   B. 73   C. 74   D. 75

3. The grade average of Nonkin is
   A. 85   B. 86   C. 87   D. 88

4. Student Ottly must attain a grade average of 90 in each
   of his years in college to be accepted into the graduate
   school of his choice.
   If, in summer school during his junior year, he takes two
   three-credit courses and receives a grade of 95 in each
   one, his grade average for his junior year will then be
   MOST NEARLY
   A. 87   B. 88   C. 89   D. 90

5. If Perry takes an additional three-credit course during
   the year and receives a grade of 95, his grade average
   will be increased to APPROXIMATELY
   A. 79   B. 80   C. 81   D. 82

TEST 3

Questions 1-5.

DIRECTIONS: Questions 1 through 5 are to be answered SOLELY on
the basis of the following information and chart.

The following table gives pertinent data for six different
applicants with regard to:

Grade averages, which are expressed on a scale running from
0 (low) to 4 (high);
   Scores on qualifying test, which run from 200 (low) to 800 (high);
   Related work experience, which is expressed in number of months;
   Personal references, which are rated from 1 (low) to 5 (high).

Applicant	Grade Average	Test Score	Work Experience	Reference
Jones	2.2	620	24	3
Perez	3.5	650	0	5
Lowitz	3.2	420	2	4
Uncker	2.1	710	15	2
Farrow	2.8	560	0	3
Shapiro	3.0	560	12	4

An administrative assistant is in charge of the initial screening
process for the program. This process requires classifying applicants
into the following four groups:

A. SUPERIOR CANDIDATES. Unless the personal reference rating
is lower than 3, all applicants with grade averages of 3.0 or higher
and test scores of 600 or higher are classified as superior candidates.

B. GOOD CANDIDATES. Unless the personal reference rating is
lower than 3, all applicants with one of the following combinations
of grade averages and test scores are classified as good candidates:
   1. Grade average of 2.5 to 2.9 and test score of 600 or
      higher;
   2. Grade average of 3.0 or higher and test score of 550 to
      599.

C. POSSIBLE CANDIDATES. Applicants with one of the following
combinations of qualifications are classified as possible candidates:
   1. Grade average of 2.5 to 2.9 and test score of 550 to 599
      and a personal reference rating of 3 or higher;
   2. Grade average of 2.0 to 2.4 and test score of 500 or
      higher and at least 21 months' work experience and a
      personal reference rating of 3 or higher;

3. A combination of grade average and test score that would otherwise qualify as *superior* or *good* but a personal reference score lower than 3.

   D. REJECTED CANDIDATES. Applicants who do not fall in any of the above groups are to be rejected.

EXAMPLE:

   Jones' grade average of 2.2 does not meet the standard for either a superior candidate (grade average must be 3.0 or higher) or a good candidate (grade average must be 2.5 to 2.9). Grade average of 2.2 does not qualify Jones as a possible candidate if Jones has a test score of 500 or higher, at least 21 months' work experience, and a personal reference rating of 3 or higher. Since Jones has a test score of 620, 24 months' work experience, and a reference rating of 3, Jones is a possible candidate. The answer is C.

   Answer Questions 1 through 5 as explained above, indicating for each whether the applicant should be classified as a
   A. superior candidate   B. good candidate
   C. possible candidate   D. rejected candidate

1. Perez   1.___

2. Lowitz   2.___

3. Uncker   3.___

4. Farrow   4.___

5. Shapiro   5.___

KEY (CORRECT ANSWERS)

TEST 1	TEST 2	TEST 3
1. B	1. C	1. A
2. C	2. D	2. D
3. B	3. C	3. D
4. D	4. B	4. C
5. A	5. B	5. B
6. C		
7. D		
8. A		
9. D		
10. D		
11. C		
12. B		

ANSWER SHEET

USE THE SPECIAL PENCIL.   MAKE GLOSSY BLACK MARKS.

	A B C D E		A B C D E		A B C D E		A B C D E		A B C D E
1	:: :: :: :: ::	26	:: :: :: :: ::	51	:: :: :: :: ::	76	:: :: :: :: ::	101	:: :: :: :: ::
2	:: :: :: :: ::	27	:: :: :: :: ::	52	:: :: :: :: ::	77	:: :: :: :: ::	102	:: :: :: :: ::
3	:: :: :: :: ::	28	:: :: :: :: ::	53	:: :: :: :: ::	78	:: :: :: :: ::	103	:: :: :: :: ::
4	:: :: :: :: ::	29	:: :: :: :: ::	54	:: :: :: :: ::	79	:: :: :: :: ::	104	:: :: :: :: ::
5	:: :: :: :: ::	30	:: :: :: :: ::	55	:: :: :: :: ::	80	:: :: :: :: ::	105	:: :: :: :: ::
6	:: :: :: :: ::	31	:: :: :: :: ::	56	:: :: :: :: ::	81	:: :: :: :: ::	106	:: :: :: :: ::
7	:: :: :: :: ::	32	:: :: :: :: ::	57	:: :: :: :: ::	82	:: :: :: :: ::	107	:: :: :: :: ::
8	:: :: :: :: ::	33	:: :: :: :: ::	58	:: :: :: :: ::	83	:: :: :: :: ::	108	:: :: :: :: ::
9	:: :: :: :: ::	34	:: :: :: :: ::	59	:: :: :: :: ::	84	:: :: :: :: ::	109	:: :: :: :: ::
10	:: :: :: :: ::	35	:: :: :: :: ::	60	:: :: :: :: ::	85	:: :: :: :: ::	110	:: :: :: :: ::

Make only ONE mark for each answer.   Additional and stray marks may be
counted as mistakes.   In making corrections, erase errors COMPLETELY.

	A B C D E		A B C D E		A B C D E		A B C D E		A B C D E
11	:: :: :: :: ::	36	:: :: :: :: ::	61	:: :: :: :: ::	86	:: :: :: :: ::	111	:: :: :: :: ::
12	:: :: :: :: ::	37	:: :: :: :: ::	62	:: :: :: :: ::	87	:: :: :: :: ::	112	:: :: :: :: ::
13	:: :: :: :: ::	38	:: :: :: :: ::	63	:: :: :: :: ::	88	:: :: :: :: ::	113	:: :: :: :: ::
14	:: :: :: :: ::	39	:: :: :: :: ::	64	:: :: :: :: ::	89	:: :: :: :: ::	114	:: :: :: :: ::
15	:: :: :: :: ::	40	:: :: :: :: ::	65	:: :: :: :: ::	90	:: :: :: :: ::	115	:: :: :: :: ::
16	:: :: :: :: ::	41	:: :: :: :: ::	66	:: :: :: :: ::	91	:: :: :: :: ::	116	:: :: :: :: ::
17	:: :: :: :: ::	42	:: :: :: :: ::	67	:: :: :: :: ::	92	:: :: :: :: ::	117	:: :: :: :: ::
18	:: :: :: :: ::	43	:: :: :: :: ::	68	:: :: :: :: ::	93	:: :: :: :: ::	118	:: :: :: :: ::
19	:: :: :: :: ::	44	:: :: :: :: ::	69	:: :: :: :: ::	94	:: :: :: :: ::	119	:: :: :: :: ::
20	:: :: :: :: ::	45	:: :: :: :: ::	70	:: :: :: :: ::	95	:: :: :: :: ::	120	:: :: :: :: ::
21	:: :: :: :: ::	46	:: :: :: :: ::	71	:: :: :: :: ::	96	:: :: :: :: ::	121	:: :: :: :: ::
22	:: :: :: :: ::	47	:: :: :: :: ::	72	:: :: :: :: ::	97	:: :: :: :: ::	122	:: :: :: :: ::
23	:: :: :: :: ::	48	:: :: :: :: ::	73	:: :: :: :: ::	98	:: :: :: :: ::	123	:: :: :: :: ::
24	:: :: :: :: ::	49	:: :: :: :: ::	74	:: :: :: :: ::	99	:: :: :: :: ::	124	:: :: :: :: ::
25	:: :: :: :: ::	50	:: :: :: :: ::	75	:: :: :: :: ::	100	:: :: :: :: ::	125	:: :: :: :: ::

ANSWER SHEET

TEST NO. _____ PART _____ TITLE OF POSITION _____

(AS GIVEN IN EXAMINATION ANNOUNCEMENT - INCLUDE OPTION, IF ANY)

PLACE OF EXAMINATION _____ (CITY OR TOWN) _____ (STATE) _____ DATE _____

RATING

USE THE SPECIAL PENCIL.   MAKE GLOSSY BLACK MARKS.

	A B C D E		A B C D E		A B C D E		A B C D E		A B C D E
1		26		51		76		101	
2		27		52		77		102	
3		28		53		78		103	
4		29		54		79		104	
5		30		55		80		105	
6		31		56		81		106	
7		32		57		82		107	
8		33		58		83		108	
9		34		59		84		109	
10		35		60		85		110	

Make only ONE mark for each answer.   Additional and stray marks may be
counted as mistakes.   In making corrections, erase errors COMPLETELY.

	A B C D E		A B C D E		A B C D E		A B C D E		A B C D E
11		36		61		86		111	
12		37		62		87		112	
13		38		63		88		113	
14		39		64		89		114	
15		40		65		90		115	
16		41		66		91		116	
17		42		67		92		117	
18		43		68		93		118	
19		44		69		94		119	
20		45		70		95		120	
21		46		71		96		121	
22		47		72		97		122	
23		48		73		98		123	
24		49		74		99		124	
25		50		75		100		125	